The School-to-Prison Pipeline
A Comprehensive Assessment

Christopher A. Mallett, PhD, JD, MSW, professor of social work, teaches research methods, statistics, program evaluation, and mental health policy graduate and undergraduate courses at Cleveland State University, Cleveland, Ohio. Dr. Mallett is licensed in Ohio as a social worker and attorney, and he has a long history of working with, advocating for, and representing vulnerable children, adolescents, and their families. His research and scholarship focus on disability law, juvenile delinquency, and young people with certain difficulties and their involvement with the juvenile justice system and school discipline protocols, specifically the impact of mental health disorders, substance abuse, special education disabilities, and trauma experiences/maltreatment victimizations. As a consultant whose expertise is nationally tapped by juvenile courts, school districts, and children's service agencies, Dr. Mallett has published more than 55 research papers, book chapters, technical assistance training briefs, and books on these topics.

The School-to-Prison Pipeline
A Comprehensive Assessment

CHRISTOPHER A. MALLETT, PhD, JD, MSW

SPRINGER PUBLISHING COMPANY
NEW YORK

Springer Publishing Company, LLC
11 West 42nd Street
New York, NY 10036
www.springerpub.com

Acquisitions Editor: Stephanie Drew
Composition: Westchester Publishing Services

ISBN: 978-0-8261-9458-9
e-book ISBN: 978-0-8261-9459-6

15 16 17 18 19 / 5 4 3 2 1

The author and the publisher of this Work have made every effort to use sources believed to be reliable to provide information that is accurate and compatible with the standards generally accepted at the time of publication. The author and publisher shall not be liable for any special, consequential, or exemplary damages resulting, in whole or in part, from the readers' use of, or reliance on, the information contained in this book. The publisher has no responsibility for the persistence or accuracy of URLs for external or third-party Internet websites referred to in this publication and does not guarantee that any content on such websites is, or will remain, accurate or appropriate.

Library of Congress Cataloging-in-Publication Data

Mallett, Christopher A.
  The school-to-prison pipeline : a comprehensive assessment / Christopher A. Mallett.
     pages cm
  Includes index.
  ISBN 978-0-8261-9458-9 (hardcopy : alk. paper) — ISBN 978-0-8261-9459-6 (ebook) 1. Juvenile justice, Administration of—United States. 2. Juvenile delinquency—United States—Prevention. 3. Problem youth—Education—United States. 4. Youth with social disabilities—Education—United States. 5. School discipline—United States. I. Title.
  HV9104.M243 2015
  364.360973—dc23
                                                                              2015015909

Special discounts on bulk quantities of our books are available to corporations, professional associations, pharmaceutical companies, health care organizations, and other qualifying groups. If you are interested in a custom book, including chapters from more than one of our titles, we can provide that service as well.
For details, please contact:
Special Sales Department, Springer Publishing Company, LLC
11 West 42nd Street, 15th Floor, New York, NY 10036-8002
Phone: 877-687-7476 or 212-431-4370; Fax: 212-941-7842
E-mail: sales@springerpub.com

Printed in the United States of America by Gasch Printing.

Contents

Preface

This book is a comprehensive assessment of the school-to-prison pipeline and is intended for stakeholders, advocates, researchers, policy makers, educators, and students. It serves as an important textbook on this topic as well as a complete resource monograph. It explains the serious problems that strict school discipline and tough-on-crime juvenile court policies have wrought on many students, disproportionately impacting some of our most vulnerable children and adolescents. The criminalization of education and school settings, along with fewer rehabilitative alternatives within the juvenile courts, has created the pipeline and also made the problems significantly worse. This book is unique in both its breadth of coverage and incorporation of empirical knowledge from the fields of education, juvenile justice/criminology, sociology/social work, and psychology to synthesize the impact and possible solutions to the entrenched school-to-prison pipeline.

This text explains how this point was reached and how to move forward to discontinue the often unintended harm being inflicted on many children and adolescents. Thus, Chapter 1 provides the overview that is necessary to understand the scope of the problems within the education and juvenile justice systems, showing how school districts and juvenile courts simultaneously shifted from rehabilitative to punitive paradigms. Chapter 2 explains that although there was a crossover impact between these two child- and adolescent-caring systems, the punitive movements were both independent and interdependent. In the school systems, and particularly in schools that are overburdened and underfinanced, many students have been increasingly suspended and expelled due to criminalizing both typical adolescent developmental behaviors and low-level–type misdemeanors: acting out in class, truancy, fighting, and other similar offenses. The increased use of zero-tolerance policies and police (safety resource officers) in the schools has exponentially increased arrests and referrals to the juvenile courts. Similarly, in the juvenile justice system, a movement toward harsher penalties and a tough-on-crime approach more than doubled the number of adolescents adjudicated delinquent and brought under court supervision.

The pipeline is a complicated problem, though certain student groups are the most at risk for being involved, sometimes targeted by authority figures, and prone to recidivism. Chapter 3 explores how these children and adolescents end up progressing through the pipeline, placing the young person at risk for school failure. These discipline-focused school punishments are significant risks, if not direct referrals, for juvenile court involvement. Alternately, within the juvenile justice system, youthful offenders who are held in detention centers and longer-term facilities include many young people whose difficulties began in the schools, and, for many of these students, within their families. Unfortunately, time spent in justice institutions is at best difficult and at worst gravely harmful for adolescents. Chapter 4 presents the common risk factors that make it more likely for students to be involved in punitive school and juvenile court systems. This is followed by a discussion of who is disproportionately involved and why this may be occurring for the following child and adolescent groups: impoverished families; those of color; trauma and maltreatment victims; those with special education disabilities; and lesbian, gay, bisexual, and transgender.

Looking forward, Chapters 5, 6, and 7 provide data-driven evidence on how to move from punitive to rehabilitative policies and improve school safety, presenting what is known to be effective in practice, and what not to do in schools and juvenile courts. In some states and jurisdictions, there have been successful changes, modifications to policies, and vastly improved outcomes for at-risk children and adolescents. These changes include minimizing the progression of students through the pipeline by using rehabilitative-focused interventions and protocols, implementing school-wide positive behavioral programs, discontinuing harsh discipline policies, improving prevention and diversion efforts, decreasing the use of detention and incarceration facilities by substituting treatment, and developing successful collaborations across the education and juvenile justice systems. The zero-tolerance movements that swept through our nation's schools and juvenile courts have not worked. However, the subsequently established school-to-prison pipeline can be dismantled.

Chapter 1:
The Punitive Generation

THE SCHOOL-TO-PRISON PIPELINE

School districts and juvenile courts in the United States were never intended to operate in a collaborative paradigm. Unfortunately, over the past 30 years, a partnership between schools and courts has developed through a punitive and harmful framework, to the detriment of many vulnerable children and adolescents. This phenomenon is often referred to as the "school-to-prison pipeline" (Kang-Brown, Trone, Fratello, & Daftary-Kapur, 2013) or "school pathways to the juvenile justice system" (Marsh, 2014). This pipeline is best understood as a set of policies and practices in schools that make it more likely for students to face criminal involvement with the juvenile courts than to attain a quality education (Advancement Project et al., 2011).

Most of the young people involved in these harsh discipline systems among the schools and juvenile courts need not be involved, for they are minimal safety risk concerns. In other words, most students pose little to no threat of harm to other students, their schools, or their communities. However, those students involved in the pipeline, and in particular those who are suspended or expelled from school or subsequently held in juvenile justice facilities, have complicated problems and poor long-term outcomes (Advancement Project et al., 2011). These problems, though, are often part of the explanation for the children's and adolescents' initial involvement in the discipline systems: poverty, trauma, mental health difficulties, and/or developmental and cognitive deficits, among others (Mallett, 2013). For those students ultimately disciplined within the school-to-prison pipeline, it is a system that is difficult to escape from (American Psychological Association Zero Tolerance Task Force, 2008).

The school-to-prison pipeline is a recent phenomenon, for punitive policies have not always existed within schools or juvenile courts. During the 19th and most of the 20th centuries, schools in the United States focused primarily on academic and learning needs while training students for postsecondary vocational occupations. On the other hand, juvenile courts were not even established until the late 19th century, and they dedicated the first 80 years of their effort to the rehabilitation of offenders, truants, and other wayward young people (Mallett, Williams, & Marsh, 2012; Steeves & Marx, 2014). This separation of duties and responsibilities between schools and the juvenile justice system shifted over the past 30 years, with simultaneous movements toward punitive policies. This resulted in policy changes from rehabilitation to a "tough on crime" approach in the juvenile courts and from education to increasing discipline within the schools, often in response to extreme school violence incidents (Marsh, 2014; Muschert & Peguero, 2010). These shifts were both independent and interdependent, resulting in the school-to-prison pipeline (Nocella, Parmar, & Stowell, 2014).

In school systems, and particularly in those schools that are overburdened and underfinanced, many students have been increasingly suspended and expelled due to criminalizing both typical adolescent developmental behaviors and low-level–type misdemeanors: acting out in class, truancy, fighting, disobedience, and other similar offenses (U.S. Department of Education, 2014a). The increased use of zero-tolerance policies and significant expansion of police (safety resource officers) in the schools have exponentially increased arrests and referrals to the juvenile courts (Advancement Project, 2005). While impacting many, these changes disproportionately ensnare a small subset of at-risk and already disadvantaged children, adolescents, and their families (Carter, Fine, & Russell, 2014; Justice Policy Institute, 2011).

Similarly, in the juvenile justice system, a movement toward harsher penalties and the tough-on-crime approach more than doubled the number of adolescents adjudicated delinquent and brought under court supervision (Scott & Steinberg, 2008). It is increasingly recognized that when truant or low-level offenders enter the juvenile courts, often referred by the school systems, their chances of both spending time in and recidivating to detention or incarceration facilities are due in large part to how the juvenile justice system operates (Petrosino, Turpin-Petrosino, & Guckenburg, 2010).

Punishment Pathways

Harsh school discipline policies lead to large numbers of primary and secondary school-aged students who experience suspension, arrests, and for some, school expulsion. Within this student group, a small number are most at risk for being captured within the school-to-prison pipeline, sometimes targeted by authority figures, and prone to recidivism (Drakeford, 2006). It is this group who often ends up staying in the pipeline, placing the young person at significant risk for school failure (U.S. Department of Education, 2014a). These school punishments, in turn, are direct student referrals for juvenile court involvement (Advancement Project, 2005).

When these school discipline actions lead to juvenile court referrals, it may result in adjudication and probation supervision. If the pipeline is not disrupted and the young person does not do well while on probation or while supervised by the court, additional harm often ensues, including detention and/or incarceration placement. Youthful offenders who are held in detention centers—these centers being a significant risk factor for incarceration—and those placed in longer-term juvenile jail facilities include many young people whose difficulties began in the schools; thus, this results in a cycle that becomes self-sustaining (Mallett, 2014). Time spent in these juvenile justice institutions is at best difficult and at worst significantly harmful for most adolescents. These facility placements impede adolescents' development into young adulthood, exacerbating social, educational, and mental health difficulties (Scott & Steinberg, 2008; Steinberg & Scott, 2003). More than half of the adolescents released from these institutions recidivate to juvenile or adult prisons within 3 years (Loughran et al., 2009; Winokur, Smith, Bontrager, & Blankenship, 2008). For those released from these institutions, their chances of completing school and finding quality vocational options are limited, and their risk of mental health problems and homelessness is significantly increased (Dmitrieva, Monahan, Cauffman, & Steinberg, 2012; Irwin & Owen, 2005). Many juvenile justice system stakeholders across jurisdictions and states are working to limit institutional placement, whereas the shift away from punishment often proves difficult, thus leaving those young people with the most complex problems in the detention and incarceration facilities (Nelson, 2008).

Prevalence of the Problems

The impact of the school-to-prison pipeline is substantial, involving millions of young people. Of the 49 million students in the United States who enrolled in the 2011 to 2012 academic year, 3.5 million students experienced in-school detention, 1.9 million students were suspended for at least 1 day, 1.6 million students were suspended more than once, and 130,000 students were expelled (U.S. Department of Education, 2014a). The extent of these problems is probably underestimated because the survey utilized samples of fewer than 3,000 of the more than 98,000 schools nationwide, making the findings projections (Fuentes, 2014; U.S. Department of Education, 2013b). Even so, this represents 2.4% of all elementary-aged students and 11.3% of all secondary school-aged students who were suspended during the 2011 to 2012 academic year (Burke & Nishioka, 2014). Comparatively, in this same academic year, only 40% more students (3.2 million) graduated from high school than those who were suspended (U.S. Department of Education, 2013a).

These annual suspension rates, which do not include in-school suspensions, are more than double the number of suspensions from the mid-1970s (Losen & Martinez, 2013). However, this increase in suspension rates is fully accounted for by increases in suspensions for minority groups, but not for Caucasians (Losen & Skiba, 2010), making it three times more likely today that a minority student is suspended compared to a Caucasian student (Losen, 2012). When reviewed longitudinally, only up to 5% of all students are suspended in any given year, whereas it is estimated that between 30% and 50% of students experience suspension between kindergarten and 12th grade, with reports as high as 60% in some middle and high schools, and, based on location, suspension is as high as 70% for certain minorities of color. To be poignant, every 2 seconds, a student is suspended from school: African American students every 4 seconds, Caucasian students every 5 seconds, Hispanic students every 7 seconds, and Asian/Pacific Islander students every 2 minutes (Children's Defense Fund, 2014). There are wide disparities across school districts, as well as a disproportionate impact on certain student populations, beyond minority status (Losen, Hewitt, & Toldson, 2014).

The juvenile justice system involves equally large numbers of adolescents as part of the school discipline systems. In 2010, more than 2.1 million young people less than 18 years of age were arrested, leading to the juvenile courts handling almost 1.3 million delinquency cases involving youthful offenders charged with criminal offenses, a 17% increase since 1985 (Hockenberry & Puzzanchera, 2014; Majd, 2011; Puzzanchera & Robson, 2014). In addition, the juvenile courts processed nearly 150,000 status offense cases, acts that were only illicit for minors and not for adults, representing a slight increase since the mid-1990s (Salsich & Trone, 2013). The largest number of status offense violations were for truancy (36%), followed by liquor law violations (22%), ungovernability (12%), running away (11%), curfew violations (10%), and others (9%) (Puzzanchera & Hockenberry, 2010; Salsich & Trone, 2013).

From this population, upward of 80,000 adolescents remain confined each day in the United States by order of a juvenile court, either in a detention center, residential facility, or incarcerated in a youthful offender prison—with the most common being a locked, long-term placement. Each year, an additional 10,000 adolescents are transferred to adult courts and held in adult jails or prisons. In total, nearly 400,000 adolescents experience some form of incarceration every year, with an additional 200,000 adolescents below the age of 18 tried in adult courts (Annie E. Casey Foundation, 2009; Campaign for Youth Justice, 2010; Hockenberry, 2014; Mendel, 2012; National Juvenile Justice and Delinquency Prevention Coalition, 2013).

Disproportionate Impact

The young people caught in the pipeline and in the juvenile courts' detention and incarceration facilities share a number of vulnerabilities. Thus, these punishment policies disproportionately involve certain at-risk groups. The first group includes children and adolescents who are poor, an experience that disproportionately involves families of color—African American, Hispanic American, and Native American minorities, depending on the community location (Mallett, 2013). In the juvenile justice system, disproportionate numbers of minority youthful offenders are found at every juvenile court processing point. This long-standing problem is referred to as "disproportionate minority contact," and when held in institutions, "disproportionate minority confinement," though more recently, it has been titled "racial and ethnic disparities" (National Council on Crime and Delinquency, 2007; Piquero, 2008). Within the schools, similar disparity problems exist with the use of suspensions, and for some expulsions, with 1 out of 4 African American secondary school students suspended every year, compared to only 1 out of 16 Caucasian students (Center for Civil Rights Remedies, 2013).

The second group includes child and adolescent victims of abuse or neglect, and those who have witnessed violence, most often, domestic violence (Cuevas, Finkelhor, Shattuck, Turner, & Hamby, 2013; Yun, Ball, & Lim, 2011). Within the pipeline, it is likely that more students who have past or current involvement with children's services are involved, compared to their nonpipeline cohort. A total of 25% to 30% of detained youthful offenders in the juvenile court systems are past victims of maltreatment; this percentage increases to 50% to 60% for those held in long-term incarceration facilities (Mallett, 2014).

The third group includes students with special education disabilities. Within the schools, one out of five students with disabilities is suspended ever year, many times greater than their nondisabled peers (Center for Civil Rights Remedies, 2013). The same impact is found in the youthful offender incarceration facilities where nearly 40% of prisoners have been identified in need of special education services—primarily learning disabilities or emotional disturbances (Holman & Ziedenberg, 2014; U.S. Department of Education, 2014a).

The fourth group includes young people who identify as lesbian, gay, bisexual, or transgender (LGBT), found disproportionately in the pipeline and throughout the juvenile justice system (Himmelstein & Bruckner, 2011; Hunt & Moodie-Mills, 2012; Muschert & Peguero, 2010; National Juvenile Justice and Delinquency Prevention Coalition, 2013). The impact within the LGBT adolescent population may also be disproportionately involving minorities and girls within both the schools and juvenile courts (Mitchum & Moodie-Mills, 2014).

The Divergence of Youth-Caring Systems

Why do these punitive school and juvenile justice policies disproportionately impact certain identified child and adolescent groups? Part of the explanation is that these commonalities are often risk factors for related school problems, delinquency behaviors, or both (Children's Law Center, 2003; Wiggins, Fenichel, & Mann, 2007). In some ways, this situation is not surprising. For example, both the child welfare and juvenile justice systems have disproportionate numbers of children and adolescents of color involved, and there is a strong link between being a victim of maltreatment and later being involved with the juvenile courts (Fluke, Harden, Jenkins, & Ruchrdanz, 2011). In addition, many maltreated children and adolescents suffer from difficult to serious mental health problems, with many not having access to effective treatment, often impacting school abilities and exacerbating academic deficits (Mallett, 2013). These multifaceted difficulties related to childhood trauma and maltreatment also increase the risk for special education disabilities and subsequently, an increased risk for involvement with the pipeline (Mears & Aron, 2003; Scarborough & McCrae, 2009).

Most of the traumatized young people who become involved with the juvenile courts and detention or incarceration facilities have at least one diagnosed mental health disorder (Schubert & Mulvey, 2014; Teplin, Abram, McClelland, Mericle, Dulcan, & Washburn, 2006). And of most concern within this institutionalized adolescent population is a smaller subset that had been identified as children who have severe emotional disturbance—the most difficult mental health disorder (Cocozza & Skowyra, 2000). Almost all children with these most difficult problems invariably end up in juvenile justice incarceration facilities. So in many ways, because of child- and youth-caring system dysfunction, overlap, and few preventative or coordinated efforts, the juvenile justice institutions have become today's child and adolescent psychiatric hospitals. These institutions have disturbingly high suicide risk rates (Hayes, 2009; Sedlak & McPherson, 2010), which the juvenile justice facilities are wholly ill-equipped to handle from a medical aspect.

Authority Through Effective Rehabilitation

There are effective ways to change the future for these children and adolescents. The pipeline can be dismantled without reducing school or community safety (Muschert, Henry, Bracy, & Peguero, 2014). There are evidence-based practices and policy changes to move from punitive to rehabilitative paradigms in schools and juvenile courts. In some states and jurisdictions, there have been significant changes, modifications to policies, and much improved outcomes for these disenfranchised children and adolescents (Davis, Irvine, & Ziedenberg, 2014; Kim, Losen, & Hewitt, 2010; U.S. Department of Education, 2014b).

A COMPREHENSIVE ASSESSMENT

Today's punitive paradigm across schools and juvenile courts is significant cause for concern not only because of the grave impact that tough-on-crime juvenile justice policies and zero-tolerance–focused schools have on the health and well-being of young people but also because of the secondary and tertiary problems affiliated with these policies and the poor long-term outcomes for many students. This book provides a comprehensive assessment of the difficulties encountered with these policies and explains the convoluted reasons for schools and courts arriving at a policy tipping point. Although there is limited movement away from these punishment-focused policies, ongoing and increased action within school districts and juvenile courts must be pursued. Otherwise, another generation of at-risk children and adolescents will be significantly harmed. For many, this damage is permanent.

The school-to-prison pipeline is complicated. This book analyzes the multifaceted problems that led to the establishment of the pipeline;

explains how the schools and juvenile justice system became punitive paradigms, reinforced and exacerbated through discipline pathways; identifies the most vulnerable groups of children and adolescents who are disproportionately impacted; shows how the youth-caring systems are often dysfunctional in addressing these problems; and highlights how stakeholders in the schools, juvenile justice system, and policy arenas can find effective rehabilitative alternatives to solve the pipeline problems—though these solutions have extensive barriers to successful implementation.

REFERENCES

Advancement Project. (2005). *Education on lockdown: The schoolhouse to jailhouse track*. Washington, DC: Author.

Advancement Project, Education Law Center–PA, FairTest, The Forum for Education and Democracy, Juvenile Law Center, & NAACP Legal Defense and Educational Fund, Inc. (2011). *Federal policy, ESEA reauthorization, and the school-to-prison pipeline*. Washington, DC: Author.

American Psychological Association Zero Tolerance Task Force. (2008). Are zero tolerance policies effective in the schools? An evidentiary review and recommendations. *American Psychologist, 63*(9), 852–862.

Annie E. Casey Foundation. (2009). *A roadmap for juvenile justice reform*. Baltimore, MD: Author.

Burke, A., & Nishioka, V. (2014). *Suspension and expulsion patterns in six Oregon school districts* (REL 2014-028). Washington, DC: U.S. Department of Education, Institute of Education Sciences, National Center for Education Evaluation and Regional Assistance, Regional Educational Laboratory Northwest.

Campaign for Youth Justice. (2010). *Key facts: Youth in the justice system, 1*(4). Washington, DC: Author.

Carter, P. L., Fine, M., & Russell, S. (2014, March). *Discipline disparities overview*. Discipline disparities series: New Research. Bloomington, IN: The Equity Project at Indiana University. Available at http://rtpcollaborative.indiana .edu/briefing-papers

Center for Civil Rights Remedies. (2013). *A summary of new research, closing the school discipline gap: Research to practice*. Washington, DC: Civil Rights Project.

Children's Defense Fund. (2014). *The state of America's children*. Washington, DC: Author.

Children's Law Center. (2003). *Education summit*. Symposium report, May 16, 2003. Washington, DC: Author.

Cocozza, J., & Skowyra, K. (2000). Youth with mental health disorders: Issues and emerging responses. *Juvenile Justice Journal, 7*(1), 3–13.

Cuevas, C. A., Finkelhor, D., Shattuck, A., Turner, H., & Hamby, S. (2013). *Children's exposure to violence and the intersection between delinquency and victimization*. Washington, DC: Office of Juvenile Justice and Delinquency Promotion, Office of Justice Programs, U.S. Department of Justice.

Davis, A., Irvine, A., & Ziedenberg, J. (2014). *Close to home: Strategies to place young people in their communities*. Oakland, CA: National Council on Crime & Delinquency.

Dmitrieva, J., Monahan, K. C., Cauffman, E., & Steinberg, L. (2012). Arrested development: The effects of incarceration on the development of psycho-social maturity. *Development and Psychopathology, 24*, 1073–1090.

Drakeford, W. (2006). *Racial disproportionality in school disciplinary practices*. Tempe, AZ: National Center for Culturally Responsible Educational Systems (NCCRES), Arizona State University.

Fluke, J., Harden, B. J., Jenkins, M., & Ruchrdanz, A. (2011). *Disparities and disproportionality in child welfare: Analysis of the research*. Washington, DC: Alliance for Racial Equality in Child Welfare.

Fuentes, A. (2014). The schoolhouse as jailhouse. In A. J. Nocella II, P. Parmar, & D. Stovall (Eds.), *From education to incarceration: Dismantling the school-to-prison pipeline* (pp. 37–53). New York, NY: Peter Lang.

Hayes, L. (2009). *Characteristics of juvenile suicide in confinement*. Washington, DC: Office of Juvenile Justice and Delinquency Prevention, Office of Justice Programs, U.S. Department of Justice.

Himmelstein, K. E. W., & Bruckner, H. (2011). Criminal-justice and school sanctions against nonheterosexual youth: A national longitudinal study. *Pediatrics, 127*(1), 49–57.

Hockenberry, S. (2014). *Juveniles in residential placement, 2011*. Washington, DC: Office of Juvenile Justice and Delinquency Prevention, Office of Justice Programs, U.S. Department of Justice.

Hockenberry, S., & Puzzanchera, C. (2014). *Juvenile court statistics, 2011*. Washington, DC: Office of Juvenile Justice and Delinquency Prevention, Office of Justice Programs, U.S. Department of Justice.

Holman, B., & Ziedenberg, J. (2014). *The dangers of detention: The impact of incarcerating youth in detention and other secure facilities*. Washington, DC: Justice Policy Institute.

Hunt, J., & Moodie-Mills, A. (2012). *The unfair criminalization of gay and transgender youth.* Washington, DC: Center for American Progress.

Irwin, J., & Owen, B. (2005). Harm and the contemporary prison. In A. Liebling & S. Maruna (Eds.), *The effects of imprisonment* (pp. 94–117). London: Willan.

Justice Policy Institute. (2011). *Education under arrest: The case against police in schools.* Washington, DC: Author.

Kang-Brown, J., Trone, J., Fratello, J., & Daftary-Kapur, T. (2013). *A generation later: What we've learned about zero tolerance in schools.* New York, NY: Vera Institute of Justice, Center on Youth Justice.

Kim, K. Y., Losen, D. J., & Hewitt, D. T. (2010). *The school-to-prison pipeline: Structuring legal reform.* New York, NY: New York University Press.

Losen, D. L. (2012). Sound discipline policy for successful schools: How redressing racial disparities can make a positive impact for all. In S. Bahena, N. Cooc, R. Currie-Rubin, P. Kuttner, & M. Ng (Eds.), *Disrupting the school-to-prison pipeline* (pp. 65–74). Cambridge, MA: Harvard Educational Review.

Losen, D. L., Hewitt, D., & Toldson, I. (2014, March). *Eliminating excessive and unfair discipline in schools: Policy recommendations for reducing disparities.* Discipline disparities series: New Research. Bloomington, IN: The Equity Project at Indiana University. Available at http://rtpcollaborative.indiana.edu/briefing-papers

Losen, D. L., & Martinez, T. (2013). *Out of school & off track: The overuse of suspensions in American middle and high schools.* Los Angeles, CA: Civil Rights Project at UCLA.

Losen, D. L., & Skiba, R. J. (2010). *Suspended education: Urban middle schools in crisis.* Los Angeles, CA: The Civil Rights Project at UCLA and the Southern Poverty Law Center.

Loughran, T., Mulvey, E., Schubert, C., Fagan, J., Pizuero, A., & Losoya, S. (2009). Estimating a dose-response relationship between length of stay and future recidivism in serious juvenile offenders. *Criminology, 47*(3), 699–740.

Majd, K. (2011). Students of the mass incarceration nation. *Howard Law Journal, 54*(2), 343–394.

Mallett, C. (2013). *Linking disorders to delinquency: Treating high risk youth in the juvenile justice system.* Boulder, CO: Lynne Rienner.

Mallett, C. (2014). The "learning disabilities to juvenile detention" pipeline: A case study. *Children & Schools, 36*(3), 147–155.

Mallett, C., Williams, M., & Marsh, S. (2012). Specialized detention facilities. In O. Thienhaus & M. Piasecki (Eds.), *Correctional psychiatry* (Vol. 2, pp. 12-2–12-24). Kingston, NJ: Civic Research Institute.

Marsh, S. (2014). *School pathways to juvenile justice system project*. Reno, NV: National Council of Juvenile and Family Court Judges.

Mears, D. P., & Aron, L. Y. (2003). *Addressing the needs of youth with disabilities in the juvenile justice system: The current state of knowledge*. Washington, DC: Urban Institute, Justice Policy Center.

Mendel, R. A. (2012). *No place for kids: The case for reducing juvenile incarceration*. Baltimore, MD: Annie E. Casey Foundation.

Mitchum, P., & Moodie-Mills, A. C. (2014). *Beyond bullying: How hostile school climate perpetuates the school-to-prison pipeline for LBGT youth*. Washington, DC: Center for American Progress.

Muschert, G. W., Henry, S., Bracy, N. L., & Peguero, A. A. (2014). *Responding to school violence: Confronting the Columbine effect*. Boulder, CO: Lynne Rienner.

Muschert, G. W., & Peguero, A. A. (2010). The Columbine effect and school antiviolence policy. *Research in Social Problems and Public Policy, 17*, 117–148.

National Council on Crime and Delinquency. (2007). *And justice for some: Differential treatment of youth of color in the justice system*. Oakland, CA: National Council on Crime and Delinquency.

National Juvenile Justice and Delinquency Prevention Coalition. (2013). *Promoting safe communities: Recommendations for the 113th Congress*. Washington, DC: Author.

Nelson, D. W. (2008). *A road map for juvenile justice reform*. Baltimore, MD: Annie E. Casey Foundation.

Nocella, A. J., Parmar, P. S., & Stowell, D. (2014). *From education to incarceration: Dismantling the school-to-prison pipeline (Counterpoints: Studies in the postmodern theory of education)*. New York, NY: Peter Lang.

Petrosino, A., Turpin-Petrosino, C., & Guckenburg, S. (2010). *Formal system processing on juveniles: Effects on delinquency*. Oslo, Norway: Campbell System Reviews.

Piquero, A. R. (2008). Disproportionate minority contact. *The Future of Children, 18*(2), 59–79.

Puzzanchera, C., & Hockenberry, S. (2010). *Juvenile court statistics, 2010*. Pittsburgh, PA: National Center for Juvenile Justice.

Puzzanchera, C., & Robson, C. (2014). *Delinquency cases in juvenile court, 2010.* Washington, DC: Office of Juvenile Justice and Delinquency Prevention, Office of Justice Programs, U.S. Department of Justice.

Salsich, A., & Trone, J. (2013). *From courts to communities: The right response to truancy, running away, and other status offenses.* New York, NY: Vera Institute of Justice.

Scarborough, A., & McCrae, J. (2009). School-age special education outcomes of infants and toddlers investigated for maltreatment. *Children and Youth Services Review, 32*(1), 80–88.

Schubert, C. A., & Mulvey, E. P. (2014). *Behavioral health problems, treatment, and outcomes in serious youthful offenders.* Washington, DC: Office of Juvenile Justice and Delinquency Prevention, Office of Justice Programs, U.S. Department of Justice.

Scott, E. S., & Steinberg, L. (2008). *Rethinking juvenile justice.* Cambridge, MA: Harvard University Press.

Sedlak, A. J., & McPherson, K. (2010). *Survey of youth in residential placement: Youth's needs and services.* Washington, DC: Westat Corporation.

Steeves, V., & Marx, G. T. (2014). Safe school initiatives and the shifting climate of trust. In G. W. Muschert, S. Henry, N. L. Bracy, & A. A. Peguero (Eds.), *Responding to school violence: Confronting the Columbine effect* (pp. 105–124). Boulder, CO: Lynne Rienner.

Steinberg, L., & Scott, E. S. (2003). Less guilty by reason of adolescence. *American Psychologist, 58*(12), 1009–1018.

Teplin, L., Abram, K., McClelland, G., Mericle, A., Dulcan, M., & Washburn, D. (2006). *Psychiatric disorders of youth in detention.* Washington, DC: Office of Justice Programs, Office of Juvenile Justice and Delinquency Prevention, U.S. Department of Justice.

U.S. Department of Education. (2013a). *Back to school statistics.* Washington, DC: National Center for Education Statistics, Institute of Education Services.

U.S. Department of Education. (2013b). *Digest of education statistics, 2012* (NCES 2014-015, Chapter 2). Washington, DC: National Center for Education Statistics.

U.S. Department of Education. (2014a). *Appendix 1: U.S. Department of Education: Director of Federal School Climate and Discipline Resources.* Washington, DC: Author.

U.S. Department of Education. (2014b). *Civil rights data collection, data snapshot: School discipline, Issue brief No. 1.* Washington, DC: Office for Civil Rights.

Wiggins, C., Fenichel, E., & Mann, T. (2007). *Developmental problems of maltreated children and early intervention options for maltreated children.* Washington, DC:

U.S. Department of Health and Human Services, Child Protective Services Project.

Winokur, K. P., Smith, A., Bontrager, S. R., & Blankenship, J. L. (2008). Juvenile recidivism and length of stay. *Journal of Criminal Justice, 36*, 126–137.

Yun, I., Ball, J. D., & Lim, H. (2011). Disentangling the relationship between child maltreatment and violent delinquency: Using a nationally representative sample. *Journal of Interpersonal Violence, 26*(1), 88–110.

Chapter 2: From Rehabilitative to Punitive Paradigms

Schools and juvenile courts have not historically been mired in the discipline dispensation techniques utilized today, but there was always a focus on controlling young people, particularly those difficult or troublesome to manage (Insley, 2001). The balance among education, discipline, and school management has faced challenges over time (Hanson, 2005; Steeves & Marx, 2014). Since the 1800s, many schools utilized corporal punishment, with remnants of these discipline techniques still incorporated as regular classroom management practice into the 1960s and 1970s (Adams, 2000). As school populations exponentially grew during this time period and corporal punishment became less acceptable and effective, other techniques were employed, including suspension and expulsion of disruptive students from schools (Hyman & McDowell, 1979). However, because of legal challenges, and in particular the *Goss v. Lopez* Supreme Court decision (419 U.S. 565, 1975), which found due process violations in the suspension and expulsion of students without hearings, schools altered their policies to include in-school suspensions. These alternative suspensions removed disruptive students from the classroom but kept them inside the school to complete their work (Heitzeg, 2014; Marsh, 2014). These more rehabilitative efforts were favored by most school administrators through the 1980s until the growth of mandatory disciplinary outcomes for disruptive students became the norm (Jones, 1996).

A number of factors impacted the schools and juvenile courts, both independently and interdependently, leading this march toward today's punitive paradigm. As reviewed and explained in the next sections, the reasons for the establishment of the school-to-prison pipeline, though with a differential impact depending on the local schools districts, juvenile courts, and communities, included a number of explanatory factors. These included the movement in the 1980s toward a tough-on-crime approach in both adult and juvenile courts, as evidenced by the "three strikes and you're out" laws (Krisberg, 2005) and the large numbers of youthful offenders transferred to adult criminal courts (Mallett, 2007); rising rates of juvenile arrests for violent crimes in the 1980s and concerns, though incorrect, that young people were increasingly dangerous (Puzzanchera & Hockenberry, 2010); passage and enactment of the Gun-Free Schools Act of 1994; the impact and aftermath of the 1999 Columbine school shooting and other school shootings (Muschert, Henry, Bracy, & Peguero, 2014); establishment of zero-tolerance disciplinary policies across most schools nationwide (Verdugo, 2002); the increased utilization and federal funding of police officers (school resource officers) in schools (Justice Policy Institute, 2011); declining school funding; the resegregation of schools by race and class (NAACP, 2005); and the focus of the No Child Left Behind (NCLB) law on test scores and related consequences (Heitzeg, 2014).

DISCIPLINE IN SCHOOLS

From Education to Discipline

Policy makers, practitioners, and involved parties do not set forth to harm children or adolescents either in schools or in juvenile justice settings. Most stakeholders and policy decisions focus on the best interests of young people, attaining these objectives through promotion of effective learning, education accomplishments, rehabilitation, and avoidance of criminological behaviors, among others. Within this framework, blame is not the intent in the analysis of the school-to-prison pipeline. However, almost all social policies have unintended consequences (Marx, 1981), as is the case with the policies that established this disciplinary regime.

In addition, no two schools are exactly alike (nor are juvenile courts), and their antiviolence policies are, thus, differentiated accordingly. Disciplinary implementation, enforcement procedures, and utilization are different according to school size, location, and demographic makeup (Arum, 2003; Kupchik & Monahan, 2006). However, a number of themes that increased punitive policies across schools have been identified: As school enrollment increases, antiviolence and discipline policies increase; urban schools have the highest proportion of discipline policies; and antiviolence policies are practiced more frequently in both the southern and western states, in schools with higher minority student populations, and in schools with higher enrollments in free or reduced-price lunch programs—these last two school characteristics are often interrelated (Muschert & Peguero, 2010).

The Rise of School Violence: Myth Versus Reality

The preponderance of school antiviolence policies across a vast majority of districts has created what has been called the "New American School," an environment of social control and fear that is more prison-like in its efforts to maintain safety (Hirschfield, 2008), and this is particularly true for many urban secondary schools (Levy-Pounds, 2014). Historically, there have been eras when youth violence was perceived as problematic, including during the 1960s and 1970s when safety concerns were often interrelated with civil rights and school population shifts, impacting minority students disproportionately in school exclusionary policies (Children's Defense Fund, 1975). However, the more recent shift toward discipline policies in the 1990s was exceptional in terms of the impact on schools and related youth-caring systems (Kang-Brown, Trone, Fratello, & Daftary-Kapur, 2013).

The 1980s and 1990s spawned fears, and media reports of young people, often minorities, committing horrific crimes, wilding events, gang violence, and concern for the emergence of the "juvenile super-predator" were wholly disproportionate to the reality of youth violence (Walker, Spohn, & DeLone, 2012; Welch, Price, & Yankey, 2002). The commission of violent crimes—homicide, aggravated assault, robbery, and rape—by young people peaked in 1994, whereas these rates have plummeted for the past 2 decades (Puzzanchera & Hockenberry, 2010). Nonetheless, state and federal legislation was enacted throughout the 1990s and early 2000s that increased punitive outcomes for many adolescents, including trying more adolescents as adults, expanding the severity of penalties, and minimizing rehabilitative alternatives (Griffin, 2008; Mallett, 2013). These policy changes and perception problems across the country set the stage for the movement toward control and discipline within the schools and, as noted, particularly in urban schools. However, when this punitive paradigm was impacted by the fallout from school shooting incidents, movements toward school lockdowns and more prison-like security environments exponentially progressed across all school districts (Cornell, 2006).

The Columbine incident of 1999 was not the first school shooting of this era, but it was the most deadly of all tragedies, had the greatest impact on public perceptions, was covered more extensively by the media, and more significantly reinforced and motivated the security environment movement within schools (Fuentes, 2014; Giroux, 2003; Muschert & Peguero, 2010). In the decade before the Columbine tragedy, there were other school shooting incidents with far less media coverage. These included incidents at Bethel Regional High School in Alaska, Pearl High School in Mississippi, Health High School in Kentucky, Frontier Middle School in Washington, and Thurston High School in Oregon (Muschert, 2009). The 2012 shootings at Sandy Hook Elementary School in Connecticut have reignited some of these disproportionate fears and increased established school violence prevention policies. Most of these shootings occurred in what many families felt were "safe" school districts—White, suburban, and middle class—leading to the increased fear that these tragic incidents could happen anywhere (Fuentes, 2014; Kupchik & Bracy, 2009). A new brand of adolescent violence or predator was now feared at hand, a transition that also reinforced and reignited the idea of a teenage super-predator (Dilulio, 1995; Hirschfield, 2010). Although these school incidents were tragic, caused the deaths of innocents, and struck fear in many parents' perceptions, schools still remain the safest place for children and adolescents. Yet, as will be seen, it is inappropriate and ineffective public policy to have small or unique tragic events direct violence prevention measures, for even across these school shootings few causative connections can be found (Carter, Fine, & Russell, 2014).

School shootings remain rare events across the country's primary and secondary schools. Since 1992, from a school population of 49 million students, the number of children or adolescents killed by homicide on school grounds remains between 11 and 34 annually (U.S. Department of Education, 2014b), with an additional 1 to 10 students who have committed suicide on school grounds, depending on the year (U.S. Department of Education, 2014a). Similarly, and in tandem with overall juvenile offender crime rates over a similar 2-decade time period, violent victimizations, student drug use, and student-related delinquency activities on school grounds have low prevalence rates and have been declining (Brooks, Schiraldi, & Ziedenberg, 2000; DeVoe et al., 2004; U.S. Department of Education, 2014b). These trends are highlighted by the significantly larger risks that children and adolescents have of being victims of violent crime outside of school (Justice Policy Institute, 2011).

For almost all children and adolescents, schools remain the safest environment. With very low rates of violent crime that occur on school grounds, and the positive impact that a nurturing and well-structured school setting provides, most students have opportunities that should allow for strong learning outcomes and social supports (Donohue, Schiraldi, & Ziedenberg, 1998; Robers, Zhang, & Truman, 2012). However, when positive structures and supports are lacking or when security measures and distrust increase throughout schools, many students are harmed, which results in poorer academic outcomes, strained social bonds with teachers and administrators, and increased risk for school failure (Sojoyner, 2014; Steeves & Marx, 2014).

Criminalization of Education

The increased punitive environment within the juvenile courts, perceptions of growing school violence, the crack cocaine epidemic that had a devastating impact on many poor communities, and worries about adolescent gangs were factors that led Congress to enact the Gun-Free Schools Act in 1994 (20 U.S.C. § 8921(b)). This federal legislation acted as a seal of approval for promoting zero-tolerance policies in school districts. Even though the law itself only made states' receipt of federal funding for K–12 education contingent on imposing a 1-year expulsion for a student found in possession of a gun on school grounds and a mandatory referral to the juvenile or adult justice system (20 U.S.C. § 8921(b)(1)(e)), the march toward school security and quick discipline had begun. Within 2 years of the passage of the law, all states had enacted compliant legislation (Brady, 2002).

Subsequent amendments to the Gun-Free Schools Act and state laws have broadened the focus from firearms to other types of weapons (Birkland & Lawrence, 2009), as well as non-weapon possession problems—use of alcohol/drugs and tobacco, fighting, and disobedience of school rules (Hirschfield, 2008). Since 1996, the proportion of schools that subsequently enacted what have come to be called zero-tolerance policies has never fallen below 75% (U.S. Department of Education, 2013), with some estimates as high as 90% (Centers for Disease Control and Prevention, 2006; Muschert & Peguero, 2010). These policies established mandatory suspensions or expulsions for an expansive range of student incidents, including violent behavior, fighting, assault, harassment, indecent exposure, vandalism, and destruction of school property, among others (Kupchik & Monahan, 2006; Verdugo, 2002). However, zero-tolerance policies also include nonviolent student behaviors, such as verbal harassment, disobedience, obscene language, and truancy (Arum, 2003; Marsh, 2014).

In many schools, these policies are supported and reinforced through the use of security guards, metal detectors, police officers working in the building, and surveillance by cameras. Security practices are not new to school districts, but they have changed over time from a focus on property crime and thefts to a concern about individual victimizations and toward today's broad security operations (Fuentes, 2014; Lawrence, 2007). During the rise of zero-tolerance policies, the use of security guards, police, and cameras has significantly risen, with higher utilization rates in urban, inner-city areas (Neiman & DeVoe, 2009; Ruddy et al., 2010). Today's school security measures impact most students: Nearly 6% of all public schools make random use of metal detectors (10% for middle schools and 13% for high schools), impacting 11% of all students; mandatory walk-through metal detectors are utilized in 2% of middle schools and in 4% of high schools; 36% of schools utilize security cameras (42% of middle schools and 64% of high schools), impacting 58% of all students; and 42% of schools employ security guards, impacting almost 65% of all students (U.S. Department of Education, 2014a). These control measures often, and in particular in low-income and inner-city public schools, create a prison-like environment (Addington, 2014; Hirschfield, 2010). The following is a disparity case in point regarding school districts and student experiences: 26% of African American students report walking through metal detectors on entering school compared with only 5.4% of Caucasian students (Toldson, 2011).

These prison-like environments, even when designed in security-friendly architecture and planning typically found in newer suburban schools, harm the learning environment for many students. In lower-income neighborhoods with more poorly funded schools, the impact of these security personnel and measures can be much harsher on students (Hirschfield, 2010; Kupchik, 2010). These environments can produce negative reactions, fears, or worries for any students about their school; however, in some schools, students may feel resentment and negative feelings toward the surveillance and oversight itself (Addington, 2009; Sipe, 2012). In fact, schools with more disruptions and disorder within the buildings and classrooms utilize more security measures, but as will be an emerging theme, it may be these security measures themselves that were contributing to the disorder (Mayer & Leone, 1999). These reactions to the safety measures may interfere with an effective learning environment (Bracy, 2010), though additional and ongoing evaluation of these environments is necessary to determine whether an improved balance between the policy objectives and student learning is possible (Addington, 2014).

Establishment of the School-to-Prison Pipeline

Zero-Tolerance Policies

The term "zero tolerance" was nationally recognized and used during the Reagan Administration's war on drugs in the mid-1980s, encapsulating both a violent drug trade occurring across many U.S. cities and foreign policy affairs in drug-importing countries (Fuentes, 2014). This war on drugs initiative and policy focus was imported to the public schools in 1986 with the passage of the Drug-Free Schools Act, a strict prohibition against drugs or alcohol possession (20 U.S.C. § 3181(a)).

In 1989, school districts in Louisville, Kentucky, and Orange County, California, enacted zero-tolerance policies calling for student expulsion for drug- and gang-related activity, as did Yonkers, New York, for school disruption. These strict-response discipline and punishment ideas became popular in education policy–making circles as well as among the general public, and by 1993, many schools began using the term "zero tolerance" as a philosophy that mandated the application of severe predetermined consequences for unsafe or unacceptable student behaviors (American Psychological Association Zero Tolerance Task Force, 2008). This law was followed by the previously discussed Gun-Free Schools Act of 1994 and its weapons prohibitions, setting the stage for zero-tolerance policies to become the norm in school management and discipline dispensation.

These policies have eliminated the consideration by school administrators for why events occur, what motivated the students' involvement, and any mitigating history that impacted the event and led to the involvement of law enforcement personnel and the removal of students from schools. These removals are often due to first-time offenses and lead to suspension or expulsion of students (Kang-Brown et al., 2013; Skiba, 2000). Although these procedural outcomes are common across many school districts, no single definition of zero tolerance exists across the country. However, there are common goals of zero-tolerance policies, including maintaining a safe school climate for students and teachers that is conducive to learning, predicated on the philosophy that removing students who engage in illicit or disruptive behavior will both deter others and improve the education climate (Skiba et al., 2006). Some authors posit a common definition when defining zero-tolerance policies and their impact on the school-to-prison pipeline:

> Zero tolerance is a philosophy or policy that mandates the application of predetermined consequences, most often

> severe and punitive in nature, that are intended to be applied regardless of the apparent severity of the behavior, mitigating circumstances, or situational context. Such an approach is intended to deter future transgressions, by sending a message that no form of a given unacceptable behavior will be tolerated under any circumstances. (Skiba et al., 2006, p. 26)

Unfortunately, these outcomes are far from achieved, and the policies themselves look to be a part of the problem.

There is legitimate concern that the enactment of the NCLB law in 2001 was juxtaposed with zero-tolerance policies and unintentionally, at least in the initial rollout of the law, exacerbated the school-to-prison pipeline. The NCLB law was implemented to hold schools accountable for student performance, with concerns for students who traditionally have performed poorly—those with disabilities, certain minority groups, students belonging to a lower socioeconomic class, and those whose first language is not English (Fuentes, 2014; Nolan, 2011). However, the punitive focus on those schools with low standardized proficiency scores has narrowed educational instruction—thus, teaching to the test—and encouraged the removal of low-performing students by referring them to alternative schools and General Education Development (GED) programs, eliminating them from attendance roles, or using zero-tolerance policies to expand arrests and expulsions (Klehr, 2009; Nichols & Berliner, 2007; Ryan, 2004).

For those students who stay enrolled, often these types of school administration actions increase disengagement from the learning environment and alienate the connections that students have with their schools, thus increasing disruptive behaviors (Kozol, 2005). Once students are removed from school, it is often difficult to overcome the barriers to reentry and successful high school completion (Advancement Project et al., 2011). One ongoing difficulty is that the NCLB Act (20 U.S.C. § 7115(b)(2)(E)), and recent state waivers to the Act lowering the original standards, failed to provide the necessary funding to address the resource disparities among the nation's schools, but did provide funding for school-based law enforcement officers and encourages the officers' involvement in problem or disruptive student discipline (Advancement Project et al., 2011). This funding trend has continued over the past decade with most (35) states providing fewer K–12 education dollars per pupil; this is problematic because states provide the majority of school district support across the country (Leachman & Mai, 2014).

Zero-tolerance policies and the criminalization of education have many causative factors and a disproportionate impact on certain students: One group includes minorities and those living in poorer communities. In particular, harmful outcomes of these strict policies have a greater impact on inner-city and lower-income school districts (Addington, 2014). Despite previous efforts at school integration, reseg-regation of public schools has been occurring across many districts (Orfield, 2009), further separating students and neighborhoods by race and class (Fry & Taylor, 2012). Students in lower-income school districts have fewer educational opportunities, are less likely to enroll in 4-year colleges, and are more likely to attend schools where a vast majority of the population are students of color (Children's Defense Fund, 2012; Palardy, 2009). Nationwide, the average African American student attends a school where nearly two of every three classmates belong to the low-income group, which is double the comparative Caucasian student rate (Orfield, Kucsera, & Siegel-Hawley, 2012). School districts that are dis-proportionately poor and minority are more likely to utilize security measures and to have police officers in their schools (Hirschfield, 2010).

Police Officers (SROs) in the Schools

Reinforcing the shifts toward discipline, the Safe Schools Act of 1994 and 1998 Amendment, both Amendments to the Omnibus Crime Control and Safe Streets Act of 1968, promoted and funded partnerships for in-school police forces, also known as school resource officers, in pri-mary and secondary schools (42 U.S.C. § 3711). These Acts were initi-ated by the Clinton Administration's reaction to the school shootings and killings at Westside Middle School in Arkansas, and they had two policy objectives: to help build school and police force collaborations and to improve school and student safety (Rich-Shea & Fox, 2014). Before these Acts, an incident such as the following was very unlikely to have occurred:

> A student was asked (by a school staff member) to remove his "do-rag" upon arriving at school prior to the start of the day. He resisted at first, but then removed it (unhappily). He then cussed out the assistant principal, who wrote him a referral for doing so. Then he was sent to the office, and he wanted to leave, but Mr. Majors (another assistant principal) stood in his way and wouldn't let him leave. The student tried to push Mr. Majors aside, and as a result he was handcuffed by the school resource office and arrested for pushing a staff member. (Kupchik, 2010, p. 79)

The idea of having police integrated within their communities was not new, as it had been introduced in the 1950s with numerous districts having officers walk in their neighborhoods. This crime management approach focused on maintaining community order and minimizing criminal activity from escalating into more serious forms (Gowri, 2003). With the progression of policing and the enactment of the 1994 Safe School Acts and subsequent amendments, police in schools became the norm for many school districts, with nearly one billion dollars spent by federal agencies during this time period, including funding from the NCLB Act, and employing more than 17,000 officers annually. By some estimates, 48% of all schools have a school resource officer on campus, with funding for officers at the federal and state levels increasing over the past few years (Justice Policy Institute, 2011; Morgan, Salomon, Plotkin, & Cohen, 2014; Thurau & Wald, 2010).

School resource officers are typically police officers from the local police district; thus, they do not answer to or are rarely employed by the local school district. The school resource officers' responsibilities vary, though a majority of their day is dedicated to law enforcement activities, followed by advising, mentoring, and teaching students (Finn, McDevitt, Lassiter, Shively, & Rich, 2005; Petteruti, 2011). This arrangement does reinforce the policy objective of the Safe Schools Acts by building stronger school and police district collaborations (Rosiak, 2009).

The Pipeline Does Not Improve School Safety

Millions of students nationwide are impacted annually by zero-tolerance policies, and hundreds of thousands of middle- and high-school students are caught every year within the school-to-prison pipeline through suspensions, arrests by school resource officers, and, for some, expulsion (Advancement Project et al., 2011; Reyes, 2006; Skiba, 2000; U.S. Department of Education, 2014b). The presence of police officers has increased student arrests on school grounds from 300% to 500% annually since the establishment of zero-tolerance policies, most of the time for nonserious offenses—unruly behaviors, disobedience, or status offenses (Advancement Project, 2005; NAACP, 2006; Theriot, 2009; Thurau & Wald, 2010). As an example, in the 2009 to 2010 academic year, 96,000 students were arrested while on school grounds and 242,000 were referred to the juvenile courts by school officials (McCurdy, 2014). With this level of impact, are the zero-tolerance policies and Safe Schools Act's objectives of making schools and students safer being met?

Unfortunately, for vested stakeholders, but particularly for students and families caught in the school-to-prison pipeline, the answer is no. Schools are safer today than at any time over the past 2 decades (Robers et al., 2012; U.S. Department of Education, 2014b), but not because of the impact that zero-tolerance policies or school resource officers have on schools. Most school discipline policies and procedures developed over the past 20 years are influenced by subjective factors, leading to inconsistent application of student codes of conduct, and, as will be reviewed later, a disproportionate impact on certain groups of students (Faffaele-Mendez, Knoff, & Ferron, 2002). Counterintuitively for many policy makers, schools that have increased their suspension and expulsion rates, hoping that the removal of problem students will improve the school environment, have found the opposite to be true: Academic achievement has declined, school and student body cohesion has become more fragile, and satisfaction with the school and its governance structures has worsened (American Psychological Association Zero Tolerance Task Force, 2008; Carter et al., 2014; Marsh, 2014).

In tandem with the philosophy of many juvenile justice system detention and incarceration facilities during the 1990s, it was believed that increased school discipline and zero-tolerance policies would have a deterrent effect on students and improve behaviors. However, increasing school suspensions has increased student misbehavior, and suspensions and expulsions have increased the likelihood for school dropout or delayed graduation (Costenbader & Markson, 1998; Henry, 2000; Justice Policy Institute, 2011). These harsh discipline policies increase education failure, isolate students socially, and restrict young adult economic options (Kupchik & Monahan, 2006; Verdugo, 2002). These discipline outcomes cause behavior and incident recidivism problems for disciplined students returning to school (Losen, Hewitt, & Toldson, 2014).

School resource officers are well thought of by many stakeholders and generally provide a feeling of safety for many inside the school, leading to some increases in crime reporting by students and some school personnel and students reporting decreases in fighting and bullying; but this is not universally found within student populations (Finn et al., 2005; Martinez, 2009). However, the impact that police officers in schools have on reinforcing zero-tolerance policies and the utilization of more formal methods of discipline is a serious concern in exacerbating and reinforcing the school-to-prison pipeline (Bazemore, Leip, & Stinchcomb, 2004; Newman, 2004; Rich-Shae, 2010). In the majority of schools where school resource officers are employed, it is often postulated, and found by some researchers, that they do more harm than good for students by increasing the criminalization of school-based, and often minor, problems (Brown, 2006; Dahlberg, 2012; Theriot, 2009). Of concern, the harsher discipline reinforcement by the presence of school resource officers may be greater for larger urban schools and schools with more at-risk and minority students (Brady, Balmer, & Phenix, 2007). The identified exception is the small number of schools where serious crime is a persistent problem (Crouch & Williams, 1995; Kupchik, 2010).

Although the presence of school resource officers may be causing little direct harm for a majority of students and the outcomes are neutral for many, they are considered a factor in the disproportionate impact of school discipline on certain student groups (American Psychological Association Zero Tolerance Task Force, 2008; Brady et al., 2007). The major policy problem is that the utilization of police officers in schools is significantly greater than the evidence of their positive impact on school safety. Thus, the officers' presence is nearly ubiquitous across most school districts, and their potential unintended and harmful consequences on the student population are potentially understated. This underappreciation across many stakeholders is because the research evidence is not complete: Too many uneven methodological standards, old data, comparison of disparate outcome definitions, and lower numbers of peer-reviewed studies have been published to provide guidance on how or whether to use school resource officers (Morgan et al., 2014).

Disconcertingly, school resource officers and school personnel involve students in the pipeline a vast majority of the time for minor or nonserious actions or behaviors, with disobedience being the most common reason (Advancement Project, 2005; Equity Project, 2014). However, even a first step into these discipline pathways can cause significant difficulties for many students. A single suspension or expulsion from school doubles the risk for a student repeating a grade, which is itself a strong risk factor for the student dropping out of high school (Kang-Brown et al., 2013; Rich-Shae & Fox, 2014). Subsequently, these outcomes are serious risks for involvement in the juvenile justice system, as evidenced by a longitudinal study of 6 million Texas students that found a discretionary school offense that did not include a weapon made juvenile court involvement three times more likely (Fabelo et al., 2011). Once involved with the juvenile courts, adolescents are significantly more likely to remain involved and to have recidivist outcomes, including detention and, for some, incarceration (Petrosino, Turpin-Petrosino, & Guckenburg, 2010).

PUNISHMENT IN THE JUVENILE COURTS

From Parens Patriae to Tough on Crime

Prior to the establishment of today's juvenile justice system, troubled children and adolescents were offered intervention efforts that focused on family control, in addition to the early use of almshouses—locked one-room buildings (Grob, 1994). By the turn of the 19th century, with the impact of increased poverty, urban growth, and immigrant influxes, new facilities were established—Houses of Refuge—in major cities to help control juvenile delinquency (Krisberg, 2005). Houses of Refuge were the first institutions that provided separate facilities for children and adolescents, apart from adult criminals and workhouses, and they also provided education along with reform efforts (Mennel, 1973). These facilities housed a broad array of young people in need, including those who were delinquent, neglected, and/or dependent. The doctrine of parens patriae (because of which the state steps in as a benevolent caretaker when necessary) supported the Houses of Refuge's efforts through the belief that the state should act as a benevolent legal parent when the family is no longer willing or able to serve the best interests of the child (Platt, 1969). This philosophy continued to guide the movement from the Houses of Refuge to the Child Savers Movement and the establishment of the juvenile courts.

The Child Savers Movement worked with the urban poor at the end of the 1800s, trying to keep children and adolescents sheltered, fed, and, when possible, employed; their efforts gradually gave way to the establishment of reform schools (Hawes, 1971; Lawrence & Hemmens, 2008). Reform schools were criticized for lacking proactive efforts to change the behavior of juvenile delinquents and for long-term housing of this population. The expansion of the Progressive Era (1880 to 1920), a time of rational optimism, brought reforms and the doctrine of parens patriae to the schools. This movement provided safeguards for children and adolescents who were charged with delinquency (including truancy and lack of supervision), with the state of Illinois establishing the first juvenile court in 1899. By 1925, 46 of the existing 48 states at the time had established juvenile or specialized courts for children and adolescents (Coalition for Juvenile Justice, 1998; Krisberg, 2005).

In conjunction with the establishment of juvenile courts, the use of correctional facilities for delinquent youthful offenders expanded from the 1940s to the 1960s. By the 1960s, a majority of those brought before the juvenile courts were, at some point, held in a detention facility or correctional facility. This detained and incarcerated population totaled more than 100,000 annually in the 1940s, rising to more than 400,000 by the 1960s. Many of these facilities were substandard, and they did not include rehabilitative services or medical care (President's Commission on Law Enforcement and Administration of Justice, 1967; Roberts, 2004).

Although juvenile courts were established as part of a reform effort to more humanely provide for the best interests of neglected, abused, and delinquent children (Binder, Geis, & Bruce, 1988), their impact was relatively limited. The continued poor treatment of system-involved youthful offenders, and the perception that a social welfare approach was doing little to curb expanding juvenile crime, resulted in more attention on issues of due process. Critics at the time argued that the juvenile courts could no longer justify their broad disposition powers and invasion of personal rights (i.e., due process) on humanitarian grounds. Youthful offenders were often treated like adult criminals, but they had none of the legal protection granted to adults (Scott & Grisso, 1997). Eventually, due process concerns came to the forefront of juvenile justice in the United States with the *Gault* decision (387 U.S. 1, 1967).

The intent of *Gault* was to balance the broad powers of the juvenile court by providing legal protection to juveniles. However, the *Gault* decision also focused attention on similarities between the juvenile and adult courts versus the differences in intent underlying the two systems (Schwartz, 2001). Although, in theory, still oriented toward rehabilitation, the new focus on due process resulted in the juvenile system orienting toward retribution as a means to address delinquency—the hallmark of the adult criminal justice system. This shift toward treating adolescents as adults, combined with the influential but misunderstood message of "nothing works" in rehabilitative youthful offenders (Martinson, 1979), set the stage for the next era of change in the juvenile justice system.

The late 1980s and early 1990s marked an aggressive swing toward societal protection as the primary goal in developing responses to crime (Scott & Grisso, 1997). As discussed, public opinion that juvenile crime was out of control, public concern about a largely fictional new class of juvenile super-predators, and a growing public attitude that juvenile courts were soft on crime fueled critical changes in the juvenile justice system that exist across many juvenile courts today: a punitive paradigm, focused on retribution and not rehabilitation. These punitive legal reforms increased juvenile detainment and incarceration as well as the wholesale transfer of many youthful offenders into the adult criminal justice system, numbering 250,000 a year (Scott & Steinberg, 2008). New punitive state laws shifted decision making from the judges to the prosecutors for many adolescents, avoiding cases or mitigating evidentiary reviews. The dismantling of the parens patriae approach within the juvenile courts continued and, in some areas, expanded the extensive use of institutional control.

The Expansion of Detention, Incarceration, and Jailing of Youthful Offenders

The incarceration of youthful offenders remains a serious problem across the juvenile justice system. Although recent reforms, state budgetary difficulties, and litigation regarding unconstitutional care and dangerous facilities have reduced the number of incarcerations over the past decade, 80,000 adolescents are still confined each day in juvenile facilities, with an additional 10,000 in adult jails and prisons (National Juvenile Justice and Delinquency Prevention Coalition, 2013). These facilities are designed within a punitive paradigm, providing minimal rehabilitative services (Mendel, 2012).

A majority of incarcerated youthful offenders are 16 to 17 years old, minority (68%), and male (87%), though the numbers of young women have been increasing slightly over the past decade. Among the ethnic minorities, approximately 60% are African American, 33% are Hispanic, and, depending on the jurisdiction, 1% to 4% are American Indian or Asian (U.S. Department of Justice, 2014). The overrepresentation of minorities within incarceration facilities, disproportionate minority confinement, is found in nearly all states, with a greater impact on minority males than females (Davis, Irvine, & Ziedenberg, 2014; U.S. Department of Justice, 2012).

Most of these youthful offenders have not been convicted of serious offenses. Recent residential surveys and FBI crime data show that only 25% of youthful offenders are incarcerated because of a violent index offense (murder, sexual assault, robbery, or aggravated assault), increasing to only 38% of those held in long-term secure institutions. The largest number of incarcerated youthful offenders (46%) committed property, drug, public order, or, especially among girls, status offenses, such as truancy, underage drinking, running away, and curfew violations. Of particular concern, 16% (ranging from 0% to 38% across states) of youth offenders were incarcerated for technical violations, such as not following court orders, probation expectations, or not attending school regularly (Hockenberry & Puzzanchera, 2014; Mendel, 2012).

The pace of incarceration reform through the juvenile justice system remains geographically disparate, with as much as a 10-fold variation in incarceration rates from state to state (Office of Juvenile Justice and Delinquency Prevention, 2014). Some jurisdictions and states have made significant reductions in their incarceration rates—Alabama, California, Connecticut, Illinois, Michigan, New York, Ohio, and Texas—whereas many others have not (Hockenberry, 2014). Certain groups—including judges, advocates, and reformers—deserve credit for moving some jurisdictions' juvenile justice paradigm away from punishment and toward rehabilitation. However, the number of youthful offender incarcerations has been declining over the past decade, whereas the rate of incarceration per arrest has been rising (National Juvenile Justice and Delinquency Prevention Coalition, 2013). As a result, this decrease in incarcerations may be due more to falling crime rates among the adolescent population than to system reforms. It is unlikely, though, that falling crime rates fully account for the changes (Butts, 2013).

Recidivism

A growing consensus has found that holding youthful offenders in any of the 591 detention centers nationwide does not meet the main functions of the juvenile courts—community safety and, for some courts, adolescent rehabilitation—and that the experience of detention itself is part of the problem (Holman & Ziedenberg, 2014; Mallett & Stoddard-Dare, 2010). Indeed, detention placement has increasingly been found to have a causal impact on increased youthful reoffending and recidivism (Justice Policy Institute, 2009; Soler, Shoenberg, & Schindler, 2009). Thus, the experience of detention makes it more likely that detained adolescents, particularly nonviolent and status offenders, will continue to engage in delinquent behavior (Holman & Ziedenberg, 2014). Though the reasons behind this are still being investigated, it is known that detained youthful offenders are more likely than nondetained offenders to further penetrate the juvenile justice system, with prior commitment being the most significant predictor of recidivism (Mallett, 2013).

Not surprisingly, with this being the impact of detention, holding adolescents in long-term incarceration facilities has no better outcomes. Placement into these facilities has either no correlation with youthful offender rearrest or recidivism rates (Loughran et al., 2009; Winokur, Smith, Bontrager, & Blankenship, 2008) or it is associated with an increased risk for offender rearrest or recidivism (Myner, Santman,

Cappelletty, & Perlmutter, 1998). As evidenced in many reviews, a large percentage, many times a majority, of incarcerated youthful offenders reoffended within 18 to 30 months of their release from these facilities (Petrosino et al., 2010). While incarcerated, many of these adolescents do not receive services that may assist in mitigating their prior offending behavior; thus, they are not provided with education or rehabilitative services that may be warranted (Annie E. Casey Foundation, 2009).

REFERENCES

Adams, T. (2000). The status of school discipline and violence. *The Annals of the American Academy of Politics and Society, 675*(1), 140–156.

Addington, L. A. (2009). Cops and cameras: Public school security as a policy response to Columbine. *American Behavioral Scientist, 52*, 1426–1446.

Addington, L. A. (2014). Surveillance and security approaches across public school levels. In G. W. Muschert, S. Henry, N. L. Bracy, & A. A. Peguero (Eds.), *Responding to school violence: Confronting the Columbine effect* (pp. 71–88). Boulder, CO: Lynne Rienner.

Advancement Project. (2005). *Education on lockdown: The schoolhouse to jailhouse track.* Washington, DC: Author.

Advancement Project, Education Law Center–PA, FairTest, Forum for Education and Democracy, Juvenile Law Center, & NAACP Legal Defense and Educational Fund, Inc. (2011). *Federal policy, ESEA reauthorization, and the school-to-prison pipeline.* Washington, DC: Author.

American Psychological Association Zero Tolerance Task Force. (2008). Are zero tolerance policies effective in the schools? An evidentiary review and recommendations. *American Psychologist, 63*(9), 852–862.

Annie E. Casey Foundation. (2009). *A roadmap for juvenile justice reform.* Baltimore, MD: Author.

Arum, R. (2003). *Judging school discipline: The crisis of moral authority.* Cambridge, MA: Harvard University Press.

Bazemore, G., Leip, L., & Stinchcomb, J. B. (2004). Boundary changes and the nexus between formal and informal social control: Truancy intervention as a case study in criminal justice expansionism. *Notre Dame Journal of Law, Ethics, and Public Policy, 18*, 521–570.

Binder, A., Geis, G., & Bruce, D. D. (1988). *Juvenile delinquency: Historical, cultural, and legal perspectives.* New York, NY: Macmillan.

Birkland, T. A., & Lawrence, R. (2009). Media framing after Columbine. *American Behavioral Scientist, 52*, 1426–1446.

Bracy, N. L. (2010). Circumventing the law: Students' rights in schools with police. *Journal of Contemporary Criminal Justice, 26*, 294–315.

Brady, K. P. (2002). Weapons of choice: Zero tolerance school discipline policies and the limitations of student procedural due process. *Children's Legal Rights Journal, 22*, 2–10.

Brady, K. P., Balmer, C., & Phenix, D. (2007). School-police partnership effectiveness in urban schools: An analysis of New York City's Impact Schools initiative. *Education and Urban Society, 39*(4), 455–478.

Brooks, K. V., Schiraldi, V., & Ziedenberg, J. (2000). *School house hype: Two years later.* Policy Report. Washington, DC: Justice Policy Institute.

Brown, B. (2006). Understanding and assessing school police officers: A conceptual and methodological comment. *Journal of Criminal Justice, 34*(6), 591–604.

Butts, J. A. (2013). *Is the decline in juvenile incarceration due to reform or falling crime rates?* New York, NY: Research and Evaluation Center, John Jay College of Criminal Justice.

Carter, P. L., Fine, M., & Russell, S. (2014, March). *Discipline disparities overview.* Discipline disparities series: New Research. Bloomington, IN: The Equity Project at Indiana University. Available at http://rtpcollaborative.indiana.edu/briefing-papers

Centers for Disease Control and Prevention. (2006). *School policy and school environment questionnaire.* Atlanta, GA: Centers for Disease Control and Prevention.

Children's Defense Fund. (1975). *School suspensions: Are they helping children?* Cambridge, MA: Washington Research Project: Children's Defense Fund.

Children's Defense Fund. (2012). *Portrait of inequality, 2012.* Washington, DC: Author.

Coalition for Juvenile Justice. (1998). *A celebration or a wake: The juvenile court after 100 years.* Washington, DC: Coalition for Juvenile Justice.

Cornell, D. G. (2006). *School violence: Fears versus facts.* Mahwah, NJ: Lawrence Erlbaum Associates.

Costenbader, V., & Markson, S. (1998). School suspension: A study with secondary school students. *Journal of School Psychology, 36*, 59–82.

Crouch, E., & Williams, D. (1995). What cities are doing to protect kids. *Educational Leadership, 52*(5), 60–62.

Dahlberg, T. L. (2012). *Arrested futures: The criminalization of school discipline in Massachusetts' three largest school districts.* New York, NY: American Civil Liberties Union.

Davis, A., Irvine, A., & Ziedenberg, J. (2014). *Stakeholders' views on the movement to reduce youth incarceration.* Oakland, CA: National Council on Crime & Delinquency.

DeVoe, J. F., Peter, K., Kaufman, P., Miller, A., Noonan, M., Snyder, T. D., & Baum, K. (2004). *Indicators of school crime and safety: 2004.* Washington, DC: U.S. Department of Education.

Dilulio, J. J., Jr. (1995). The coming of the superpredators. *Weekly Standard, 1*(11), 23–32.

Donohue, E., Schiraldi, V., & Ziedenberg. (1998). *School house hype: School shootings and the real risks kids face in America.* Washington, DC/Covington, KY: Justice Policy Institute and Children's Law Center.

Equity Project at Indiana University. (2014, March). *Discipline disparities series: Key findings.* Discipline disparities series: New Research. Bloomington, IN: The Equity Project at Indiana University. Available at http://rtpcollaborative.indiana.edu/briefing-papers

Fabelo, T., Thompson, M. D., Plotkin, M., Carmichael, D., Marchbanks, M. P. III, & Booth, E. A. (2011). *Breaking schools' rules: A statewide study of how school discipline relates to students' success and juvenile justice involvement.* New York, NY; College Station, TX: Council of State Governments Justice Center; Public Research Policy Research Institute of Texas A & M University.

Faffaele-Mendez, L. M., Knoff, H. M., & Ferron, J. M. (2002). School demographic variables and out-of-school suspension rates: A quantitative and qualitative analysis of a large, ethnically diverse school district. *Psychology in the Schools, 39*(3), 259–277.

Finn, P., McDevitt, J., Lassiter, M., Shively, M., & Rich, T. (2005). *Case studies of 19 school resource officer (SRO) programs.* Washington, DC: National Institute of Justice, U.S. Department of Justice.

Fry, R., & Taylor, P. (2012). *The rise of residential segregation by income.* Washington, DC: Pew Research Center.

Fuentes, A. (2014). The schoolhouse as jailhouse. In A. J. Nocella II, P. Parmar, & D. Stovall (Eds.), *From education to incarceration: Dismantling the school-to-prison pipeline.* New York, NY: Peter Lang.

Giroux, H. A. (2003). Racial injustice and disposable youth in the age of zero tolerance. *Qualitative Studies in Education, 16*(4), 553–564.

Gowri, A. (2003). Community policing is an epicycle. *Policing: An International Journal of Police Strategies and Management, 26*(4), 591–611.

Griffin, P. (2008). *Different from adults: An updated analysis of juvenile transfer and blended sentencing laws, with recommendations for reform.* Pittsburgh, PA: National Center for Juvenile Justice.

Grob, G. N. (1994). *The mad among us: A history of the care of America's mentally ill.* New York: The Free Press.

Hanson, A. L. (2005). Have zero tolerance school discipline policies turned into a nightmare? The American dream's promise of equal educational opportunity grounded in *Brown v. Board of Education. UC Davis Journal of Juvenile Law and Policy, 9*(2), 289–379.

Hawes, J. (1971). *Children in urban society: Juvenile delinquency in nineteenth century America.* New York, NY: Oxford University Press.

Heitzeg, N. A. (2014). Criminalizing education: Zero tolerance policies, police in the hallways, and the school to prison pipeline. In A. J. Nocella II, P. Parmar, & D. Stovall (Eds.), *From education to incarceration: Dismantling the school-to-prison pipeline.* New York, NY: Peter Lang.

Henry, S. (2000). What is school violence? An integrated definition. *Annals of the American Academy of Political and Social Science, 567,* 16–29.

Hirschfield, P. J. (2008). Preparing for prison? The criminalization of school discipline in the USA. *Theoretical Criminology, 12*(1), 79–101.

Hirschfield, P. J. (2010). School surveillance in America: Disparate and unequal. In T. Monahan & R. D. Torres (Eds.), *Schools under surveillance: Cultures of control in public education* (pp. 38–54). New Brunswick, NJ: Rutgers University Press.

Hockenberry, S. (2014). *Juveniles in residential placement, 2011.* Washington, DC: Office of Juvenile Justice and Delinquency Prevention, Office of Justice Programs, U.S. Department of Justice.

Hockenberry, S., & Puzzanchera, C. (2014). *Juvenile court statistics, 2011.* Washington, DC: Office of Juvenile Justice and Delinquency Prevention, Office of Justice Programs, U.S. Department of Justice.

Holman, B., & Ziedenberg, J. (2014). *The dangers of detention: The impact of incarcerating youth in detention and other secure facilities.* Washington, DC: Justice Policy Institute.

Hyman, I. A., & McDowell, E. (1979). *Corporal punishment in American education.* Philadelphia, PA: Temple University Press.

Insley, A. (2001). Suspending and expelling children from educational opportunity: Time to reevaluate zero tolerance policies. *American University Law Review, 50,* 1039–1074.

Jones, V. (1996). Classroom management. In J. Sikula, T. Buttery, & E. Guiton (Eds.), *Handbook of research on teacher education.* New York, NY: Macmillan.

Justice Policy Institute. (2009). *The costs of confinement: Why good juvenile justice policies make good fiscal sense.* Washington, DC: Justice Policy Institute.

Justice Policy Institute. (2011). *Education under arrest: The case against police in schools.* Washington, DC: Justice Policy Institute.

Kang-Brown, J., Trone, J., Fratello, J., & Daftary-Kapur, T. (2013). *A generation later: What we've learned about zero tolerance in schools.* New York, NY: Vera Institute of Justice, Center on Youth Justice.

Klehr, D. G. (2009). Addressing the unintended consequences of No Child Left Behind and zero tolerance: Better strategies for safe schools and successful students. *Georgetown Journal on Poverty, Law, and Policy, 16*, 585–597.

Kozol, J. (2005). *The shame of the nation: The restoration of apartheid schooling in America.* New York, NY: Three Rivers Press.

Krisberg, B. (2005). *Juvenile justice: Redeeming our children.* Thousand Oaks, CA: Sage.

Kupchik, A. (2010). *Homeroom security: School discipline in an age of fear.* New York, NY: New York University Press.

Kupchik, A., & Bracy, N. L. (2009). To protect, serve, and mentor: Police officers in public schools. In T. Monahan & R. D. Torres (Eds.), *Schools under surveillance: Cultures of control in public education* (pp. 21–37). New Brunswick, NJ: Rutgers University Press.

Kupchik, A., & Monahan, T. (2006). The new American school: Preparation for post-industrial discipline. *British Journal of Sociology of Education, 27*, 617–632.

Lawrence, R., & Hemmens, C. (2008). *Juvenile justice: A text reader.* Thousand Oaks, CA: Sage.

Lawrence, R. G. (2007). *School crime and juvenile justice* (2nd ed.). New York, NY: Oxford University Press.

Leachman, M., & Mai, C. (2014). *Most states funding schools less than before the recession.* Washington, DC: Center on Budget and Policy Priorities.

Levy-Pounds, N. (2014). Warehousing, imprisoning, and labelling youth "minorities." In A. J. Nocella II, P. Parmar, & D. Stovall (Eds.), *From education to incarceration: Dismantling the school-to-prison pipeline* (pp. 131–144). New York, NY: Peter Lang.

Losen, D. L., Hewitt, D., & Toldson, I. (2014, March). *Eliminating excessive and unfair discipline in schools: Policy recommendations for reducing disparities.* Discipline disparities series: New Research. Bloomington, IN: The Equity Project at Indiana University. Available at http://rtpcollaborative.indiana.edu/briefing-papers

Loughran, T., Mulvey, E., Schubert, C., Fagan, J., Pizuero, A., & Losoya, S. (2009). Estimating a dose-response relationship between length of stay and future recidivism in serious juvenile offenders. *Criminology, 47*(3), 699–740.

Mallett, C. (2007). Death is not different: The transfer of juvenile offenders to adult criminal courts. *Criminal Law Bulletin, 43*(4), 523–547.

Mallett, C. (2013). *Linking disorders to delinquency: Treating high risk youth in the juvenile justice system.* Boulder, CO: Lynne Rienner.

Mallett, C., & Stoddard-Dare, P. (2010). Predicting secure detention placement for African American juvenile offenders: Addressing the disproportionate minority confinement problem. *Journal of Ethnicity in Criminal Justice, 8*(2), 91–103.

Marsh, S. (2014). *School pathways to juvenile justice system project.* Reno, NV: National Council of Juvenile and Family Court Judges.

Martinez, S. (2009). A system gone berserk: How are zero-tolerance policies really affecting schools? *Preventing School Failure, 53*(3), 153–157.

Martinson, R. (1979). New findings, new views: A note of caution regarding sentencing reform. *Hofstra Law Review, 7,* 243–258.

Marx, G. T. (1981). Ironies of social control: Authorities as contributors to deviance through escalation, nonenforcement and covert facilitation. *Social Problems, 28*(3), 221–246.

Mayer, M. J., & Leone, P. E. (1999). A structural analysis of school violence and disruption: Implications for creating safer schools. *Education and Treatment of Children, 22*(3), 333–356.

McCurdy, J. (2014). Targets for arrest. In A. J. Nocella II, P. Parmar, & D. Stovall (Eds.), *From education to incarceration: Dismantling the school-to-prison pipeline* (pp. 86–101). New York, NY: Peter Lang.

Mendel, R. A. (2012). *No place for kids: The case for reducing juvenile incarceration.* Baltimore, MD: Annie E. Casey Foundation.

Mennel, R. (1973). *Thorns and thistles.* Hanover, NH: University of New Hampshire Press.

Morgan, E., Salomon, N., Plotkin, M., & Cohen, R. (2014). *The school discipline consensus report: Strategies from the field to keep students engaged in school and out of the juvenile justice system.* Washington, DC: Council of State Governments Justice Center.

Muschert, G. W. (2009). Frame-changing in the media coverage of a school shooting: The rise of Columbine as a national concern. *Social Science Journal, 46*(1), 164–170.

Muschert, G. W., Henry, S., Bracy, N. L., & Peguero, A. A. (2014). *Responding to school violence: Confronting the Columbine effect.* Boulder, CO: Lynne Rienner Publishers.

Muschert, G. W., & Peguero, A. A. (2010). The Columbine effect and school anti-violence policy. *Research in Social Problems and Public Policy, 17,* 117–148.

Myner, J., Santman, J., Cappelletty, G., & Perlmutter, B. (1998). Variables related to recidivism among juvenile offenders. *International Journal of Offender Therapy and Comparative Criminology, 42*, 65–80.

NAACP. (2005). *Interrupting the school to prison pipeline.* Washington, DC: Author.

NAACP. (2006). *Arresting development: Addressing the school discipline crisis in Florida.* Florida State Conference NAACP. Washington, DC: Advancement Project.

National Juvenile Justice and Delinquency Prevention Coalition. (2013). *Promoting safe communities.* Washington, DC: National Juvenile Justice and Delinquency Prevention Coalition.

Neiman, S., & DeVoe, J. F. (2009). *Crime, violence, discipline, and safety in US public schools: Findings from the school survey on crime and safety.* Washington, DC: U.S. Department of Education.

Newman, K. (2004). *Rampage: The social roots of school shootings.* New York, NY: Basic Books.

Nichols, S. L., & Berliner, D. C. (2007). *Collateral damage: How high-stakes testing corrupts America's schools.* Cambridge, MA: Harvard Educational Press.

Nolan, K. (2011). *Police in the hallways: Discipline in an urban high school.* Minneapolis: University of Minnesota Press.

Office of Juvenile Justice and Delinquency Prevention. (2014). *OJJDP statistical briefing book.* Washington, DC: Office of Justice Programs, U.S. Department of Justice.

Orfield, G. (2009). *Reviving the goal of an integrated society: A 21st century challenge.* Los Angeles: UCLA Civil Rights Project.

Orfield, G., Kucsera, J., & Siegel-Hawley, G. (2012). *E Pluribus . . . separation: Deepening double segregation for more students.* Los Angeles, CA: UCLA Civil Rights Project.

Palardy, G. (2009). High school socioeconomic segregation and student attainment. *American Educational Research Journal, 50*(4), 714–754.

Petrosino, A., Turpin-Petrosino, C., & Guckenburg, S. (2010). *Formal system processing on juveniles: Effects on delinquency.* Oslo, Norway: Campbell System Reviews.

Petteruti, A. (2011). *"Education under arrest": The case against police in schools.* Washington, DC: Justice Policy Institute.

Platt, M. (1969). *The child savers.* Chicago, IL: University of Chicago Press.

President's Commission on Law Enforcement and Administration of Justice. (1967). *Task force report: Corrections.* Washington, DC: Government Printing Office.

Puzzanchera, C., & Hockenberry, S. (2010). *Juvenile court statistics, 2010.* Pittsburgh, PA: National Center for Juvenile Justice.

Reyes, A. H. (2006). *Discipline, achievement, and race: Is zero tolerance the answer?* Lanham, MD: Rowman and Littlefield.

Rich-Shae, A. M. (2010). Adolescent youth and social control: The changing role of public schools. *Dissertation Abstracts International.* (UMI No. 3427444).

Rich-Shae, A. M., & Fox, J. A. (2014). Zero-tolerance policies. In G. W. Muschert, S. Henry, N. L. Bracy, & A. A. Peguero (Eds.), *Responding to school violence: Confronting the Columbine effect* (pp. 89–104). Boulder, CO: Lynne Rienner.

Robers, S., Zhang, J., & Truman, J. (2012). *Indicators of school crime and safety: 2011.* Washington, DC: National Center for Education Statistics, Institute of Education Services.

Roberts, A. R. (2004). Treating juveniles in institutional and open settings. In A. R. Roberts (Ed.), *Juvenile justice sourcebook: Past, present, and future* (pp. 129–146). New York, NY: Oxford University Press.

Rosiak, J. (2009). *Developing safe schools partnerships with law enforcement.* Washington, DC: National Center for Mental Health Promotion and Youth Violence Prevention.

Ruddy, S. A., Bauer, L., Neiman, S., Hryczaniuk, C. A., Thomas, T. L., & Parmer, R. J. (2010). *2007–08 school survey on crime and safety (SSOCS): Survey documentation for restricted-use data file uses.* Washington, DC: U.S. Department of Education.

Ryan, J. E. (2004). The perverse incentives of the No Child Left Behind Act. *New York University Law Review, 79,* 932–945.

Schwartz, R. G. (2001). Juvenile justice and positive youth development. In P. L. Benson & K. J. Pittman (Eds.), *Trends in youth development: Visions, realities and challenges* (pp. 231–267). Boston, MA: Kluwer Academic.

Scott, E. S., & Grisso, T. (1997). The evolution of adolescence: A developmental perspective on juvenile justice reform. *Journal of Criminal Law & Criminology, 88,* 137–189.

Scott, E. S., & Steinberg, L. (2008). Adolescent development and the regulation of youth crime. *The Future of Children, 18*(2), 16–33.

Sipe, P. (2012). Newjack: Teaching in a failing middle school. In S. Bahena, N. Cooc, R. Currie-Rubin, P. Kuttner, & M. Ng (Eds.), *Disrupting the school-to-prison pipeline* (pp. 32–41). Cambridge, MA: Harvard Educational Review.

Skiba, R. J. (2000). *Zero tolerance, zero evidence: An analysis of school disciplinary practice.* Indiana Education Policy Center, Policy Research Report #SRS2. Bloomington, IN: Indiana University.

Skiba, R. J., Reynolds, C. R., Graham, S., Sheras, P., Conoley, J. C., & Garcia-Vasquez, E. (2006). *Are zero tolerance policies effective in the schools? An evidentiary review and recommendations.* Washington, DC: American Psychological Association Zero Tolerance Task Force.

Sojoyner, D. M. (2014). Changing the lens: Moving away from the school to prison pipeline. In A. J. Nocella II, P. Parmar, & D. Stovall (Eds.), *From education to incarceration: Dismantling the school-to-prison pipeline* (pp. 54–66). New York, NY: Peter Lang.

Soler, M., Shoenberg, D., & Schindler, M. (2009). Juvenile justice: Lessons for a new era [Symposium Issue]. *Georgetown Journal on Poverty Law and Policy, 16,* 483–541.

Steeves, V., & Marx, G. T. (2014). Safe schools initiatives and the shifting climate of trust. In G. W. Muschert, S. Henry, N. L. Bracy, & A. A. Peguero (Eds.), *Responding to school violence: Confronting the Columbine effect* (pp. 105–124). Boulder, CO: Lynne Rienner.

Theriot, M. T. (2009). School resource officers and the criminalization of student behavior. *Journal of Criminal Justice, 37,* 280–287.

Thurau, L., & Wald, J. (2010). Controlling partners: When law enforcement meets discipline in public schools. *New York Law School Law Review, 54,* 977–1020.

Toldson, I. A. (2011). *Breaking barriers 2: Plotting the path away from juvenile detention and toward academic success for school-age African American males.* Washington, DC: Congressional Black Caucus Foundation, Inc., Center for Policy Analysis and Research.

U.S. Department of Education. (2013). *Back to school statistics.* Washington, DC: National Center for Education Statistics, Institute of Education Services.

U.S. Department of Education. (2014a). *Appendix 1: U.S. Department of Education: Director of Federal School Climate and Discipline Resources.* Washington, DC: Author.

U.S. Department of Education. (2014b). *Indicators of school crime and safety, 2014.* Washington, DC: National Center for Education Statistics, Institute of Education Services.

U.S. Department of Justice. (2012). *Disproportionate minority contact technical assistance manual* (4th ed.). Washington, DC: Office of Juvenile Justice and Delinquency Prevention, Office of Justice Programs, U.S. Department of Justice.

U.S. Department of Justice. (2014). *OJJDP statistical briefing book*. Washington, DC: Office of Juvenile Justice and Delinquency Prevention, Office of Justice Programs, U.S. Department of Justice.

Verdugo, R. R. (2002). Race-ethnicity, social class, and zero-tolerance policies: The cultural and structural wars. *Education and Urban Society, 35*(1), 50–75.

Walker, S., Spohn, C., & DeLone, M. (2012). *The color of justice: Race, ethnicity and crime in America* (6th ed.). Belmont, CA: Wadsworth.

Welch, M., Price, E. A., & Yankey, N. (2002). Moral panic over youth violence: Wilding and the manufacture of menace in the media. *Youth and Society, 34*(1), 3–30.

Winokur, K. P., Smith, A., Bontrager, S. R., & Blankenship, J. L. (2008). Juvenile recidivism and length of stay. *Journal of Criminal Justice, 36*, 126–137.

Chapter 3: Punishment Pathways Exacerbate the Problems

The schools' reactionary movement into zero-tolerance policies and the juvenile courts' regressive tough-on-crime approach over the past 20 years have drawn millions of at-risk children and adolescents into a punitive paradigm quagmire. These policies were established, as many policies are, without solid empirical support (Marx, 1981), and today, children and adolescents impacted by them are experiencing many unintended consequences. However, the population of young people captured within the punitive paradigms, as well as the narrower school-to-prison pipeline, often were already facing difficulties or obstacles within their families, schools, or communities (Mallett, 2013). Once these at-risk children and adolescents become formally involved with either the school disciplinary system or the local juvenile courts, outcomes are often harmful. In fact, once the disciplinary systems are triggered for a student or youthful offender, the risks for continued involvement are significantly exacerbated (Petrosino, Turpin-Petrosino, & Guckenburg, 2010).

STUDENTS IN THE SCHOOL-TO-PRISON PIPELINE

From the Classroom to the Courtroom

Students disciplined through zero-tolerance policies are often first-time offenders for nonviolent incidents. Nonetheless, these children and adolescents are placed at a higher risk of escalating disciplinary policies, including suspensions and expulsions (Kang-Brown, Trone, Fratello, & Daftary-Kapur, 2013; Skiba, 2000). It is quite clear that students who are suspended from school have a significantly greater chance of becoming involved with the juvenile justice system, even though a majority of these suspensions are due to disobedience or minor infractions of school discipline protocols (U.S. Department of Education, 2014). Longitudinal research validates much of what has been anecdotally identified and hypothesized (Fabelo et al., 2011)—that these suspensions are often a result of inflexible zero-tolerance policies, a belief in the discipline philosophy, and school resource officers' presence (Advancement Project et al., 2011). Case examples of students captured within the pipeline highlight what the more rigorous data-driven methodology has been attempting to identify for the past decade:

> A 17-year-old high school junior shot a paper clip with a rubber band at a classmate, missed, and broke the skin of a cafeteria worker. The student was expelled from school. (Heitzeg, 2014, p. 21)

> An 11-year-old girl in Orlando, Florida, was Tasered by a police officer, arrested, and faced charges of battery on a security resource officer, disrupting a school function, and resisting with violence. She had pushed another student. (Heitzeg, 2014, p. 22)

> A 14-year-old girl was arrested and charged with battery for pouring a carton of chocolate milk on the head of a classmate. The girl explained that she heard that the victim was "talking about her." Local police state that they believed "the quickest way to resolve it was to charge her." (Advancement Project, 2005, p. 13)

> A ten-year old honor roll student was expelled in 1998 when she accidently brought her mother's lunch box to school and obediently reported to her teacher that it contained a paring knife. (Insley, 2001, p. 1040)

> A 14-year-old girl was arrested in school in Wauwatosa, Wisconsin, after refusing to stop texting on her cell phone in class. A school resource officer's report says that student refused to stop texting during class after a teacher told her

to stop and the student told the resource officer she didn't have a phone after she was pulled out of the classroom . . . The officer noted that the student is "known to me and the administration based on prior negative contacts" . . . after the arrest, the student was suspended for a week. (McCurdy, 2014, pp. 93–94)

A 16-year-old transgender student attending Hercules High School in California, who claimed that fellow students bullied her for years, was recently charged with misdemeanour battery after getting into a schoolyard fight. Despite video footage capturing the altercation between the girl and three other teenagers, she was the only student to be criminally charged. The other three students involved only received out-of-school suspensions. (Mitchum & Moodie-Mills, 2014, p. 18)

A high school student was arrested and charged with second degree breach of peace for a shouting argument with his girlfriend. Bridgeport students and parents protested the over-reliance on law enforcement in schools after 140 students were arrested during the first six weeks of the 2004–2005 school year. (Advancement Project, 2005, p. 13)

These students, as well as thousands of others, are neither posing serious risks to the student body nor posing safety concerns for the schools they attend. However, within today's punitive paradigm, mitigating circumstances are not necessarily part of the investigation or punishment decision. Counterintuitively, some education researchers have found that students who misbehave and are the targets of discretionary zero-tolerance policies do well academically; they also found that the policy prescriptions themselves may lead to school disengagement by the child or adolescent (Hoffman, Erickson, & Spence, 2013). Being disengaged or removed from school is a significant risk factor for poor peer choices, and for some, delinquent behaviors (Mallett, 2013; Skiba et al., 2006).

Involvement in school discipline procedures and corresponding suspensions or expulsions not only impact students in some obvious ways—missing instructional time and opportunities to learn, falling behind academically, and forming negative attitudes or perceptions concerning schools and the school personnel—but also greatly increase the risk for grade retention, which is particularly harmful for middle and high school students (Jimerson, Anderson, & Whipple, 2002; Skiba, Arrendonda, & Rausch, 2014). Just one suspension in the ninth grade has been found to double the risk for failing subsequent academic courses in high school (Balfanz, Byrnes, & Fox, 2015; Kirk & Sampson, 2013), also increasing the risk of dropping out of school by 20% (Marchbanks et al., 2015). Being retained in grade level significantly increases the risk of dropping out of high school (Kang-Brown et al., 2013). The risk of dropping out of high school is also doubled if a young person is arrested either on or off schools grounds, and it is four times greater if the young person is formally involved with the juvenile courts (Gagnon & Leone, 2002; Sweeten, 2006). Juvenile justice system involvement reinforces the school-to-prison pipeline because the young people who are supervised by the courts have an increased risk for being held in detention, for being incarcerated, and for recidivism to placement (Petrosino et al., 2010).

Targets for Arrest

School punishments are not equitably distributed across most schools, because low-income students and children and adolescents of color (among other student groups) are much more likely to be punished in school than others (McNulty-Eitle & Eitle, 2004; Skiba, Michael, Nardo, & Peterson, 2000). In 2012, the U.S. Department of Education identified that in school districts with more than 50,000 students, African American students represented 24% of enrollment but 35% of on-campus arrests, with lower, but still disparate rates for Hispanic students (McCurdy, 2014). Even after controlling for other explanations—misbehavior, academic performance, attitudes, parental attention, school characteristics, and socioeconomic status—this disparity was found to be most likely a result of unfair targeting of the students (Carter, 2005; Kupchik, 2010; Payne & Welch, 2010; Equity Project, 2014).

Students of color in schools that have higher proportions of African American students are more likely to receive punitive and not rehabilitative discipline responses from the school, even after controlling for other possible reasons—socioeconomic status, delinquency rates, gender, staff training, and urbanicity (Addington, 2014; Majd, 2011; Skiba & Williams, 2014). These disparity arrest and punishment rates correlate to the increased police presence in schools, with some finding the power of the school resource officers becoming greater than that of the teachers and administrators of the school, thus criminalizing more student problems (Stinchcomb, Bazemore, & Riestenberg, 2006). Thus, since a vast majority of students are punished under zero-tolerance policies because of discretionary offenses, negative perceptions or worries by the school and police personnel increase their risk for trouble through minor misbehaviors. This often exacerbates the disadvantages faced by impoverished students and students of color, entangling them within the pipeline (Kupchik, 2010; Payne & Welch, 2010). In addition, longitudinal reviews have found that suspensions from school tend to precede serious delinquency for African American and Latino students, and that delinquent behaviors are often triggered by academic disengagement (Center for Civil Rights Remedies, 2013).

Evidence is strong that students with special education disabilities are similarly targeted for school discipline problems and that racial disparity exists across special education student populations as well (Rivkin, 2010). Students of color have been disproportionately found in the diagnosis of certain special education categories: mental retardation and severe emotional disturbances (Harry & Klinger, 2006; Smith & Erevelles, 2004), thus causing many to conclude that referral bias from school personnel is a causal factor (Adams & Meiners, 2014). A student with any special education disability is almost three times more likely to receive an out-of-school suspension (20%) compared with those without a disability (7%), with the most common disability types for suspended students being learning disabilities and severe emotional disturbances (Fabelo et al., 2011; Kang-Brown et al., 2013).

These increased school discipline policies have, based on more recent data collection, directly or indirectly targeted a disproportionate number of lesbian, gay, bisexual, and transgender (LGBT) students. LGBT students are almost three times more likely to experience harsh disciplinary treatment than their non-LGBT peers, even though misbehavior and disobedience to rules among these two groups are not significantly different (Himmelstein & Bruckner, 2011). The LGBT students are often pushed out of the classroom environment because of a hostile school climate, which includes bullying, verbal abuse, and threats, among other behaviors (Majd, Marksamer, & Reyes, 2009; Mitchum & Moodie-Mills, 2014).

As discussed, harsh and inflexible discipline on the basis of zero-tolerance policies does not incorporate mitigating information, historical context, or other family or student factors in determining the decisions of the school administration or school resource officers. These decisions are, for most incidents, predetermined, and for many disadvantaged and at-risk students, they only make their school experiences and chances for graduation more difficult. These at-risk students already face challenges in their daily academic efforts. Becoming targets of indiscriminate policies only complicates these young people's lives. As will be reviewed later, these young people have significant risks for becoming involved in the juvenile justice system, but the one-way disciplinary pipeline only heightens these students' chances for being formally involved with the juvenile courts. Fortunately, most of these discipline policies and disparities are because of differences in school policy, school leadership, and other factors that are under the control of educators and policy makers (Fabelo et al., 2011).

Delinquency Adjudication

Juvenile courts receive many referrals for young people because of criminal behaviors, status offenses, and family problems or violence, among other reasons. From more than two million arrests of young people annually, a near majority become formally involved and, thus, are adjudicated delinquent by juvenile courts nationwide (Majd, 2011; Puzzanchera & Robson, 2014). Delinquency adjudication is an official court order providing legal control over a child or adolescent, often leading to the assignment of a probation officer and ongoing supervision (Mallett, 2013). However, as reviewed, most of the school referrals and arrests that are brought to the juvenile courts are for minor offenses, misdemeanors such as disobedience (talking back to teachers or administrators), disturbing the peace, or fighting (aggravated battery), thus allowing adolescent misbehaviors and disruptions to be criminally prosecuted (Advancement Project, 2005). Within the zero-tolerance policy movement, today, 14 states have laws that criminalize "disturbing schools," a vague term that allows for the prosecution of many forms of misbehavior and disobedience by students (Majd, 2011).

Once young people are adjudicated delinquent and come under formal supervision, they are court ordered to perform certain activities, refrain from other activities or ongoing negative choices, or change certain outcomes. These court orders often set up the adolescent for failure because of resistance to ongoing supervision, the inability to meet the court-order expectations, or other intervening or confounding problems (Sulok, 2007). For example, if a student has a truancy history and triggers the school disciplinary system for a referral to the local juvenile court, then the young person is often court ordered to attend school. This does little to address any underlying or mitigating reason as to why the young person is not attending school; it simply states that the student must do so. These acts of truancy could be because the student is a target of severe bullying based on sexual orientation, or they may be because the parents in the home are substance users, thus providing little to no structure or incentive for the student to attend school regularly.

Under these circumstances, the juvenile court may never discover the reasons for the lack of school attendance only the fact that the outcome is still truancy. Thus, the court personnel may find the young person in violation of the court order, a potentially serious problem. Under the current federal and state policy, local courts are allowed to detain or incarcerate a young person solely for violation of a court order—a technical violation not adhering to a judge's order, not a criminal violation or a new offense (National Center for Youth Law, 2008). This punitive juvenile court response of acting on a technical violation—not following a court order—accounts for more than 35% of the youthful offenders held in detention and for 16% of those offenders incarcerated in juvenile facilities (Mendel, 2012; Puzzanchera, 2011).

DETAINED AND INCARCERATED YOUTHFUL OFFENDERS

Almost all young people who end up in the nation's detention and incarceration facilities have troubled lives. Their difficulties span across a range of life experiences that occur within the families, neighborhoods, communities, and schools, and they are directly linked to offending behaviors and delinquency (Hawkins et al., 2000). These experiences place many of these children and adolescents on the pathway to detention and incarceration. The profile of youthful offenders in juvenile detention and incarceration facilities tells us much about how they ended up in these locked facilities: disproportionately poor youth of color, traumatic and maltreated childhoods, school difficulties, mental health problems, and special education disabilities. The disproportionate, and often comorbid, impact of these problems for this institutionalized population is extreme when compared with that for their noninstitutionalized and nondelinquent peers.

Most children and adolescents neither suffer from nor experience maltreatment victimizations, violent traumas, special education disabilities, or mental health problems. If a child or adolescent experiences one of these difficulties, it is most often a singular experience (Mallett, 2013). Only a small percentage (less than 1%) of this population will be victims of maltreatment, have a learning disability (3%–4%), be diagnosed with a serious mental health disorder (5%–9%), or have an active substance abuse problem (4%–5%) (New Freedom Commission on Mental Health, 2003; Substance Abuse and Mental Health Services Administration, 2013a, 2013b; U.S. Department of Education, 2014; U.S. Department of

TABLE 3.1 Maltreatment, Education Disabilities,
and Mental Health Disorders

Problem Area	Detained/Incarcerated Youthful Offender Population	Adolescent Population
Maltreatment victimization	26–60	1
Special education disabilities (learning disabilities and severe emotional disturbances)	28–45	4–6
Serious mental health disorders (including substance abuse)	25–70	3–9

Health and Human Services, 2013). However, reviews of detained and incarcerated youthful offenders have found significantly higher incidences of these experiences within this population—from 2 (some mental health disorders) to as many as 60 times (see Table 3.1) the rates found in the child and adolescent population (Abram et al., 2013; Langrehr, 2011; Leone & Weinberg, 2010; Sedlak & McPherson, 2010; Teplin, Abram, Washburn, Welty, Hershfield, & Dulcan, 2013).

Maltreatment victimization rates indicate the substantiated cases of abuse and neglect as reported by the U.S. Department of Health and Human Services; learning disabilities and severe emotional disturbances are found in the identified students who are under an individualized education plan as directed by the Individuals with Disabilities Education Act (U.S. Department of Education, 2014); and mental health/substance abuse disorders are diagnosed psychiatric problems as defined by the *Diagnostic and Statistical Manual of Mental Disorders* (American Psychiatric Association, 2013). These problems and difficulties are much more common in the serious youthful offender population; this could be compared with the adolescent population (ages 12–17) in the United States, where significantly lower rates are found across all problem and difficulty areas.

Adolescents held in detention and incarceration facilities are at risk of developing and continuing these patterns into adulthood, even if their initial placement in these facilities was not for serious offenses (Dodge, Dishion, & Landsford, 2006; Howell, 2003). As is evident from the detained and incarcerated youthful offender population, this group is disproportionately impacted by maltreatment and related trauma, mental health problems, and learning/academic disabilities. For many, these difficulties are part of the explanation for why these young people become formally involved with the juvenile courts.

Maltreatment/Trauma

Children and adolescents who have been maltreated or who have experienced related traumas are more likely to engage in delinquent activities and offending behaviors, compared with children and adolescents without a maltreatment history (Loeber & Farrington, 2001; Verrecchia, Fetzer, Lemmon, & Austin, 2010; Yun, Ball, & Lim, 2011). Due to the significant differences in outcomes of offending acts (e.g., arrest, conviction, delinquency adjudication), including whether official records or youthful offender self-reports were used, the link between maltreatment and delinquency may be underestimated (Maxfield, Weiler, & Widom, 2000). There is significant empirical support recognizing the strong link between trauma, subsequent mental health difficulties, and involvement with the juvenile justice system detention and incarceration facilities (Abram et al., 2013; Hooks, 2012).

All maltreatment types—physical abuse, sexual abuse, and neglect—have been linked to later antisocial behavior, violent crimes, and court involvement (Grogan-Kaylor, Ruffolo, Ortega, & Clarke, 2008; Lemmon, 2009; Yun et al., 2011), even in the presence of other risk factors (Loeber & Farrington, 2001; Widom & Maxfield, 2001). Research is clear that repeated maltreatment, no matter the type, has a key impact on youthful offending behavior (Arata, Langhinrichsen-Rohling, Bowers, & O'Brien, 2007). Such repeat victimization predicts the initiation, continuation, and severity of delinquent acts, and it is associated with serious, chronic, and violent offending behaviors (Hamilton, Falshaw, & Browne, 2002; Smith & Thornberry, 1995).

Learning Disabilities

Children at risk for academic failure in elementary school often have unidentified learning problems; those who fail are at increased risk for later offending behaviors (Hawkins et al., 2000). It is speculated that adolescents with unidentified learning disabilities are disproportionately represented among those who are suspended, expelled, and/or drop out of high school (Keleher, 2000). These out-of-school outcomes are risk factors for delinquent and criminal activities, often serious offending (Advancement Project, 2005; Sum, Khatiwada, McLaughlin, & Palma, 2009).

However, even for those adolescents who have been identified with learning disabilities, the risk for delinquency is higher (Mears & Aron, 2003). Adolescents with learning disabilities compared with those adolescents without such learning disabilities have two to three times greater risk of being involved in offending activities, as well as higher offending recidivism rates, though the explanations for this disparity are multifactored (Matta-Oshima, Huang, Jonson-Reid, & Drake, 2010; Wang, Blomberg, & Li, 2005).

Mental Health and Substance Abuse Disorders

Mental health problems and disorders are linked to youthful offending behaviors and delinquency, though it is not clear whether this link is direct or whether these difficulties lead to other risk factors, poor decision making, or the interaction of various other risks (Grisso, 2008; Schubert & Mulvey, 2014; Shufelt & Cocozza, 2006). Still, reviews have consistently found that children and adolescents who are involved with mental health services have a significantly higher risk for later juvenile court involvement (Rosenblatt, Rosenblatt, & Biggs, 2000; Vander-Stoep, Evans, & Taub, 1997). Those young people with both behavioral disorders and substance use disorders are particularly at risk for both delinquency and not completing high school (Chassin, Flora, & King, 2004; Schubert & Mulvey, 2014).

In reviews that investigated the link from specific childhood mental health difficulties to juvenile court involvement, a number of pathways have been established. Developmental studies have found behavioral and emotional problems to be predictive of later delinquency and substance abuse (Hawkins et al., 2000). Early childhood aggressive behaviors have been found to be predictive of later delinquent behaviors and activities, and attention and hyperactivity problems have been found to be linked to later high-risk taking and more violent offending behavior (Grisso, 2008). In addition, childhood depression and attention deficit hyperactivity disorder have been found to be linked to later delinquency, evidenced through physical aggression and stealing behaviors (Wasserman et al., 2003).

For adolescents who are detained or incarcerated, a number of pathways from earlier mental health problems or demographic profiles have been identified. Adolescent mental health and delinquent populations were found to be at higher risk for detention or incarceration with a diagnosis of alcohol problems or conduct disorder in middle school, reported use and abuse of substances, and being African American or Hispanic—a potential tie-in with the disproportionate minority confinement problem (Scott, Snowden, & Libby, 2002). These two populations, adolescents with mental health problems and those involved in the juvenile justice system institutions, often differ little, and many spend time across both service delivery systems (Chayt, 2012; Teplin et al., 2006;

Teplin et al., 2013). Today's juvenile detention and correctional facilities have become the default mental health treatment centers or hospitals for many young people with psychological and/or behavioral disorders (Boesky, 2002; Hooks, 2012). A case in point was a 2003 Government Accountability Office study that found that more than 12,700 families relinquished custody of their children to gain necessary mental health service for them, with 9,000 of these custody outcomes to the juvenile justice system (Koppelman, 2005).

Comorbidity

One of the common themes and risks identified across many of these difficulties is poverty. Zero-tolerance policies are found throughout the nation's schools, whereas higher security measures, more strict punitive policies, and a stronger school-to-prison pipeline have been found in larger, urban schools with student populations that are often disproportionately poor and of color (Justice Policy Institute, 2011; Losen, 2012). However, poverty, with its powerful impact, is an interactive problem, acting as a causative, intervening, and/or explanatory variable, depending on the research focus. In fact, poverty is increasingly found not to be an explanation for why students are disproportionately found in the school-to-prison pipeline. The answer is more complicated, but the explanatory reasons are the school environments, teachers, administrators, and school resource officers (Equity Project, 2014; Skiba & Williams, 2014).

Poverty impacts young people in many ways, increasing risks for numerous problematic and nefarious outcomes. Children and adolescents who grow up in low-income families are more likely to be retained or held back a grade level in school (Bradley & Corwyn, 2002); not graduate from high school (Brooks-Gunn & Duncan, 1997; Wald & Martinez, 2003); to have both internalizing (i.e., depression and anxiety) and externalizing (i.e., conduct disorder) behavior problems (Koball et al., 2011; Moore & Redd, 2002); to develop learning disabilities (Mears & Aron, 2003); and to engage in delinquent activities (Hawkins et al., 2000; Loeber & Farrington, 1998).

These adolescent difficulties also become more complex and more difficult to unravel because of frequent comorbidities. Court-involved adolescents often have multiple disabilities and/or disorders occurring both over time and at the same time, a situation that may greatly compound the negative outcomes (Dembo, Wareham, Poythress, Meyers, & Schmeidler, 2008). The comorbidity conundrum is not only an underinvestigated phenomenon but also one that may strongly affect the school-to-prison pipeline as well as youthful offender behaviors.

When such comorbid phenomena have been studied, difficult and complicated adolescent and family problems have been identified. In one investigation of delinquent youthful offenders, it was found that 32% had a special education disability; 39% had a diagnosed mental health disorder; 32% had an active substance abuse problem; 56% had been victims of maltreatment; and more than 40% had two or more of these problems, with higher comorbid prevalence rates found for those who were detained or incarcerated (Mallett, 2009). In a similar review of a jurisdiction's mental health system and juvenile court, 20% of adolescents receiving mental health services had a recent arrest record, whereas 30% of adolescents who were arrested received mental health services (Rosenblatt et al., 2000). In one study of the mental health problems of adolescents who were transferred from the juvenile to the criminal courts in Chicago, more than 43% of the youthful offenders had two or more psychiatric diagnoses (Washburn et al., 2008). Similarly, a review of youthful offenders who stayed in the juvenile courts found that 79% of adolescents with one mental health disorder also met criteria for a second disorder (Shufelt & Cocozza, 2006), and when this population has co-occurring behavioral and emotional problems they are at a higher risk for committing violent offenses (Hoeve, McReynolds, & Wasserman, 2013).

Of significant concern are the adolescents who are seriously emotionally disturbed, identified with multiple mental health disorders and related problems that continue into adulthood. This group almost always has contact with the juvenile justice system, represents up to 20% of youthful offenders within incarceration facilities, and continues to have offending problems and eventual involvement with the criminal courts (Cocozza & Skowyra, 2000). It is estimated that one of every ten adolescents who are seriously emotionally disturbed has both an impairing mental health disorder and an active substance abuse problem: a dual diagnosis, which is particularly difficult to address in treatment (Chassin, 2008).

Failure of Early Screening and Assessment

This population of adolescents who end up in the juvenile justice detention and incarceration facilities, many funneled through the school-to-prison pipeline, are disadvantaged at best and traumatized, severely disabled, and serious offenders at worst. The correctional institutions have become the placement of last resort across most of the youth-caring systems, used by schools, mental health providers, and the police because so few alternative or rehabilitative options exist when these young people run up against the punitive paradigm. This paradigm pervades many of the systems and, as reviewed, becomes a pathway moving vulnerable children and adolescents toward fairly bleak outcomes. Often, at the front end of these outcomes is the failure to correctly or accurately identify the early risks, a dearth of screenings and assessments used during the children and adolescents' youth-caring systems involvement, and/or the utilization of inappropriate or empirically unsound assessment tools (Baird et al., 2013; National Council on Crime and Delinquency, 2014).

These assessments are important and identify problems and risk factors of children and adolescents' school and home lives. School systems are required by federal law (IDEA; 34 C.F.R. § 300.8(a)(1)) to assess all students believed to have a possible special education disability—the "child find obligation" (34 C.F.R. § 300.111). However, these reviews have been found to be problematic for a number of reasons: inaccurate assessment and outcome; accurate assessment but, as already noted, students with special education disabilities are at higher risk for disciplined and pipeline involvement; and not identifying related or compounding factors that are impacting the students' academic or behavioral problems (Mallett, 2011; Mears & Aron, 2003). Knowing that most of the young people caught within the pipeline and those who end up in juvenile justice institutions have multiple risks and disabilities, it would be imperative for the schools and juvenile justice system personnel to improve early identification and prevention efforts to minimize further penetration of the students into disciplinary actions (Washington State Institute for Public Policy, 2007). These disciplinary paradigms disproportionately impact certain students, and with the comorbidity across certain risk factors and outcomes, it should be possible to more sensibly and accurately identify many of these young people before they enter the school-to-prison pipeline and, for some, are suspended or expelled.

Although significant empirically supported screening and assessment instruments are available, which can help inform decisions by school (teachers, counselors, administrators) and juvenile court personnel (intake workers, probation officers, magistrates, judges), a less coherent and haphazard decision process is all too often the norm in determining the balance of a students' dangerousness, blameworthiness, and likely future behavior (Mulvey & Iselin, 2008). Often, school systems and juvenile courts make uninformed decisions based on zero-tolerance policies and traditions, without a serious use of actuarial or screening instruments (National Council on Crime and Delinquency, 2014).

Within the schools and many juvenile court institutions, there is limited utilization of standardized instruments that can screen for these risks. However, screening, as opposed to assessment, is a brief process used by professionals, or even nonprofessionals, to identify problems that are in need of further assessment—they are timely and relatively inexpensive (Grisso, Barnum, Fletcher, Cauffman, & Peuschold, 2001). Knowing that most students involved in disciplinary actions have troubles related to mental health, family dysfunction, trauma, and academic difficulties, it is possible to identify many of those at risk through these screenings (Rapp-Palicchi & Roberts, 2004).

Rehabilitative Alternatives Are Not the Norm

A majority of juvenile justice detention and incarceration facilities use punitive approaches; however, recognition is growing that a rehabilitative environment better achieves important public policy goals of decreasing youth recidivism and, subsequently, increasing community safety (U.S. Department of Justice, 2014). There is evidence that incarceration facilities that identify youthful offender problems and provide disability treatment services and quality education programs can have a significant impact on decreasing re-offending outcomes (Garrido & Morales, 2007; Holman & Ziedenberg, 2014). However, a majority of serious youthful offenders across the nation are still in large training schools, facilities with low-quality education, and rehabilitative alternatives (Hockenberry & Puzzanchera, 2014). As discussed, such facilities generally provide little to no rehabilitative care for these adolescents with disabilities, often do not meet the education or special education needs of the youthful offender, and can be overcrowded and unsafe environments (Sedlak & McPherson, 2010).

Many of the tens of thousands of adolescents who remain every day in detention and incarceration facilities have become the most difficult to rehabilitate, because their problems remain the most complex. Most jurisdictions have not made progress, and their institutions continue to have a punitive focus, whereas those that have decreased their institutionalized offender populations face some daunting issues. For those young men and women still confined in these facilities, many have long histories of multiple mental health disorders and related difficulties, often substance abuse and trauma that continue into young adulthood (MacArthur Foundation, 2012). For the students that are both intentionally and unintentionally caught within the school-to-prison pipeline, these institutionalized placements are harmful for many reasons (Dodge et al., 2006). Considering that a majority of students who end up within the pipeline do so because of low-level or status offenses (Advancement Project, 2005), these outcomes are unduly and unreasonably harsh. For most adolescents, these discipline outcomes are life changing and harmful.

DISCIPLINE OUTCOMES ARE HARMFUL AND DANGEROUS

Adolescent Development

Ongoing research has clearly delineated that adolescents are different from young adults across most developmental pathways—biology, cognition, emotion, and interpersonal relationships (Scott & Steinberg, 2008). Adolescents' decision making is limited in scope and is impacted by immaturity, impulsivity, and an underdeveloped ability to appreciate consequences (Giedd, 2004; Somerville & Casey, 2010; Steinberg, Dahl, Keating, Kupfer, & Masten, 2006). Although older adolescents are capable of adult cognitive capacities, their ability to use these decision-making steps is not fully applicable due to their lack of life experiences. An inhibiting factor is adolescents' focus on the present and less ability to have a future orientation, having a limited appreciation of the long-term consequences of decision making (Greene, 1986).

In addition, adolescents are vulnerable to external coercion and peer pressure, due to their unformed character development (Scott & Steinberg, 2008). These peer influences often peak at the age of 14 and decline into young adulthood, and they are particularly influential in group situations (Moffitt, 1993). This influence, along with adolescents' increased risk taking that often includes the minimizing of the risk and the overinflation of rewards, leads many to make poor decisions in schools, neighborhoods, and communities. Resisting peer pressure can have many negative and ostracizing outcomes for young people (Fagan, 2000; Steinberg, 2007). So in many ways, policies that are focused on discipline outcomes, including, for example, school expulsions for ongoing attendance problems and truancy and harsh sentencing for criminal or delinquent activity, may have little to no deterrent effect on adolescents (Mallett, 2013). Of note, researchers have consistently found that most adolescents involved in school discipline problems or delinquent activities will actually grow out of these antisocial tendencies as their character develops and they become young adults (Piquero, Farrington, & Blumstein, 2003).

These diminished capacities have been recognized in numerous Supreme Court decisions over the past decade finding adolescence itself a mitigating factor in harsh sentencing decisions. These court decisions have ended some of the harshest sentences for youthful offenders, including the death penalty and mandatory life imprisonment without parole, finding them to violate the Eighth Amendment's cruel and unusual punishment clause (*Graham v. Florida*, 130 S. Ct. 2011, 2030, 2010; *Miller v. Alabama*, 132 S. Ct. 2455, 2012; *Roper v. Simmons*, 543 U.S. 441, 2005).

Nonetheless, certain student groups and at-risk adolescents are disciplined early in their development during middle and early high school, thus escalating disproportionate risks for ongoing punitive outcomes, including, for some, formal juvenile court involvement. Initial involvement in the pipeline, particularly at earlier ages, poses great risk for students. Being suspended as a freshman in high school doubles the risk for school dropout, with more than one-third of males, disproportionately African American, who are suspended for more than 10 days ultimately sentenced to a juvenile correctional facility (Shollenberg, 2015). In addition, suspension or expulsion for a discretionary school violation makes juvenile court involvement almost three times more likely (Fabelo et al., 2011). The delinquent activities for these young people always followed their first suspension, showing a clear correlative connection within the pipeline (Equity Project, 2014).

Many times, alternative education schools are utilized as placements for children and adolescents who are at risk for school problems, failure, or disciplinary concerns. These are not positive solutions for many students and may exacerbate the problems. In one review of elementary school students in an alternative school, more than half were placed in the local juvenile detention within 4 years, with more than 40% of middle-school students in an alternative school placed in the detention center within 2 years, disproportionately African American students (Vanderhaar, Petrosko, & Munoz, 2015). These racial disparities are found across many alternative schools, and their suspended student populations mirror the disparity within the juvenile court referrals, even after controlling for other possible explanations (Nicholson-Crotty, Birchmeier, & Valentine, 2009).

In addition, a first-time arrest during high school, with many such arrests originating on school grounds, makes dropping out of school nearly twice as likely (Kaba & Edwards, 2011). If the arrest is followed by formal juvenile court involvement and a court appearance, this student drop-out risk is four times more likely (Sweeten, 2006). Ultimately, when a student drops out of high school, the risk of lifetime incarceration increases more than threefold (Martin & Halperin, 2006). Even without an adult incarceration experience, formal juvenile delinquency adjudication may impede young adults from accessing student loans, being accepted for military service, or receiving public or subsidized housing (Pinard, 2006).

Mental Health

Many adolescents struggle with the transition into young adulthood, a time of stress and problematic outcomes for those involved in the school and juvenile court discipline pathways, as well as for those who are at risk for involvement (Arnett, 2000). The adolescents who are the most at risk for poor adult outcomes are those with mental health problems and those who had contact with one of the youth-caring systems—juvenile courts, mental health, and/or child welfare (U.S. Department of Health and Human Services, 2009). A significant majority of mental health problems have an onset before age 20, with many beginning during middle adolescence, and diagnoses of serious mental health disorders are found to be the most prevalent during later adolescence (Substance Abuse and Mental Health Services Administration, 2013b). These trends and prevalence rates are similar for young people struggling with substance use or abuse problems (Substance Abuse and Mental Health Services Administration, 2013b), with serious comorbidity problems across diagnoses making treatment and rehabilitation particularly difficult for the mental health system, schools, and, by default, the juvenile courts (Holman & Ziedenberg, 2014; Zajac, Sheidow, & Davis, 2013).

Juvenile Detention and Incarceration

When young people become involved with and progress through the juvenile justice system, detention and incarceration are the outcome for many. As discussed, a majority of these institutionalized youthful offenders have a multitude of problems, often comorbid, across mental health, educational, and trauma difficulties (Mallett, 2013; Teplin et al., 2006). However, these detention and incarceration placements have almost no rehabilitative value, and for most adolescents, the experiences increase their difficulties and risks for recidivism. The reasons are varied, but they are the result of the institutions' punitive paradigm.

While incarcerated, many of these adolescents do not receive services that may assist in mitigating the prior offending behavior; thus, they are not provided with rehabilitative programming for mental health, education, or trauma difficulties that may be warranted, thus often exacerbating the problems (Holman & Ziedenberg, 2014). Most incarceration facilities are not equipped to meet even the minimal rehabilitative needs of the adolescents placed within the institution, let alone youthful offenders with serious comorbid mental health problems, trauma-related disabilities, and/or special education disabilities (Annie E. Casey Foundation, 2012). Almost two-thirds of youthful offenders released from juvenile justice facilities end up dropping out of high school, with a disproportionate impact on those with special education disabilities (Feierman, Levick, & Mody, 2010).

Juvenile incarceration also lessens adolescents' abilities to function independently because of the rigid expectations of the justice facility, and social and coping skills are diminished for similar reasons—particularly for those adolescents held in isolation or solitary confinement (American Civil Liberties Union, 2013; Dmitrieva, Monahan, Cauffman, & Steinberg 2012). Many education systems within state incarceration facilities receive failing grades, do not address gaps in the adolescents' school abilities, and do not provide appropriate services for those with learning disabilities (Balfanz, Spiridakis, Neild, & Legters, 2003; Sedlak & McPherson, 2010). Incarceration facilities separate the adolescents from their families and are often dangerous and violent environments—factors in poor young adult outcomes (Mears & Aron, 2003; U.S. Department of Justice, 2012). Thus, over time, once released from juvenile facilities, these youthful offenders have ongoing difficulties as they age, including unemployment or underemployment; poor marital outcomes; adult criminal records; drug additions; increased suicide risk; and involvement as adults in the child welfare system, often leading to abuse or neglect charges (Giordano, Cernkovich, & Lowery, 2004; Giordano, Cernkovich, & Rudolph, 2002; Lewis, Yeager, Cobham-Portorreal, Klein, Showalter, & Anthony 1991; Lewis, Yeager, Lovely, Stein, & Cobham-Portorreal, 1994).

Criminal Justice

There are also problems within the adult incarceration facilities for the tens of thousands of adolescents transferred annually to the criminal justice system. Youthful offenders found in the adult criminal justice facilities are more likely to engage in future violence when compared with similarly situated offenders in the juvenile justice system (Mulvey & Shubert, 2012). In addition, those young people in adult prisons are more likely to be physically and sexually abused, and to commit suicide (Centers for Disease Control and Prevention, 2007). Similarly, during the tough-on-crime policy approach of the 1990s and 2000s, rehabilitative and educational alternatives or programs within these institutions had been significantly decreased, or eliminated altogether, providing few alternatives for those willing to change while incarcerated (Gordon & Weldon, 2003; Petteruti & Walsh, 2008; Pew Center on the States, 2011; Vacca, 2004). Without alternatives or rehabilitative programming, the environment and difficulties encountered while incarcerated often impose new learned behaviors on inmates, increasing antisocial activities and criminal knowledge; this is particularly true for younger offenders (Dodge & Pettit, 2003).

These harms, traumas, and difficulties do not end for the adolescent after leaving the juvenile justice or criminal justice systems (Aizer & Doyle, 2013; Greenwood, 2008). A number of factors predict future involvement with the adult criminal courts, including youthful offenders whose offending behaviors start early and continue through late adolescence; those who commit more offenses, primarily against people, and violent types, and are more frequently adjudicated delinquent; and those whose offense severity escalates over time (Loeber & Farrington, 2008). In some jurisdictions, youthful offenders who were incarcerated in juvenile facilities, compared with those who received nonincarcerated sentences, were three times more likely to be incarcerated in adult facilities (De Li, 1999). If more serious youthful offenders do not desist these negative patterns, but continue their involvement with the criminal courts as adults, their prospects are bleak (Pew Center on the States, 2011; Spelman, 2000; Trulson, Haerle, DeLisi, & Marquart, 2011). A recent national review of 40 states, representing 90% of all released inmates, found that 44% of those inmates returned to prison within 3 years (Pew Center on the States, 2011). Such high recidivism rates in adult incarceration facilities have remained fairly stable over the past 2 decades (Langan & Levin, 2002). Risk factors for re-offending and returning to adult criminal facilities include being a younger adult offender, male, and single; having low educational attainment; and having an increased number of convictions over time (Loeber & Farrington, 2008; Uggen, 2000). These re-offending risks often start, for many adolescents, with their involvement in the school-to-prison pipeline.

Ex-prisoners face substantial barriers to reintegration and reentry to their communities upon their release from adult incarceration facilities (Pager, 2003; Western, Kling, & Weiman 2001). Incarceration may perpetuate criminal activities because of socioeconomic harm caused by the imprisonment of offenders, their families, and communities (Hirschfield & Piquero, 2010). Employment is a primary link for the ex-prisoners' successful reentry into the community (Bellair & Kowalski, 2011); however, there is commonly a mismatch within the communities to which the offenders return between employment opportunities and the ex-prisoners' vocational skill set. Often, there are not enough low-level jobs in the communities that the ex-prisoners return to, leaving few, if any, alternatives to crime (Solomon, Visher, LaVigne, & Osborne, 2006). Some of these barriers explain the significant risk for and high levels of homelessness experienced by ex-offenders released from jails and prisons. Though the data are not complete, ex-offender populations of some cities have a 30% to 50% rate of experiencing homelessness within 1 year of their release from the prisons (National Healthcare for the Homeless Council, 2012).

REFERENCES

Abram, K. M., Teplin, L. A., King, D. C., Longworth, S. L., Emanuel, K. M., Romero, E. G., . . . Olson, N. D. (2013). *PTSD, trauma, and comorbid psychiatric disorders in detained youth.* Washington, DC: Office of Juvenile Justice and Delinquency Prevention, Office of Justice Programs, U.S. Department of Justice.

Adams, D., & Meiners, E. (2014). Who wants to be special? Pathologization and the preparation for bodies for prison. In A. J. Nocella II, P. Parmar, & D. Stovall (Eds.), *From education to incarceration: Dismantling the school-to-prison pipeline* (pp. 145–164). New York, NY: Peter Lang.

Addington, L. A. (2014). Surveillance and security approaches across public school levels. In G. W. Muschert, S. Henry, N. L. Bracy, & A. A. Peguero (Eds.), *Responding to school violence: Confronting the Columbine effect* (pp. 71–88). Boulder, CO: Lynne Rienner.

Advancement Project. (2005). *Education on lockdown: The schoolhouse to jailhouse track.* Washington, DC: Author.

Advancement Project, Education Law Center–PA, FairTest, The Forum for Education and Democracy, Juvenile Law Center, & NAACP Legal Defense and Educational Fund, Inc. (2011). *Federal policy, ESEA reauthorization, and the school-to-prison pipeline.* Washington, DC: Juvenile Law Center, NAACP Legal Defense and Educational Fund, Inc.

Aizer, A., & Doyle, J. J., Jr. (2013). *Juvenile incarceration, human capital, and future crime: Evidence from randomly assigned judges.* NBER Working Paper Series. Cambridge, MA: National Bureau of Economic Research.

American Civil Liberties Union. (2013). *Alone and afraid: Children held in solitary confinement and isolation in juvenile detention and correctional facilities.* New York, NY: Author.

American Psychiatric Association. (2013). *Diagnostic and statistical manual of mental disorders* (5th ed.). Washington, DC: American Psychiatric Publishing.

Annie E. Casey Foundation. (2012). *Expanding JDAI's focus to reduce commitments and placements.* Baltimore, MD: Author.

Arata, C. A., Langhinrichsen-Rohling, J., Bowers, D., & O'Brien, N. O. (2007). Differential correlates of multi-type maltreatment among urban youth. *Child Abuse and Neglect: The International Journal, 31,* 393–415.

Arnett, J. J. (2000). Emerging adulthood: A theory of development from the late teens through the twenties. *The American Psychologist, 55*(5), 469–480.

Baird, C., Healy, T., Johnson, K., Bogie, A., Dankert, E. W., & Scharenbroch, C. (2013). *A comparison of risk assessment instruments in juvenile justice.* Madison, WI: National Council on Crime and Delinquency.

Balfanz, R., Byrnes, V., & Fox, J. (2015). Sent home and put off-track: The antecedents, disproportionalities, and consequences of being suspended in the ninth grade. In D. J. Losen (Ed.), *Closing the school discipline gap: Research for policymakers.* New York, NY: Teachers College.

Balfanz, R., Spiridakis, K., Neild, C., & Legters, N. (2003). High-poverty secondary school and juvenile justice systems: How neither helps the other and how that could change. *New Directions for Youth Development, 99,* 71–89.

Bellair, P. E., & Kowalski, B. R. (2011). Low-skill employment opportunity and African American-white difference in recidivism. *Journal of Research in Crime and Delinquency, 48*(2), 176–208.

Boesky, L. (2002). *Juvenile offenders with mental health disorders.* Lanham, MD: American Correctional Association.

Bradley, R. H., & Corwyn, R. F. (2002). Socioeconomic status and child development. *Annual Review of Psychology, 53,* 371–399.

Brooks-Gunn, J., & Duncan, G. J. (1997). The effects of poverty on children. *The Future of Children: Children and Poverty, 7,* 55–71.

Carter, P. L. (2005). *Keepin' it real: School success beyond black and white.* New York, NY: Oxford University Press.

Center for Civil Rights Remedies. (2013). *A summary of new research, closing the school discipline gap: Research to practice.* Washington, DC: Civil Rights Project.

Centers for Disease Control and Prevention. (2007). Effects on violence of laws and policies facilitating the transfer of youth from the juvenile to the adult system. *MMWR, 56*(RR-9).

Chassin, L. (2008). Juvenile justice and substance abuse. *The Future of Children, 18*(2), 165–184.

Chassin, L., Flora, D. B., & King, K. M. (2004). Trajectories of substance use and substance use disorders from adolescence to adulthood: The effects of parent alcoholism and personality. *Journal of Abnormal Psychology, 113*, 483–498.

Chayt, B. (2012). *Juvenile justice and mental health: A collaborative approach.* Chicago, IL: John D. and Catherine T. MacArthur Foundation.

Cocozza, J., & Skowyra, K. (2000). Youth with mental health disorders: Issues and emerging responses. *Juvenile Justice Journal, 7*(1), 3–13.

De Li, S. (1999). Legal sanctions and youths' status achievement: A longitudinal study. *Justice Quarterly, 16*, 377–401.

Dembo, R., Wareham, J., Poythress, N., Meyers, K., & Schmeidler, J. (2008). Psychosocial functioning problems over time among high-risk youth: A latent class transition analysis. *Crime and Delinquency, 54*(4), 644–670.

Dmitrieva, J., Monahan, K. C., Cauffman, E., & Steinberg, L. (2012). Arrested development: The effects of incarceration on the development of psychosocial maturity. *Development and Psychopathology, 24*, 1073–1090.

Dodge, K. A., Dishion, T. J., & Landsford, J. E. (2006). *Deviant peer influences in programs for youth.* New York, NY: Guilford Press.

Dodge, K. A., & Pettit, G. S. (2003). A biopsychosocial model of the development of chronic conduct problems in adolescence. *Developmental Psychology, 39*, 349–371.

Equity Project at Indiana University. (2014, March). *Discipline disparities series: Key findings.* Discipline disparities series: New Research. Bloomington, IN: The Equity Project at Indiana University. Available at http://rtpcollaborative.indiana.edu/briefing-papers

Fabelo, T., Thompson, M. D., Plotkin, M., Carmichael, D., Marchbanks, M. P. III, & Booth, E. A. (2011). *Breaking schools' rules: A statewide study of how school discipline relates to students' success and juvenile justice involvement.* New York, NY; College Station, TX: Council of State Governments Justice Center; Public Research Policy Research Institute of Texas A & M University.

Fagan, J. (2000). Contexts of choice by adolescents in criminal events. In T. Grisso & R. Schwartz (Eds.), *Youth on trial.* Chicago, IL: University of Chicago Press.

Feierman, J., Levick, M., & Mody, A. (2010). The school-to-prison pipeline . . . and back: Obstacles and remedies for the re-enrollment of adjudicated youth. *New York Law School Review, 54*, 1115–1129.

Gagnon, J. C., & Leone, P. E. (2002). Alternative strategies for school violence prevention. *New Directions for Youth Development, 92*, 101–125.

Garrido, V., & Morales, L. A. (2007). *Serious (violent and chronic) juvenile offenders: A systematic review of treatment effectiveness in secure corrections.* Philadelphia, PA: The Campbell Collaboration Reviews of Intervention and Policy Evaluations (CT-RIPE), Campbell Collaboration.

Giedd, J. N. (2004). Structural magnetic resonance imaging of the adolescent brain. *Annals of the New York Academy of Sciences, 1021,* 83.

Giordano, P. C., Cernkovich, S. A., & Lowery, A. R. (2004). A long-term follow-up of serious adolescent female offenders. In M. Putallaz & K. L. Bierman (Eds.), *Aggression, antisocial behavior, and violence among girls: A developmental perspective* (pp. 186–202). New York, NY: Guilford Press.

Giordano, P. C., Cernkovich, S. A., & Rudolph, J. L. (2002). Gender, crime, and desistance: Toward a theory of cognitive transformation. *American Journal of Sociology, 107*(4), 990–1064.

Gordon, H., & Weldon, B. (2003). Impact of career and technical education programs on adult offenders: Learning behind bars. *Journal of Correctional Education, 54*(4), 200–209.

Greene, A. (1986). Future-time perspective in adolescence: The present of things future revisited. *Journal of Youth and Adolescence, 15,* 99–113.

Greenwood, P. (2008). Prevention and intervention programs for juvenile offenders. *The Future of Children, 18*(2), 185–210.

Grisso, T. (2008). Adolescent offenders with mental disorders. *The Future of Children, 18*(2), 143–162.

Grisso, T., Barnum, R., Fletcher, K., Cauffman, E., & Peuschold, D. (2001). Massachusetts youth screen instruments for mental health needs of juvenile justice youths. *Journal of the American Academy of Child and Adolescent Psychiatry, 40,* 541–548.

Grogan-Kaylor, A., Ruffolo, M. C., Ortega, R. C., & Clarke, J. (2008). Behavior of youth involved in the child welfare system. *Child Abuse and Neglect: The International Journal, 32,* 35–49.

Hamilton, C. E., Falshaw, L., & Browne, K. D. (2002). The link between recurrent maltreatment and offending behavior. *International Journal of Offender Therapy and Comparative Criminology, 46,* 75–94.

Harry, B., & Klinger, J. (2006). *Why are so many minority students in special education? Understanding race and disability in schools.* New York, NY: Teachers College.

Hawkins, J. D., Herrenkohl, T. I., Farrington, D. P., Brewer, D., Catalano, R. F., Harachi, T. W., & Cothern, L. (2000). *Predictors of youth violence.* Washington, DC: Office of Juvenile Justice and Delinquency Prevention, Office of Justice Programs, U.S. Department of Justice.

Heitzeg, N. A. (2014). Criminalizing education: Zero tolerance policies, police in the hallways, and the school to prison pipeline. In A. J. Nocella II, P. Parmar, & D. Stovall (Eds.), *From education to incarceration: Dismantling the school-to-prison pipeline* (pp. 11–36). New York, NY: Peter Lang.

Himmelstein, K. E. W., & Bruckner, H. (2011). Criminal-justice and school sanctions against nonheterosexual youth: A national longitudinal study. *Pediatrics, 127*(1), 49–57.

Hirschfield, P. J., & Piquero, A. R. (2010). Normalization and legitimization: Modeling stigmatizing attitudes toward ex-offenders. *Criminology, 48*(1), 27–55.

Hockenberry, S., & Puzzanchera, C. (2014). *Juvenile court statistics, 2011.* Washington, DC: Office of Juvenile Justice and Delinquency Prevention, Office of Justice Programs, U.S. Department of Justice.

Hoeve, M., McReynolds, L. S., & Wasserman, G. A. (2013). The influence of adolescent psychiatric disorder on young adult recidivism. *Criminal Justice and Behavior, 40*(3), 289–301.

Hoffman, J. P., Erickson, L. D., & Spence, K. R. (2013). Modeling the association between academic achievement and delinquency. *Criminology, 51*(3), 629–660.

Holman, B., & Ziedenberg, J. (2014). *The dangers of detention: The impact of incarcerating youth in detention and other secure facilities.* Washington, DC: Justice Policy Institute.

Hooks, J. (2012). *Mental health and the juvenile justices system.* Columbus, OH: Correctional Institution Inspection Committee.

Howell, J. C. (2003). *Preventing and reducing juvenile delinquency: A comprehensive framework.* Thousand Oaks, CA: Sage.

Insley, A. (2001). Suspending and expelling children from educational opportunity: Time to reevaluate zero tolerance policies. *American University Law Review, 50*, 1039–1074.

Jimerson, S. R., Anderson, G. E., & Whipple, A. D. (2002). Winning the battle and losing the way: Examining the relation between grade retention and dropping out of high school. *Psychology in the Schools, 39*(4), 441–457.

Justice Policy Institute. (2011). *Education under arrest: The case against police in schools.* Washington, DC: Author.

Kaba, M., & Edwards, F. (2011). *Policing Chicago public schools: A gateway to the school-to-prison pipeline.* Chicago, IL: Project NIA: Building Peaceful Communities.

Kang-Brown, J., Trone, J., Fratello, J., & Daftary-Kapur, T. (2013). *A generation later: What we've learned about zero tolerance in schools.* New York, NY: Vera Institute of Justice, Center on Youth Justice.

Keleher, T. (2000). *Racial disparities related to school zone tolerance policies.* Testimony to the U.S. Commission on Civil Rights, February 18, 2000. Oakland, CA: Applied Research Center.

Kirk, D. S., & Sampson, R. L. (2013). Juvenile arrest and collateral educational damage in the transition to adulthood. *Sociology of Education, 86*(1), 36–62.

Koball, H., Dion, R., Gothro, A., Bardo, M., Dworsky, A., Lansing, J., . . . Manning, A. E. (2011). *Synthesis of research and resources to support at-risk youth,* OPRE Report #2011-22. Washington, DC: Office of Planning, Research and Evaluation, Administration for Children and Families, U.S. Department of Health and Human Services.

Koppelman, J. (2005). *Mental health and juvenile justice: Moving toward more effective systems of care.* National Health Policy Reform, Issue Brief No. 805. Washington, DC: George Washington University.

Kupchik, A. (2010). *Homeroom security: School discipline in an age of fear.* New York, NY: New York University Press.

Langan, P. A., & Levin, D. J. (2002). *Recidivism of prisoners released in 1994.* Washington, DC: Bureau of Justice Statistics, U.S. Department of Justice.

Langrehr, K. J. (2011). Racial distinctions in the psychosocial histories of incarcerated youth. *Psychological Services, 8*(1), 23–35.

Lemmon, J. H. (2009). How child maltreatment affects dimensions of juvenile delinquency in a cohort of low-income urban males. *Justice Quarterly, 16*, 357–376.

Leone, P., & Weinberg, L. (2010). *Addressing the unmet educational needs of children and youth in the juvenile justice and child welfare systems.* Washington, DC: Center for Juvenile Justice Reform, Georgetown University.

Lewis, D. O., Yeager, C. A., Cobham-Portorreal, C. S., Klein, N., Showalter, C., & Anthony, A. (1991). A follow-up of female delinquents: Maternal contributions to the perpetuation of deviance. *Journal of the American Academy of Child and Adolescent Psychiatry, 30*(2), 197–201.

Lewis, D. O., Yeager, C. A., Lovely, R., Stein, A., & Cobham-Portorreal, C. S. (1994). A clinical follow-up of delinquent males: Ignored vulnerabilities, unmet needs, and the perpetuation of violence. *Journal of the American Academy of Child and Adolescent Psychiatry, 33*(4), 518–528.

Loeber, R., & Farrington, D. P. (Eds.). (1998). *Serious and violent juvenile offenders: Risk factors and successful interventions.* Thousand Oaks, CA: Sage.

Loeber, R., & Farrington, D. P. (2001). The significant concern of child delinquency. In R. Loeber & D. P. Farrington (Eds.), *Child delinquents: Development, intervention, and service needs* (pp. 1–22). Thousand Oaks, CA: Sage.

Loeber, R., & Farrington, D. P. (2008). *From juvenile offending to young adult offending*. IJ-CX-K-42. Washington, DC: National Institute of Justice, Office of Justice Programs, U.S. Department of Justice.

Losen, D. L. (2012). Sound discipline policy for successful schools: How redressing racial disparities can make a positive impact for all. In S. Bahena, N. Cooc, R. Currie-Rubin, P. Kuttner, & M. Ng (Eds.), *Disrupting the school-to-prison pipeline* (pp. 45–74). Cambridge, MA: Harvard Educational Review.

MacArthur Foundation. (2012). *Juvenile justice and mental health: A collaborative approach*. Chicago, IL: Models for Change: Systems Reform in Juvenile Justice.

Majd, K. (2011). Students of the mass incarceration nation. *Howard Law Journal*, *54*(2), 343–394.

Majd, K., Marksamer, J., & Reyes, C. (2009). *Hidden justice: Lesbian, gay, bisexual and transgender youth in juvenile courts*. San Francisco, CA: National Center for Lesbian Rights.

Mallett, C. (2009). Disparate juvenile court outcomes for disabled delinquent youth: A social work call to action. *Child and Adolescent Social Work Journal*, *26*, 197–207.

Mallett, C. (2011). *Seven things juvenile courts should know about learning disabilities*. Reno, NV: National Council of Juvenile and Family Court Judges.

Mallett, C. (2013). *Linking disorders to delinquency: Treating high risk youth in the juvenile justice system*. Boulder, CO: Lynne Rienner.

Marchbanks, M. P., III, Blake, J., Booth, E., Carmichael, A., Seibert, A. L., & Fabelo, T. (2015). The economic effects of exclusionary discipline on grade retention and high school dropout. In D. J. Losen (Ed.), *Closing the school discipline gap: Research for policymakers*. New York, NY: Teachers College.

Martin, N., & Halperin, S. (2006). *Whatever it takes: How twelve communities are reconnecting out-of-school youth*. Washington, DC: American Youth Policy Form.

Marx, G. T. (1981). Ironies of social control: Authorities as contributors to deviance through escalation, nonenforcement and covert facilitation. *Social Problems*, *28*(3), 221–246.

Matta-Oshima, K. M., Huang, J., Jonson-Reid, M., & Drake, B. (2010). Children with disabilities in poor households: Association with juvenile and adult offending. *Social Work Research*, *34*(2), 102–113.

Maxfield, M. G., Weiler, B. L., & Widom, C. S. (2000). Comparing self-reports and official records of arrest. *Journal of Quantitative Criminology*, *16*(1), 87–110.

McCurdy, J. (2014). Targets for arrest. In A. J. Nocella II, P. Parmar, & D. Stovall (Eds.), *From education to incarceration: Dismantling the school-to-prison pipeline* (pp. 86–101). New York, NY: Peter Lang.

McNulty-Eitle, T., & Eitle, D. J. (2004). Inequality, segregation, and the over-representation of African Americans in school suspension. *Sociological Perspectives, 47,* 269–287.

Mears, D. P., & Aron, L. Y. (2003). *Addressing the needs of youth with disabilities in the juvenile justice system: The current state of knowledge.* Washington, DC: Urban Institute, Justice Policy Center.

Mendel, R. A. (2012). *No place for kids: The case for reducing juvenile incarceration.* Baltimore, MD: Annie E. Casey Foundation.

Mitchum, P., & Moodie-Mills, A. C. (2014). *Beyond bullying: How hostile school climate perpetuates the school-to-prison pipeline for LBGT youth.* Washington, DC: Center for American Progress.

Moffitt, T. (1993). Adolescence-limited and life-course-persistent antisocial behavior: A developmental taxonomy. *Psychological Review, 100,* 674–701.

Moore, K., & Redd, Z. (2002). *Children in poverty: Trends, consequences and policy options.* Child Trends Research Brief. Washington, DC: Child Trends.

Mulvey, E. P., & Iselin, A. R. (2008). Improving professional judgments of risk and amenability in juvenile justice. *The Future of Children, 18*(2), 35–58.

Mulvey, E. P., & Shubert, C. A. (2012). *Transfer of juveniles to adult court: Effects of a policy in one court.* Washington, DC: Office of Juvenile Justice and Delinquency Prevention, Office of Justice Programs, U.S. Department of Justice.

National Center for Youth Law. (2008). *The incarceration of status offenders under the valid court order exception to the Juvenile Justice and Delinquency Prevention Act.* First National Conference on Homeless Youth and the Law, Washington, DC.

National Council on Crime and Delinquency. (2014). *NCCD compares juvenile justice risk assessment instruments: A summary of the OJJDP-funded study.* Oakland, CA.

National Healthcare for the Homeless Council. (2012). *Criminal justice, homelessness, and health: 2012 policy statement.* Nashville, TN: Author.

New Freedom Commission on Mental Health. (2003). *Achieving the promise: Transforming mental health care in America, final report.* Washington, DC: U.S. Department of Health and Human Services.

Nicholson-Crotty, S., Birchmeier, Z., & Valentine, D. (2009). Exploring the impact of school discipline on racial disproportion in the juvenile justice system. *Social Science Quarterly, 90*(4), 1003–1018.

Pager, D. (2003). The mark of a criminal record. *American Journal of Sociology, 108,* 937–975.

Payne, A. A., & Welch, K. (2010). Racial threat and punitive school discipline. *Social Problems, 25,* 26–39.

Petrosino, A., Turpin-Petrosino, C., & Guckenburg, S. (2010). *Formal system processing on juveniles: Effects on delinquency.* Oslo, Norway: Campbell System Reviews 2010 (1).

Petteruti, A., & Walsh, N. (2008). *Jailing communities: The impact of jail expansion and effective public safety strategies.* Washington, DC: Justice Policy Institute.

Pew Center on the States. (2011). *State of recidivism: The revolving door of America's prisons.* Washington, DC: Pew Charitable Trusts.

Pinard, M. (2006). The logistical and ethical difficulties of informing juveniles about the collateral consequences of adjudication. *Nevada Law Journal, 6,* 1111–1129.

Piquero, A. R., Farrington, D., & Blumstein, A. (2003). The criminal career paradigm. In M. Tonry & N. Morris (Eds.), *Crime and justice: An annual review of research 30.* Chicago, IL: University of Chicago Press.

Puzzanchera, C. (2011). *Juvenile arrests, 2011.* Washington, DC: Office of Juvenile Justice and Delinquency Prevention, Office of Justice Programs, U.S. Department of Justice.

Puzzanchera, C., & Robson, C. (2014). *Delinquency cases in juvenile court, 2010.* Washington, DC: Office of Juvenile Justice and Delinquency Prevention, Office of Justice Programs, U.S. Department of Justice.

Rapp-Palicchi, L., & Roberts, A. R. (2004). Mental illness and juvenile offending. In A. R. Roberts (Ed.), *Juvenile justice sourcebook: Past, present, and future* (pp. 289–308). New York, NY: Oxford University Press.

Rivkin, D. H. (2010). Decriminalizing students with disabilities. *New York Law School Law Review, 54,* 909–942.

Rosenblatt, J. A., Rosenblatt, A. R., & Biggs, E. E. (2000). Criminal behavior and emotional disorder: Comparing youth served by the mental health and juvenile justice systems. *Journal of Behavioral Health Services and Research, 27*(2), 227–237.

Schubert, C. A., & Mulvey, E. P. (2014). *Behavioral health problems, treatment, and outcomes in serious youthful offenders.* Washington, DC: Office of Juvenile Justice and Delinquency Prevention, Office of Justice Programs, U.S. Department of Justice.

Scott, E. S., & Steinberg, L. (2008). Adolescent development and the regulation of youth crime. *The Future of Children, 18*(2), 16–33.

Scott, M., Snowden, L., & Libby, A. M. (2002). From mental health to juvenile justice: What factors predict this transition? *Journal of Child and Family Studies, 11*(3), 299–311.

Sedlak, A. J., & McPherson, K. (2010). *Survey of youth in residential placement: Youth's needs and services.* Washington, DC: Westat Corporation.

Shollenberg, T. O. (2015). Racial disparities in school suspension and subsequent outcomes: Evidence from the National Longitudinal Survey of Youth, 1997. In D. J. Losen (Ed.), *Closing the school discipline gap: Research for policymakers.* New York, NY: Teachers College.

Shufelt, J. L., & Cocozza, J. J. (2006). *Youth with mental health disorders in the juvenile justice system: Results from a multi-state prevalence study.* Delmar, NY: National Center for Mental Health and Juvenile Justice.

Skiba, R. J. (2000). *Zero tolerance, zero evidence: An analysis of school disciplinary practice.* Indiana Education Policy Center, Policy Research Report #SRS2. Bloomington, IN: Indiana University.

Skiba, R. J., Arrendonda, M. I., & Rausch, M. K. (2014, March). *New and developing research on disparities in discipline.* Discipline disparities series: New Research. Bloomington, IN: The Equity Project at Indiana University. Available at http://rtpcollaborative.indiana.edu/briefing-papers

Skiba, R. J., Michael, R. S., Nardo, A. C., & Peterson, R. (2000). *The color of discipline: Sources of racial and gender disproportionality in school punishment.* Indiana Education Policy Center, Research Report SRS1. Bloomington, IN: Indiana University.

Skiba, R. J., Reynolds, C. R., Graham, S., Sheras, P., Conoley, J. C., & Garcia-Vasquez, E. (2006). *Are zero tolerance policies effective in the schools? An evidentiary review and recommendations.* Washington, DC: American Psychological Association Zero Tolerance Task Force.

Skiba, R. J., & Williams, N. T. (2014, March). *Are black kids worse? Myths and facts about racial differences in behavior.* Discipline disparities series: New Research. Bloomington, IN: The Equity Project at Indiana University. Available at http://rtpcollaborative.indiana.edu/briefing-papers

Smith, C. A., & Thornberry, T. O. (1995). The relationship between childhood maltreatment and adolescent involvement in delinquency. *Criminology, 33*(4), 451–481.

Smith, R. M., & Erevelles, N. (2004). Toward an enabling education: The difference that disability makes. *Educational Researcher, 23*(8), 31–36.

Solomon, A. L., Visher, C., LaVigne, N. G., & Osborne, J. (2006). *Understanding the challenges of prisoner reentry: Research findings from the Urban Institute's prisoner reentry portfolio.* Washington, DC: Urban Institute.

Somerville, L. H., & Casey, B. (2010). Developmental neurobiology of cognitive control and motivational systems. *Current Opinion in Neurobiology, 20*(2), 236–241.

Spelman, W. (2000). The limited importance of prison expansion. In A. Blumstein & J. Wallman (Eds.), *The crime drop in America* (pp. 125–153). New York, NY: Cambridge University Press.

Steinberg, L. (2007). Risk-taking in adolescence: New perspectives from brain and behavioral science. *Current Directions in Psychological Science, 16,* 55–59.

Steinberg, L., Dahl, R., Keating, D., Kupfer, D. J., & Masten, A. S. (2006). The study of development psychopathology in adolescence: Integrating affective neuroscience with the study of context. In D. Cicchetti & D. J. Cohen (Eds.), *Developmental psychopathology* (2nd ed., pp. 710–741). Hoboken, NJ: John Wiley.

Stinchcomb, J. B., Bazemore, G., & Riestenberg, N. (2006). Beyond zero tolerance: Restoring justice in secondary schools. *Youth Violence and Juvenile Justice, 4,* 123–147.

Substance Abuse and Mental Health Services Administration. (2013a). *Behavioral health, United States, 2012.* Washington, DC: Center for Behavioral Health Statistics and Quality, U.S. Department of Health and Human Services.

Substance Abuse and Mental Health Services Administration. (2013b). *National survey on drug use and health.* Washington, DC: Center for Mental Health Services, U.S. Department of Health and Human Services.

Sulok, M. M. (2007). Extended jurisdiction juvenile prosecution: To resolve or not to revoke. *Loyola University Chicago Law Review, 215,* 270–295.

Sum, A., Khatiwada, I., McLaughlin, J., & Palma, S. (2009). *The consequences of dropping out of high school: Joblessness and jailing for high school dropouts and the high cost to taxpayers.* Boston, MA: Center for Labor Market Studies, Northeastern University.

Sweeten, G. (2006). Who will graduate? Disruption of high school education by arrest and court involvement. *Justice Quarterly, 23,* 462–473.

Teplin, L., Abram, K., McClelland, G., Mericle, A., Dulcan, M., & Washburn, D. (2006). *Psychiatric disorders of youth in detention.* Washington, DC: Office of Justice Programs, Office of Juvenile Justice and Delinquency Prevention, U.S. Department of Justice.

Teplin, L. A., Abram, K. M., Washburn, J. J., Welty, L. J., Hershfield, J. A., & Dulcan, M. K. (2013). *The Northwestern juvenile project: Overview.* Washington, DC: Office of Juvenile Justice and Delinquency Prevention, Office of Justice Programs, U.S. Department of Justice.

Trulson, C. R., Haerle, D. R., DeLisi, M., & Marquart, J. W. (2011). Blended sentencing, early release, and recidivism of violent institutionalized delinquents. *The Prison Journal, 91*(3), 255–278.

Uggen, C. (2000). Work as a turning point in the life course of criminals: A duration model of age, employment, and recidivism. *American Sociological Review*, *65*, 529–546.

U.S. Department of Education. (2014). *35th annual report to Congress on the implementation of the Individuals with Disabilities Education Act, 2014*. Washington, DC: Office of Special Education and Rehabilitative Services, Office of Special Education Programs.

U.S. Department of Health and Human Services. (2009). *ASPE Research Brief: The mental health of vulnerable youth and their transition to adulthood: Examining the role of the child welfare, juvenile justice, and run-away/homeless systems*. Washington, DC: U.S. Government Printing Office.

U.S. Department of Health and Human Services. (2013). *Child maltreatment 2012*. Washington, DC: U.S. Government Printing Office.

U.S. Department of Justice. (2012). *Sexual victimization in juvenile facilities reported by youth, 2012*. Washington, DC: Office of Juvenile Justice and Delinquency Prevention, Office of Justice Programs, U.S. Department of Justice.

U.S. Department of Justice. (2014). *Changing lives: Prevention and intervention to reduce serious offending*. Washington, DC: Office of Juvenile Justice and Delinquency Prevention, Office of Justice Programs, U.S. Department of Justice.

Vacca, J. S. (2004). Education prisoners are less likely to return to prison. *The Journal of Correctional Education*, *55*, 297–305.

Vanderhaar, J. E., Petrosko, J. M., & Munoz, M. (2015). Reconsidering the alternatives: The relationship between suspension, disciplinary alternative school placement, subsequent juvenile detention, and the salience of race. In D. J. Losen (Ed.), *Closing the school discipline gap: Research for policymakers*. New York, NY: Teachers College.

Vander-Stoep, A., Evans, C., & Taub, J. (1997). Risk of juvenile justice system referral among children in a public mental health system. *Journal of Mental Health Administration*, *24*, 428–442.

Verrecchia, P. J., Fetzer, M. D., Lemmon, J. H., & Austin, T. L. (2010). An examination of direct and indirect effects of maltreatment dimensions and other ecological risk on persistent youth offending. *Criminal Justice Review, 35*(2), 220–243.

Wald, M., & Martinez, T. (2003). *Connected by 25: Improving the life chances of the country's most vulnerable 14–24 year-olds*. William and Flora Hewlett Foundation Working Paper, Menlo Park, CA.

Wang, X., Blomberg, T. G., & Li, S. D. (2005). Comparison of the educational deficiencies of delinquent and nondelinquent students. *Evaluation Review: A Journal of Applied Social Research, 29*(4), 291–312.

Washburn, J., Teplin, L., Voss, L., Simion, C., Abram, K., & McClelland, G. (2008). Psychiatric disorders among detained youths: A comparison of youths processed in juvenile court and adult criminal court. *Psychiatric Services, 59*(9), 965–973.

Washington State Institute for Public Policy. (2007). *Evidence-based juvenile offender programs: Program description, quality assurance, and cost.* Olympia, WA: Author.

Wasserman, G. A., Keenan, K., Tremblay, R. E., Cole, J. D., Herrenkohl, T. I., Loeber, R., & Petechuk, D. (2003). *Risk and protective factors of child delinquency.* Washington, DC: Office of Juvenile Justice and Delinquency Prevention, U.S. Department of Justice.

Western, B., Kling, J., & Weiman, D. (2001). The labor market consequences of incarceration. *Crime and Delinquency, 47*(3), 410–427.

Widom, C. S., & Maxfield, M. (2001). *An update on the "cycle of violence."* Washington, DC: National Institute of Justice, U.S. Department of Justice.

Yun, I., Ball, J. D., & Lim, H. (2011). Disentangling the relationship between child maltreatment and violent delinquency: Using a nationally representative sample. *Journal of Interpersonal Violence, 26*(1), 88–110.

Zajac, K., Sheidow, A. J., & Davis, M. (2013). *Transition age youth with mental health challenges in the juvenile justice system.* Washington, DC: American Institutes for Research.

Chapter 4: Disproportionate Impact on Vulnerable Children and Adolescents

A majority of students in this country's primary and secondary schools are impacted by the criminalization of education—security guards, school resource officers, security cameras, inflexible discipline codes, and subsequent school punishment rigidity (Lawrence, 2007; U.S. Department of Education, 2014a). Most students experience these security and discipline-focused measures throughout their school day as a normative routine. However, this punitive environmental norm is harmful to the learning, academic environment, and socio-emotional development of many students, as well as to the overall school climate (American Psychological Association Zero Tolerance Task Force, 2008; Bracy, 2010). These measures, counterintuitively to many, make schools less safe (Carter, Fine, & Russell, 2014).

This generation's shift toward strict and controlling school discipline and subsequent establishment of the school-to-prison pipeline had neither well-planned policies nor equitable outcomes. The use of certain security measures within schools—cameras, metal detectors, security guards, and school resource officers—is more commonly found in urban, inner-city environments and in neighborhoods that more often struggle with poverty and its insidious impact on families (Neiman & DeVoe, 2009; Ruddy et al., 2010). The discipline protocols and prison-like school environments in these schools are likely to harm the students more harshly than schools with fewer discipline measures or less discipline protocol rigidity (Hirschfield, 2010). However, the pipeline has been established across most schools. Two students' stories, the first from a lower-income school district and the second from a suburban, higher-income school district, are as follows:

By most accounts, Marlon Morgan is a great kid. The soft-spoken junior plays basketball for Saguaro High School. He was nominated for Youth of the Year last year by a branch of the Boys and Girls Clubs of Scottsdale. So why were his classmates wearing "Free Marlon" t-shirts last week? The 17-year-old had just been arrested on campus during lunch for wearing his baseball cap sideways instead of to the front and refusing to turn it the other way. Morgan, who is Black, believes he was singled out. Other teens in the same room were wearing their hats that way. . . . Morgan was having lunch when Saguaro security guards approached him about his hat. It is against school policy to wear hats sideways because it can be a sign of disrespect for authority, the police report said, but Morgan said that the rule is enforced selectively. According to a police report, he pointed to several White students whose hats were on sideways. (Kupchik, 2010, p. 159)

An LGBT youth of color faced constant bullying from peers (and) did not report the abuse to school staff because, as she put it, "No one (was) going to do anything." "After months and months of harassment she blew up and really hurt another student. She ended up getting extended suspension so, you know, she just dropped out. She was sixteen at the time and just didn't see the point of that anymore. And she felt like she wasn't going to be supported in the school." In this case "extended suspension" amounted to 45 days, as opposed to the 10 days of suspension her bully received. This lack of protection from harassment and bullying, exposure to violence, along with differential and harsh discipline ultimately resulted in the students departure from school altogether. While seemingly a choice, such departure is part of a larger pattern of school push-out. (Burdge, Licona, & Hyemingway, 2014, p. 11)

These two students were disciplined for disobedience and non-compliance to rigid rules stated in the schools' student codes of conduct, and without review of mitigating information to understand why the incidents occurred. Established zero-tolerance policies within school districts and the regiment of disciplinary actions within schools have an inequitable and unfair impact on certain students, not only on minority and/or lesbian, gay, bisexual, or transgender (LGBT) adolescents, as will be discussed throughout this chapter. Many of these children and adolescents are already vulnerable and at risk for difficulties because of certain individual, family, or community-based characteristics, experiences, or harms (Mallett, 2013).

RISK FACTORS

School Discipline/Pipeline

The children and adolescents who are involved in the broad school discipline protocols and the smaller number subsequently caught within the school-to-prison pipeline share many commonalities and experiences that place them at higher risk for these outcomes. As will be seen, most to all of these school discipline risks are also factors for adolescents' involvement with the juvenile courts.

Poverty

More than one in five children grow up in poverty, and all, minority and Caucasian, are more likely to start school academically behind their peers, less likely to graduate from high school, and more likely to be poor as adults (Holzer, Schanzenbach, Duncan, & Ludwig, 2007). The south has the highest number of the nation's poor children (42.1%) and the highest child poverty rate (24.2%), though there are significant state-by-state variations. Children of color are disproportionately poor, with the youngest children the most at risk: Nearly one in three children of color was poor in 2012. African American children were the poorest (39.6%), followed by Native Americans/Native Alaskan children (36.8%), and Hispanic children (33.7%) (Children's Defense Fund, 2014; U.S. Department of Health and Human Services, 2013a). The families of these children have more difficulty in finding and accessing safe housing and in securing mental health care when needed (U.S. Government Accountability Office, 2007).

Poverty impacts education outcomes for children, particularly for children of color, who fare worse than nonminority children. Nearly three quarters of lower-income fourth- and eighth-grade students cannot read or compute at grade level, compared to only half of higher-income students. A 78% of public school students graduated high school in 4 years in 2010, dropping to 70% for Hispanic students and 66% for African American students. A more troubling fact, and at risk for the school-to-prison pipeline, is that young children from poor families, compared to those from nonpoor families, are two times more likely to have behavioral, developmental, or social delays (Children's Defense Fund, 2014). Many families living in poverty or near poverty also experience homelessness, and 1.2 million public school students were identified as homeless during the 2011 to 2012 school year. If children experience homelessness, they are twice as likely to have moderate-to-severe health problems, to repeat a school grade, to be suspended or expelled, and to drop out of high school (National Low Income Housing Coalition, 2013).

Maltreatment/Trauma

Involvement in the school-to-prison pipeline disproportionately includes a number of child and adolescent groups, including but not limited to minorities of color and children living in poverty (Piquero, 2008; Center for Civil Rights Remedies, 2013). This disproportionate involvement of minority and poor families is also found in the child welfare system, a correlative link across child and adolescent risk factors. In other words, poverty and ethnicity are factors contributing to a greater chance of a family being involved with a children's service agency because of abuse or neglect.

However, this involvement is not because poor or minority families maltreat their children more often than nonminority families do; there are other explanations (Drake & Zuravin, 1998; Lu et al., 2004; U.S. Government Accountability Office, 2007). A child's or family's race has been found to be a significant influence on the child welfare professionals' decisions at almost every decision-making stage, even when controlling for race and poverty. This makes it more than twice as likely for African American and non-Hispanic Indian families to be involved. In addition, the services and rehabilitative programming offered to these minority families are fewer than those offered to nonminority families, particularly the case for kincare family placements, leading to poorer outcomes for children (Hill, 2005).

Foster care is one of these difficult outcomes for many children and adolescents. In 2000, African American children represented 38% of the foster-care population while comprising only 16% of the general child and adolescent population; however, through concerted federal and state efforts, this disparity has lessened since 2004. However, it is still twice as likely that an African American or non-Hispanic Indian child, compared to a Caucasian child, will be placed in a foster-care home (Summers, Wood, & Donovan, 2013). In addition, these foster-care placements are typically 9 months longer for minority children and adolescents—22 months compared to 31 months (U.S. Government Accountability Office, 2007). In addition, in 2012, more than 23,000 adolescents aged out of foster care, because they turned 18 years old and had not returned home, been adopted, or been placed with a legal guardian. This group of young people, also disproportionately minority, is at increased risk for not graduating from high school, becoming homeless, and/or involved with the juvenile or criminal justice system (Children's Defense Fund, 2014).

Maltreatment Impact on School Performance

Academic success and transitions from primary to secondary school are markedly more difficult for many children and adolescents who have been victims of maltreatment. Abuse and neglect may impact children's abilities to learn, decrease cognitive and language capacities (Smithgall, Gladden, Howard, Goerge, & Courtney, 2004), increase risk for special education disabilities, and decrease standardized testing outcomes (Egeland, 1997; Mears & Aron, 2003). Most directly, maltreated children and adolescents have poorer academic outcomes (Leiter, 2007). With this being the case, most researchers reviewed maltreatment as a distinct variable; while fewer researchers investigated the impact a specific type of abuse or neglect had on school performance, many researchers controlled for known influences on school performance, including poverty, family characteristics, social and peer influences, and neighborhoods (Boden, Horwood, & Fergusson, 2007; Staudt, 2001). These children and adolescents are at a significant academic disadvantage.

Primary School

Maltreated children are more likely to have poorer grades and be held back a grade level (Shonk & Cicchetti, 2001; Kelly, Thornberry, & Smith, 1997), particularly in kindergarten and first grade (Rowe & Eckenrode, 1999). This was also found for children in the school year after they entered out-of-home care (Smithgall et al., 2004). It is not clear how the child welfare agency as well as family involvement impact these school delays and being held back, though frequent moves and changes can make or exacerbate educational difficulties (Ayassee, 1995; National Youth in Care Network, 2001).

Cognitive and language delays, apparent at the school enrollment age, are greater for maltreated children when compared with nonmaltreated children from lower socioeconomic backgrounds, and much greater when compared with nonmaltreated children from higher socioeconomic backgrounds (Wiggins, Fenichel, & Mann, 2007). On average, these maltreated students enter school one-half year behind on academic performance (Smithgall et al., 2004) and have poorer academic performance and adaptive functioning at ages 6 and 8 (Kurtz, Gaudin, Wodarski, & Howing, 1993; Zolotor et al., 1999). These students also have higher absenteeism rates (Lansford et al., 2002; Leiter, 2007; Leiter & Johnsen, 1997). The impact of neglect on children's academic outcomes has been consistently found to be harmful, and particularly in grades and overall academic skills (Leiter, 2007). Three-quarters of children (and adolescents) involved with the child welfare system is because of neglect (U.S. Department of Health and Human Services, 2013b).

It should be noted, though, that many children experience more than one type and one occurrence of maltreatment, with the cumulative and interactive effects of these multiple experiences complicating the research findings (Mallett, 2013; Margolin & Gordis, 2000). Some researchers have identified that the severity of abuse has a negative impact on verbal abilities and verbal IQ (Perez & Widom, 1994). The more serious or pervasive the maltreatment, the greater the risk for the child's decline in school performance, including absenteeism and grades; however, experiencing maltreatment at an earlier age may lead to behavior problems and increased placement into special education programs (Leiter & Johnsen, 1997; Leiter, 2007). Maltreated children are less inclined to engage in independent activities, require more external motivations, and show less academic engagement (Koenig, Cichetti, & Rogosch, 2000; Shonk & Cicchetti, 2001). They also show less effective work habits and discipline and receive lower math and English grades during elementary school (Rowe & Eckenrode, 1999).

Maltreated children, and particularly children in foster care, are more likely to be diagnosed with a special education disability during earlier school years—upward of 35% (Children's Law Center, 2003; Scarborough & McCrae, 2009). Children in foster care also have poorer academic achievement compared with their peers. Specifically, these children have been found to be far below their grade level in reading comprehension—96% behind—and mathematics—95% behind (Hyames & de Hames, 2000). In addition, children in foster care were half as likely to be performing at grade level (Conger & Rebeck, 2001) and upward of 50% were held back one grade (Children's Law Center, 2003). Children in out-of-home care do not seem to fall further behind in reading achievement while in care, but the achievement gap remains (Smithgall et al., 2004).

Secondary School

Maltreatment has also been found to negatively impact older students' academic outcomes (Courtney et al., 2004; Wodarski et al., 1990). More intense, or long-lasting maltreatment, was found to be associated with having a low grade point average and problems in completing homework assignments, though the impact was moderated by cognitive deficits (Slade & Wissow, 2007). Older maltreated adolescents also report being three or four grade levels behind in reading abilities, and significantly more had repeated at least one grade (Courtney, Terao, & Bost, 2004). In one survey of out-of-home care, middle-school students were three times more likely to be identified in need of special education services, with almost all students with learning disabilities scoring below national reading norms (Smithgall et al., 2004).

Many maltreated adolescents score significantly lower in standardized and required proficiency examinations (Egeland, 1997): One-fourth in the bottom quartile passed the Iowa Test of Basic Skills in Chicago (Smithgall et al., 2004); one-fourth of the Ohio ninth-grade students in foster care passed the mathematics and science tests, and only one-half passed the reading proficiency tests (Coleman, 2004); and Washington state adolescents in foster care scored on average 15 to 20 points lower in the statewide achievement tests than their nonmaltreated peers (Burley & Halpern, 2001). Some researchers have found that maltreated students have significantly lower high school graduation rates when compared with nonmaltreated students (Boden, Horwood, & Ferguson, 2007; Buehler, Orme, Post, & Patterson, 2000; McGloin & Widom, 2001; Thornberry, Ireland, & Smith, 2001). Children and adolescents in foster care are particularly at risk, with approximately 46% not completing high school (Children's Law Center, 2003).

Cross-System Risks

Many child and adolescent disabilities, and related difficulties such as academic problems and mental health disorders, come to the attention of systems designed to identify the problem, intervene, and provide treatment. However, the risks and links across the child- and adolescent-caring systems and possible juvenile court involvement have been known for some time. Adolescent mental health and delinquent populations were found to have risk factors for detention or incarceration, which included being African American or Hispanic—another tie-in with the disproportionate minority confinement problem—having a diagnosis of alcohol problems or conduct disorder in middle school, reported use and abuse of substances, and receiving prior mental health services (Scott, Snowden, & Libby, 2002; Watts & Wright, 1990). Other reviews have substantiated an increased risk of juvenile justice system detainment for minorities, drug use, and public mental health insurance coverage of the adolescent; however, the questions remain whether drug use is a predictor of delinquency or whether delinquency predicts drug use (Brunelle, Brochu, & Cousineau, 2000; Mallett, 2012).

Children and adolescents who received mental health system services prior to juvenile court involvement were at risk, when compared to their peers who were not involved with the juvenile courts, for drug and/or alcohol abuse, conduct disorder, and physical abuse (Rosenblatt, Rosenblatt, & Biggs, 2000); as well as had a two to three times greater risk for juvenile court involvement (Breda, 2003; Vander-Stoep, Evans, & Taub, 1997). These two populations, children and adolescents with emotional disturbances and those involved in the juvenile justice system, differ little across service delivery systems. In other words, these populations intersect, sharing members and also have similarly identified needs and problems (Melton & Pagliocca, 1992; Teplin et al., 2006).

Delinquency/Juvenile Court

Children and adolescents typically experience increased risk for involvement with the juvenile courts as a result of a combination of risk factors, rather than any single experience, leading to offending behaviors and delinquency. These risks often include poverty, family dysfunction, violence, trauma, academic and learning problems, mental health difficulties, and unstable and disorganized neighborhoods, among others (Howell, 2003). The concern here is about the risk and impact that trauma, maltreatment, mental health problems, and special education disabilities have on delinquency outcomes, since these problems are found disproportionately within the school-to-prison pipeline and also in the juvenile court detention and incarceration facilities (Abram et al., 2013; Cuevas et al. 2013; Langrehr, 2011; Leone & Weinberg, 2010; Sedlak & McPherson, 2010; Teplin et al., 2006).

A significant number of delinquency risk and predictive models have been developed, including separation into demographic/historical factors (Heilbrun, 1997), criminology and clinical frameworks (Monahan et al., 2001), and an ecological model (U.S. Department of Health and Human Services, 2001). The ecological model is of the most use here because of its focus on the etiology and interrelations of the risk factors.

This model typology separates these risks as they relate to the individual, family, and community (DeMatteo & Marczyk, 2005; Hawkens et al., 2000). However, many of these difficulties are yet intertwined with other problems. In other words, researchers are still working to determine which children and adolescents are more at risk for which difficulty or disability, and from there are trying to understand how these difficulties affect or cause offending behaviors and delinquency.

Individual Risk Factors

Factors that increase the likelihood that an individual child or adolescent will develop a special education disability, in particular learning disabilities, include living in poverty, family dysfunction, being adopted, male gender, and low household educational attainment (Altarac & Saroha, 2007). Identified and unidentified special education disabilities, in turn, are risk factors for delinquent behaviors and delinquency (Mallett, 2008; Mears & Aron, 2003; Sum, Khatiwada, McLaughlin, & Palma, 2009). Students with learning disabilities are two to three times more at risk than their nondisabled peers to be involved with offending activities both on and off school grounds, to be arrested while in school, and to have higher recidivism rates (Matta-Oshima, Huang, Jonson-Reid, & Drake, 2010; Wang, Blomberg, & Li, 2005).

Maltreatment victimization—neglect, physical abuse, and sexual abuse—has a wide range of harmful outcomes and increases the risk for further problems. The harmful outcomes may include poor cognitive development (Guterman, 2001; Wiggins, Fenichel, & Mann, 2007), mental health problems, and drug use or abuse (Kelly, Thornberry, & Smith, 1997; Wiebush, Freitag, & Baird, 2001). Physical abuse of children often results in depression and posttraumatic stress disorder (Kilpatrick et al., 2003); sexual abuse with again posttraumatic stress and anxiety-related disorders; and neglect with anxiety and behavior problems (Turner, Finklehor, & Ormrod, 2006). Many mental health problems, including a history of early aggression (ages 6–13), hyperactivity, and substance abuse or dependence, are also risk factors for youthful offending behaviors (Chassin, 2008; Grisso, 2008; Hawkens et al., 1998). As noted earlier, maltreatment has a profound educational impact on many children and adolescents, including lower academic performance and grades, falling behind in grade levels, lower standardized testing and proficiency scores, and a significantly higher risk for learning disabilities and emotional disturbances (Courtney et al., 2004; Smithgall et al., 2004).

Children and adolescents who have been maltreated are more likely to engage in offending and delinquent behaviors compared to those without maltreatment histories (Maxfield, Weiler, & Widom, 2000). Adolescents who have been victims of physical abuse and neglect have stronger links to delinquency, though researchers are still trying to determine the etiology and differential impact that these types of maltreatment typologies have on delinquent activities and offending behaviors (Mallett, Stoddard-Dare, & Seck, 2009; Yun, Ball, & Lim, 2011).

Females are more likely than males to have been victims of sexual abuse, and they are equally likely to have experienced physical abuse (Hennessey, Ford, Mahoney, Ko, & Siegfried, 2004; U.S. Department of Health and Human Services, 2013b). The cumulative impact of maltreatment, in addition to other risks often associated with this maltreatment, such as substance abuse and school difficulties, may affect females more negatively than males (Howell, 2003; National Center for Child Traumatic Stress, 2009). It is known that repeat maltreatment victimization predicts the earlier initiation and often greater severity of delinquent acts (Stewart, Livingston, & Dennison, 2008). In fact, when other risks are accounted for, this link appears to be the strongest in predicting serious or chronic youthful offending behavior (Lemmon, 2006; Smith, Ireland, & Thornberry, 2005).

Family Risk Factors

Living in poverty is associated with many child and adolescent difficulties across schools, mental health, and behavior problems, as well as has a strong link to delinquency adjudication (Hawkens et al., 2000; Loeber & Farrington, 1998). Poverty increases the likelihood that the family environment will be more unstable for children. Family dysfunction and instability, when measured in terms of witnessing violent treatment of family members, is a risk for later adolescent delinquency (Dembo et al., 2000; Felitta et al., 2008). In addition, criminal activity, particularly by parents (Dong et al., 2004), early parental loss (Farrington, 1997), parent/child separation (DeMatteo & Marczyk, 2005), and residential instability (Felitta et al., 2008; Hawkens et al., 1998) are risk factors for delinquent activities, emotional problems, substance use and abuse, poor academic outcomes, and maltreatment victimization. As can be seen, risk factors for some areas are outcomes for other problems and vice versa, providing further evidence of the complex interplay of causation and the difficulties in both studying and effectively intervening in these child and adolescent comorbid issues.

Community Risk Factors

The less well organized and cohesive the community, the greater the risk for poor child and adolescent outcomes. Crime, including drug-selling, and low-income housing in the community are linked to delinquent behaviors, as is the exposure to violence within the community. Witnessing violence has been associated with aggressive behavior, poor school performance, and increased mental health difficulties, including depression, anxiety, and trauma (Gorman-Smith & Tolan, 1998; Margolin & Gordis, 2000; Schwartz & Gorman, 2003). These more violent communities are often disproportionately composed of minority populations and the poor (Kracke & Hahn, 2008). The interrelationship of risks across the individual, family, and community is often confounding.

Resiliency: Avoiding the Pipeline and Delinquency

Children and adolescents will react to these individual, family, and community risk factors in varying ways. Some are highly resilient to such experiences, whereas others are greatly affected and troubled. The term "resilient" has been operationalized in a number of ways, though considerable debate remains on how best to study this concept (Luthar, 2003; Rutter, 2006). "Resiliency" has, for instance, been defined as the capacity for children and adolescents to thrive in the face of these risks and difficulties, avoiding many of their deleterious effects. A second definition states that "resiliency" is the process of, or capacity for, a successful adaption despite the circumstances (Masten, Best, & Garmezy, 1990). Regardless of how the term is defined, many children and adolescents are simply able to withstand the challenge of numerous problems and risk factors without sustaining harmful long-term consequences (Fergus & Zimmerman, 2004).

The degree of resilience that an individual has depends on a complex interaction of risk factors, balanced with protective factors (Buffington, Pierkhising, & Marsh, 2010). Protective factors are often considered and measured as the absence of risk factors (Hawkens et al., 2000). However, specific protective factors have been identified that may minimize certain childhood and adolescent risks. For example, a strong relationship with a positive parent or parental figure may be protection enough for a child to overcome maltreatment experiences and subsequent school and academic difficulties. Or the school that the child attends may provide enough of a support system that the dysfunctional family system does not greatly impact development. Or the family environment may provide a stable enough home that even a very low-income and violent neighborhood will not significantly impede the child's development (Fraser, 2004).

When measuring and identifying childhood resiliency factors that protect from family dysfunction, poverty, and related difficulties, a significant interplay is observed among heritable factors, individual characteristics, and experiences over time (Collishaw et al., 2007). These may include individual cognitive factors such as self-regulation abilities and intelligence, biological factors such as stress and reactivity, interpersonal factors such as peer affiliations, and family-related factors, including parenting abilities (Caspi et al., 2002).

In a number of reviews of children who have experienced trauma and maltreatment, some specific protective factors were identified: above-average cognitive abilities and learning styles, an internal locus of control, the presence of spirituality, external attributions of blame from traumatic events, and emotional support (Heller, Larrieu, D'Imperio, & Boris, 1999; McGee, Wolfe, & Olson, 2001). The presence of these protective factors, or other factors yet to be identified, may be the reason for growing evidence that the mental health of a substantial minority of maltreated children is relatively unaffected by their adversity (American Bar Association, 2014; McGloin & Widom, 2001). Children and adolescents who are not maltreated but who are exposed to other risk factors are also at risk for the development of mental health difficulties, substance abuse problems, learning/academic problems, and subsequent delinquency. Nonetheless, many of these children are also resilient, adapt, and develop well into adolescence without significant trouble (Luthar, 2003; National Center for Children in Poverty, 2000).

Thus, in the end, it is still difficult to predict how an individual child or adolescent will respond to these risk factors and harmful experiences. And as reviewed next, certain groups of young people are the most at risk for involvement within these discipline systems—either the risks and cumulative impact of comorbid difficulties are too great, or they possess few protective or resilient traits to avoid these harmful outcomes.

DISPROPORTIONATE IMPACT

It is clear that there are common experiences and difficulties for being involved in school discipline and the juvenile justice system across certain vulnerable children and adolescents, with similar risks within their families, in schools, with peers, and in neighborhood settings. These risks, experiences, and problems make it much more likely for young people to have school problems, peer issues, family difficulties, and police and juvenile court involvement—and for some, this means involvement in the school-to-prison pipeline.

This pipeline disproportionately impacts and involves certain child and adolescent groups: those who experience poverty, students of color, students who have special education disabilities, children and adolescents who have been traumatized or maltreated, and young people who identify as LGBT. School discipline is not evenly distributed; it is these students who more often experience suspensions, expulsions, and school-based arrests, making school failure and dropping out of school more likely. However, most existing research finds that these students neither misbehave more nor are more prone to causing school-based problems; the explanation is more often unfair targeting of these children and adolescents by school and police personnel (Carter, Fine, & Russell, 2014; Kupchik, 2010). The unfair targeting and disciplining of these students run counter to the principles of education and skill development: academic training, behavior modification, and socialization toward young adulthood (Devine, 1996). By increasing school discipline and removal, the very students that today's No Child Left Behind law is intended to help—those who are disadvantaged (Title I)—cannot be helped.

Impoverished Children and Adolescents

Lower-income and poor students, who are also disproportionately children and adolescents of color (U.S. Department of Health and Human Services, 2013a), are more likely to be punished in school, and with harsher discipline, than middle-class students (McCarthy & Hoge, 1987; McNulty-Eitle & Eitle, 2004). More specifically, almost 22% of those below the age of 18 were living in poverty in 2012 (more than 16 million), an increase of 34% since 2000. More than one in three Hispanic and African American children and adolescents were poor compared to one in eight Caucasian children and adolescents, with a greater disparity for those living in extreme poverty—one in five African American and one in seven Hispanic children (Children's Defense Fund, 2013; U.S. Department of Commerce, 2013).

Although students in poverty are overrepresented in populations that experience more school discipline, poverty is not an explanatory or a correlative reason for these outcomes. The relationship between poverty and school disruption or behavioral disorders is quite small (Fabelo et al., 2011; Skiba et al., 2011; Skiba & Williams, 2014). In other words, significant racial disparities in school suspension and expulsions have been consistently found after controlling for poverty (Noltmeyer & McLoughlin, 2010; Skiba, Michael, Nardo, & Peterson, 2000; Wu, Pink, Crain, & Moles, 1982). Schools are the safest environment for children and adolescents, and they can maintain security in poor, middle-class, or wealthy neighborhoods, for safety is based on school climate, relationships, academic supports, and trust across stakeholders. Poverty, and other related neighborhood problems such as crime, is less important than these school supports in keeping children and adolescents in school and academically successful (Carter, Fine, & Russell, 2014; U.S. Department of Education, 2014b).

Students who are the most impacted by these punitive policies—both in schools and in juvenile courts—are low-income males of color. In school settings, it is particularly true that minority students are treated more harshly in under-resourced urban schools. Specifically, schools with a greater proportion of African American students have increased zero-tolerance policies and use harsher, compared to milder, discipline measures. In these school environments, for many students, there is a cumulative impact, with the use of more than one discipline measure in many situations (Welch & Payne, 2010). In addition, these schools are less likely to be communally organized, a framework that has been found to be an effective alternative to harsh discipline policies (Payne, 2012; Payne, Gottfredson, & Gottfredson, 2008).

However, poverty and living in more disorganized communities, including higher crime rates, greatly increase the risk for children and adolescents to become involved in delinquent activities and the juvenile courts. Part of the explanation for higher delinquency risks is that poorer and more disorganized neighborhoods have weaker social controls, increasing residents' isolation, which causes higher neighborhood turnover (Hawkens et al., 2000; Shader, 2001). Although this link has been established, there still remains a paucity of reviews that attempt to determine how many of the youthful offenders involved in the juvenile courts come from poor families, or what proportion of adjudicated or detained youthful offenders are from poor families. Although the risk from poverty to delinquent activities is established, national or longitudinal studies of the courts are marred by different reporting expectations and lack of local courts' data collection or sharing (Mallett, 2013). However, when reviewing the overrepresentation of children and adolescents of color in both the school discipline pipeline and formal juvenile court involvement, the answer becomes clear. In particular, there is strong evidence when investigating the juvenile courts' detention and incarceration facilities.

Children and Adolescents of Color

Over the past three decades, reviews have found minority students to be significantly more at risk than Caucasian students for school discipline, harsher outcomes, and involvement in the school-to-prison pipeline (Advancement Project et al., 2011). These are not new problems for African American students, though historical investigations are less complete for other minority groups, including Hispanic and Native American students. Nonetheless, since 1975, African American students have been suspended from school at two to three times the rates of Caucasian students, with some finding significantly higher disparities (Children's Defense Fund, 1975; Fabelo et al., 2011; Gregory, Skiba, & Noguera, 2010; Losen & Martinez, 2013; Massachusetts Advocacy Center, 1986; Morgan, Salomon, Plotkin, & Cohen, 2014; Rausch & Skiba, 2004; U.S. Department of Education, 2000).

These disparities are found across the continuum of school procedures, school locations, and school districts. More specifically, African American students, particularly males, are three and a half times more likely to be suspended or expelled than their peers, with one in five African American male students being suspended out of school for at least one day during the 2012 school year (U.S. Department of Education, 2014a). As noted, these disparities cannot be explained by higher rates of student misbehavior or the difficulties of living in poverty (Carter, Fine, & Russell, 2014; Nicholson-Crotty, Birchmeier, & Valentine, 2009; Skiba, Shure, & Williams, 2012). These disparities are also found, though to lesser degrees, for Hispanic and Native American students as well as for English language learning students, depending on the location of the school district (Center for Civil Rights, 2013). Nationwide, African American students constitute 18% of students but represent 39% of expulsions and 42% of referrals to law enforcement while in school; in more disparate contrast, African American and Hispanic students constitute 42% of students but account for 72% of those arrested for school-related offenses (Losen, Hewitt, & Toldson, 2014).

Case in point, a recent and important review of 364 elementary and middle schools found that African American students were more than twice as likely as their Caucasian peers in elementary school to be referred to the office for problem behaviors and nearly four times more likely in middle school. In addition, African American and Hispanic students were more likely than their Caucasian peers to be suspended out of school or expelled for the same or similar infraction of school discipline policies (Skiba et al., 2011). In certain reviews, and where racial disparities exist, African American and other minority students, compared to Caucasian students, were more often disciplined for more subjective infractions or misbehaviors—disrespect, loitering, and excessive noise, among others (American Psychological Association Zero Tolerance Task Force, 2008; Skiba, Michael, Nardo, & Peterson, 2002). This is poignant because a majority of suspensions and expulsions are due to nonserious actions or behaviors, with disobedience—defiance and/or disruptive behavior—being the most common reason (Equity Project, 2014; Wald, 2014).

In recent research from the Discipline Disparities Research-to-Practice Collaborative, a longitudinal study of Florida schools found that 39% of African American students, 26% of Hispanic students, and 22% of Caucasian students had experienced suspension, with African American students having longer suspension time frames even after controlling for the impact of poverty (Balfanz, Byrnes, & Fox, 2015). Gender was also found to have an impact on these disparate discipline outcomes. Although males are significantly more likely than females to be suspended or expelled, generally around twice the risk, African American males are the most at risk for school-based arrest and suspension, though African American females are at a higher risk than Hispanic or Caucasian females for these same discipline outcomes (Darensbourg, Perez, & Blake, 2010; Skiba, Arrendonda, & Rausch, 2014).

There are also disproportionate impacts on youthful offenders of color who are involved with the juvenile courts. Adolescents of color are overrepresented at each decision-making point within the juvenile justice system, from arrest to charges to disposition, with the greatest disparities the further a youthful offender penetrates the system. This problem is known as disproportionate minority contact (Piquero, 2008). African American youthful offenders are referred to the juvenile courts for delinquency adjudication at a rate of 140% greater than are Caucasian youthful offenders (Puzzanchera & Robson, 2014). And if adjudicated and probation-supervised youthful offenders continue through the juvenile justice system to residential placement, the disparity is stark: African Americans and Hispanics represent one-third of this country's adolescent population, but more than two-thirds are held in the juvenile incarceration facilities (Hockenberry & Puzzanchera, 2014; National Council on Crime and Delinquency, 2007).

More specifically, these incarcerated youthful offenders are older adolescents (16- and 17-year olds), minority (68%), and male (87%). Of the youthful offenders incarcerated who are minorities, approximately 60% are African American, 33% are Hispanic, and, depending on the jurisdiction, between 1% and 4% are American Indian or Asian (Office of Juvenile Justice and Delinquency Prevention, 2014). These disparities are found in nearly all states with a greater impact on minority males than on females (Office of Juvenile Justice and Delinquency Prevention, 2014). To highlight the risk, an African American youthful offender is six times more likely to be incarcerated and a Hispanic youthful offender is three times more likely than a Caucasian youthful offender, even when controlling for other explanatory variables (Kempf-Leonard, 2007; Piquero, 2008).

Students With Special Education Disabilities

Students with special education disabilities, as prescribed and directed by the Individuals with Disabilities Education Act (IDEA), are entitled to receive free, appropriate public education in the least restrictive education environment. Children and adolescents across a wide range of difficulties are protected by this federal law, but many are being inappropriately removed from the classroom and schools through harsh discipline practices (Advancement Project et al., 2011). The primary concern for those who are overrepresented in the pipeline and the juvenile courts are students with emotional disturbances and/or learning disabilities (Mallett, 2011; Mears & Aron, 2003). As discussed earlier, it is well established that students with learning disabilities have a two to three times greater risk than students without these disabilities of being involved in offending and delinquent activities and of having higher recidivism rates (Matta-Oshima et al., 2010; Wang et al., 2005). The risk for students of color to be diagnosed with learning disabilities is significantly greater: Hispanics are almost 20% more likely, African Americans are more than 40% more likely, and American Indians are 80% more likely (U.S. Department of Education, 2014a).

Most reviews of students with special education disabilities find that they represent a larger percentage of the suspended and expelled student population—20% to 24% compared with the typical 11% to 14% of the population that students with special education disabilities represent within their school district (Fabelo et al., 2011; Harry & Klingner, 2006; Kansas Department of Education, 2004; Losen & Gillespie, 2012; Losen & Martinez, 2013). These discipline disparities have been found to be an outcome of higher rates of student misbehaviors and disruptions; however, misbehavior was found to have no impact on these differences, indicating a need for more investigations to determine if bias or targeting of students is occurring (American Psychological Association Zero Tolerance Task Force, 2008).

In particular, students with certain impairing mental health problems—diagnosed under the IDEA as an emotional disturbance—are found to be the most at risk for school discipline within the special education student population, with some researchers finding almost three-fourths of this group suspended or expelled during their high school years (Wagner, Kutash, Duchnowski, Epstein, & Sumi, 2005), and others finding these discipline outcomes to be between 7 and 12 times more likely for students with emotional disturbances compared to students without them (Cooley, 1995). In some jurisdictions, African American students with emotional disturbance disabilities are the most at risk, with significantly higher numbers being suspended or expelled than Caucasian students with disabilities in studies conducted in Texas and Los Angeles (Fabelo et al., 2011; Losen & Gillespie, 2012). This student group with emotional problems is more likely to be placed in restrictive settings, has high school dropout rates, and 50% have at least one arrest as young adults, during and after high school (Merrell & Walker, 2004).

Significantly large numbers of youthful offenders involved with the juvenile courts have special education disabilities, particularly those in detention and incarceration facilities—between 28% and 43% (Kvarfordt, Purcell, & Shannon, 2005; Rozalski, Deignan, & Engel, 2008; Wang et al., 2005; White & Loeber, 2008). Among those adolescents with special education disabilities in these locked facilities, 48% had an identified emotional disturbance, 39% had a specific learning disability, 10% had mental retardation (developmental disabilities), and 3% had other health impairments (Burrell & Warboys, 2000; Quinn, Rutherford, Leone, Osher, & Poirier, 2005).

A smaller subset of this child and adolescent population with mental health disabilities, between 5% and 10%, develops serious emotional disturbances that cause substantial impairment in functioning at home, at school, and/or in the community. This group with serious emotional disturbances does not differ significantly in terms of age, ethnicity, or gender from the general child and adolescent population (Freidman, Katz-Leavy, Mandersched, & Sondheimer, 1996; Substance Abuse and Mental Health Services Administration, 2013). However, these severely impaired young people have challenges in accessing mental health services, have trouble in school settings, and are often formally involved with the juvenile courts (Armstrong, Dedrick, & Greenbaum, 2003; Bazelon Center for Mental Health Law, 2003). This small number of adolescents who are considered seriously emotionally disturbed typically have long histories of multiple mental health disorders that will normally persist into adulthood, and they constitute an estimated 15% to 20% of the youthful offenders in juvenile justice detention and incarceration facilities (Cocozza & Skowyra, 2000; Mallett, 2013).

In addition to this subgroup of offending adolescents, many are diagnosed with other mental health problems. Common mental health disorders found within juvenile justice correctional facility populations include depressive disorders (13%–40%), psychotic disorders (5%–10%), anxiety disorders (approximately 25%), attention deficit hyperactivity disorder (ADHD) (approximately 20%), disruptive behavior disorders (30%–80%), and substance use disorders (30%–70%) (Abram et al., 2013; Goldstein, Olubadewo, Redding, & Lexcen, 2005; Grisso, 2008; Kinscherff, 2012).

Maltreatment and Trauma Victims

The link from maltreatment and trauma to the school-to-prison pipeline is indirect. This is the case for two reasons. One, maltreatment and related traumas have multiple harmful impacts on children and adolescents, both at the time of the incidents and over time and through comorbidity of difficulties. And two, because of research methodological challenges that have complied with the dearth of literature and published investigations, other links and risks are more readily apparent or easily discerned. Here, the links and risk factors are presented, with a prima facie conclusion that maltreatment is at minimum a strong correlative thread for many students both into and through the pipeline.

As reviewed earlier, maltreatment and related traumas have profound impacts on many child and adolescent school outcomes. The more serious, earlier in life, or pervasive the maltreatment, the greater the risk for special education disabilities (Leiter, 2007; Smithgall et al., 2004), a disability group that is of itself at a much higher risk for involvement in school discipline and in the pipeline (Center for Civil Rights Remedies, 2013). In addition, any maltreatment victimization, be it neglect, physical abuse, or sexual abuse, often leads to other school-related difficulties, thus making the transition from primary to secondary school more difficult (Smithgall et al., 2004); it also results in poorer academic outcomes (Mears & Aron, 2003; Shonk & Cicchetti, 2001), failure of a school grade, cognitive and language delays (Wiggins, Fenichel, & Mann, 2007), higher absenteeism rates (Lansford et al., 2002), lower standardized testing scores (Coleman, 2004), and lower high school graduation rates (Boden, Horwood, & Fergusson, 2007; Thornberry, Ireland, & Smith, 2001). Children and adolescents in foster care who are disproportionately African American and non-Hispanic Indian (Summers, Wood, & Donovan, 2013) are at even higher risk for a number of these and related difficulties: special education disabilities, not graduating high school, homelessness, and juvenile and/or criminal court involvement (Children's Defense Fund, 2014; Scarborough & McCrae, 2009).

The links from maltreatment, particularly for child victims, to school difficulties are clear. The literature on school discipline and the number of groups who are at higher risk for involvement in the pipeline is also self-evident—children and adolescents in poverty, students of color, and students with special education disabilities (among others). Thus, maltreatment may be a strong, and for many children, a direct link to disproportionate school discipline because of these trauma-related problems. In addition, it is speculated by many child-welfare experts that the identified and substantiated cases of child maltreatment are significantly undercounted—with the actual number of victimizations being many times greater than the annual approximate count of 800,000 (Child Help, 2014; U.S. Department of Health and Human Services, 2013b). If so, maltreatment and its subsequent harm on school outcomes may also be a hidden explanatory or correlative link to students' eventual involvement in the pipeline. It is one possible reason that the juvenile courts have a surprisingly disproportionate number of youthful offenders with maltreatment backgrounds.

When this disproportionality is evaluated, it is identified that between 26% and 60% of adjudicated delinquent adolescents have been found with past or concurrent maltreatment victimizations (Bender, 2009; Ford, Chapman, Hawke, & Albert, 2007; Mallett, Stoddard-Dare, & Seck, 2009; Sedlak & McPherson, 2010; Stouthamer-Loeber, Wei, Homish, & Loeber, 2002). This maltreatment to delinquency link has been fairly well established, though with some gaps in knowledge. Through the use of longitudinal and group comparison designs, maltreatment victims have been found much more likely to be arrested, though this varied by gender, race, and maltreatment type (Maxfield & Widom, 1996), to be involved with more serious delinquent activities (Lemmon, 1999; Smith & Thornberry, 1995), and for the continuation of criminal involvement (Lemmon, 2006).

Though maltreatment is a significant risk factor for later juvenile court involvement, it is important to highlight that a majority of children and adolescents who are victims never become involved with the juvenile courts (Yun, Ball, & Lim, 2011; Widom, 2003). However, as noted, victims of maltreatment are significantly overrepresented among those involved with the juvenile courts and, in particular, among those youthful offenders who are detained and incarcerated in facilities where more than half of the residents have been victims (Currie & Tekin, 2006; Lemmon, 2006). Thus, it is not surprising that there is strong empirical support confirming the links across child and adolescent trauma, mental health difficulties, and placement in juvenile justice detention and incarceration facilities (Abram et al., 2013; Hooks, 2012).

The correlation across child maltreatment, schools, and juvenile delinquency is a serious, though under-investigated, concern. Research is gradually revealing how victimization experiences may contribute to the child's and adolescent's pathway into delinquency. However, this remains a complex matter because of the hidden and unidentified victims, differential impact of maltreatment, maltreatment victimization types, and diverse harmful outcomes, and because a number of maltreatment outcomes are, in their own turn, also significant youthful offending risk factors. Further investigations are warranted, and in particular, reviewing the link between the school and the juvenile justice system.

LGBT Students

Students who identify as LGBT have been found to be at greater risk for involvement in school discipline and, for some, the juvenile courts and detention and incarceration facilities (Losen, Hewitt, & Toldson, 2014). In the past few years, researchers have identified this student group to have a heightened risk for involvement in the pipeline; this may be due to more students having found ways to identify as LGBT and, subsequently, researchers have been investigating the problems for this group. Thus, there is limited, though compelling evidence.

> Asante Colman, a seventeen-year-old junior at Charles City High School in Charles City County, Virginia, was suspended for three days after refusing an order from a school official to take off a pair of high heels he was wearing. "I'm not advertising. I'm being myself," said Colman. "I want to be able to be a regular student. A gay regular student that attends CCHS." (Mitchum & Moodie-Mills, 2014, p. 11)

LGBT students experience exclusionary discipline—suspensions and expulsion—and hostile school environments more often than their peers, increasing the risk for arrests and juvenile court involvement (Skiba, Arrendonda, & Rausch, 2014). One nationally representative research sample of LGBT-identifying students found a 30% to 150% greater risk, dependent on outcome of interest, for school expulsion, juvenile arrest, and conviction, with a particularly higher risk for girls, even after controlling for other explanatory variables (Himmelstein & Bruckner, 2011). School environments have been found to be hostile and unsafe for many LGBT-identifying students, leading some to become confrontational and aggressive to maintain safety (Kosciw, Greytak, Diaz, & Bartkiewicz, 2010; Savage & Schanding, 2013).

Other LGBT-identifying students avoid the difficulties, hostilities, and challenges and have increased absenteeism rates, because of the unsafe school environment, with many having poorer academic outcomes, grades, and school engagement as a result of these and other problems (Kosciw, Palmer, Kull, & Greytak, 2013; Murdoch & Bolch, 2005; Russell, Kostroski, Horn, & Saewyc, 2010). In-school victimizations for LGBT students have been associated with harmful psychological effects, such as depression and other mental health difficulties, including high rates of suicide compared to their peers (Himmelstein & Bruckner, 2011; Human Rights Watch, 2009; Tooney, Ryan, Diaz, & Russell, 2011). Within the LGBT student community, the most recent school climate report found that 63% felt unsafe because of their sexual orientation, 38% were physically harassed, 18% were physically assaulted, and 32% skipped a day of school in the previous month due to feeling unsafe (Kosciw, Greytak, Barkiewicz, & Palmer, 2012). These difficulties may also begin for many of these young people at home, where there is a significantly increased risk for family violence once adolescents announce their sexual orientation as non-heterosexual (Estrada & Marksamer, 2006), as well as disproportionate numbers of LGBT adolescents who run away from home (Burwick, Oddo, Durso, Friend, & Gates, 2014). Homelessness is a significant predictor for a young person to be involved with the juvenile justice system, and approximately 40% of homeless adolescents are LGBT (Majd, Marksamer, & Reyes, 2009).

> My mom (told the judge that I was gay). She told him I wouldn't go to school and I got kicked out. (But the problem was) I was getting harassed at school. My probation officer lied and said it wasn't as bad (at school) as it was. (Mitchum & Moodie-Mills, 2014, p. 8)

As LGBT students are disproportionately impacted by school discipline, greater numbers are undoubtedly moving through the school-to-prison pipeline. Though this area is a recently investigated phenomenon, for the same research limitations enumerated earlier, it is probably not a new situation in the juvenile courts. Historical myths that LGBT adolescents are rare or nonexistent in the juvenile courts have given way to epidemiology of the adolescent population. Emerging evidence has found that LGBT adolescents are twice as likely to be arrested and detained for status and other nonviolent offenses (Irvine, 2010), and that between 13% and 15% of youthful offenders formally processed in the juvenile courts and being held in the detention centers are LGBT (Beck, Cantor, Hartge, & Smith, 2013; Majd, Marksamer, & Reyes, 2009). A disproportionate number, approximately 60%, of these arrested and detained LGBT adolescents are Black or Hispanic, mirroring or expanding the racial and ethnic disparities (Hunt & Moodie-Mills, 2012; Piquero, 2008).

In fact, family rejection and school harassment continue to be factors that increase the numbers of LGBT adolescents in the juvenile justice system, with this lack of support perpetuating offending and truancy recidivism (Advancement Project, 2005; Fedders, 2006). LGBT adolescents are also nearly three times more likely to report being victims of childhood physical or sexual abuse, with boys more at risk than girls (Friedman et al., 2011). Following family rejection during adolescence, drug use was three times more likely and suicide was eight times more likely for LGBT young people (Ryan, Huebner, Diaz, & Sanchez, 2009). In addition, one review found that the risk for home removal by a children's service agency and placement in a group or foster home was twice as likely for LGBT adolescents than for maltreated non-LGBT adolescents (Irvine, 2010). As discussed, the link from maltreatment to the juvenile courts is well established, and the comorbidity of difficulties and its impact on these adolescents has become a serious policy concern over the past decade.

Suicide in the Juvenile Justice Institutions

The comorbid impact of maltreatment, school difficulties, bullying, mental health problems, and a punitive juvenile justice system have resulted in harmful detention and incarceration facilities where many young people spend, often significant, lengths of time. These facilities, with some variance across local and state jurisdictions, have become today's child and adolescent psychiatric hospitals, a role they are ill-equipped to handle. Whether because of the structure of the facilities, the serious and significant comorbid problems the youthful offenders are dealing with, or a combination of the two, these detention and incarceration facilities are unsafe places (Holman & Ziedenberg, 2014; U.S. Department of Justice, 2012). In particular, the incarceration experience itself increases this risk for suicide both during and after release (Hayes, 2009). In addition to incarceration, there are other suicide risk factors that these adolescents may experience:

a family or individual history of suicide, a history of depression, serious alcohol or drug abuse, loss (trauma), and easy access to lethal methods (Centers for Disease Control and Prevention, 2009; Evans, Hawton, & Rodham, 2004).

In a comprehensive review of youthful offenders in custody, 22% reported that they had tried to kill themselves during their lifetime, a significantly higher risk than nonoffending adolescents (Sedlak & McPherson, 2010). A national study of court-ordered juvenile offenders in placement found that 110 completed suicides occurred between 1995 and 1999. Of the 79 cases with complete information, it was found that 42% of the suicides took place in secure juvenile court facilities and training schools, 37% in detention centers, 15% in residential treatment centers, and 6% in reception or diagnostic centers (Hayes, 2009). A similar review of youthful offenders in juvenile detention facilities in the 1980s found a suicide rate that was almost five times higher than for adolescents in the general population (Memory, 1989). With a recent investigation of detained youthful offenders, it was found that more than 11% had attempted suicide during their young lives (Abram et al., 2014). In addition, thoughts of suicide ranged from 15% to 50% for incarcerated youthful offenders (Abram et al., 2014), whereas large reviews of those adolescents in custody or detention found that between 25% and 30% reported suicidal thoughts (Cauffman, 2004; Putnins, 2005; Sedlak & McPherson, 2010). Researchers have begun to analyze how facility characteristics may be related to suicide attempts and deaths (Gallagher & Dobrin, 2005; Thompson, Ho, & Kingree, 2007), with some finding that facilities that house larger populations of youthful offenders and those that had locked sleeping room doors had the highest risk of suicide (Gallagher & Dobrin, 2006).

Because the youthful offender detained and incarcerated population is disproportionately minority and male, it is important to note that adolescent males are more likely to die from suicide attempts, as well as use more violent means, though adolescent females are more likely to report attempting suicide (Centers for Disease Control and Prevention, 2013; Penn, Esposito, Schaeffer, Fritz, & Spirito, 2003). Native American/Alaskan Native and Hispanic adolescents have been found to have the highest rate of suicide deaths (Centers for Disease Control and Prevention, 2013) and suicidal ideation (Graham & Corcoran, 2003), whereas Caucasian adolescent females reported more incidents of suicide or self-injury than their African American counterparts (Holsinger, K. & Holsinger, A., 2005). Many of these adolescents suffer from mental health and substance abuse problems, which places them at high risk for suicidal ideation, attempts, and completions (Douglas, Herbozo, Poythress, Belfrage, & Edens, 2006; Gould, Greenberg, Velting, & Shaffer, 2003). Serious mental health problems have been found to affect more than one in four juvenile justice system-involved adolescents (Shufelt & Cocozza, 2006) and more than half of those in detention and incarceration facilities (Abram et al., 2013; Teplin et al., 2006).

These adolescent difficulties and comorbidities, interrelated to the incarceration experience, need to address whether the risk of harm and ongoing recidivism is to be minimized. However, predicting suicide risk is difficult, for risk factors vary in their impact and intensity. Even when other risk factors—age, ethnicity, gender, alcohol and drug problems, depression, and impulsivity—were accounted for, delinquency was still related to suicidal ideation and attempts until 1 year later, and to suicidal ideation until 7 years later (Thompson, Ho, & Kingree, 2007). Youthful offenders with an arrest history are more likely to report a suicide attempt than those without an arrest history (Tolou-Shams, Brown, Gordon, & Fernandez, 2007). In addition, demonstrating the impact of comorbid problems, young people in juvenile justice facilities who have experienced maltreatment as children are more than twice as likely to have attempted suicide as their peers who had experienced maltreatment but were not in these facilities (Croysdale, Drerup, Bewsey, & Hoffman, 2008). In addition, those who committed suicide had experienced rates of maltreatment that were 2 to 10 times greater than the general child and adolescent population (Hayes, 2009). In a stark finding, 63% of adolescents who had completed suicide in Utah between 1996 and 1999 had contact with the juvenile justice system (Gray et al., 2002). The risk of suicide for the young people involved with the juvenile courts and its detention and incarceration facilities is a significant problem.

WHY THE DISPROPORTIONATE IMPACT?

The question remains: Why are these children and adolescents, many already troubled and vulnerable, disproportionately impacted by increased school discipline protocols, school-to-prison pipeline involvement, and, for some, juvenile court supervision, detention, or incarceration? Although the answer remains necessary for local school district and juvenile court stakeholders to determine because most jurisdictions, and even states, have unique circumstances, there remain themes and larger contexts that should be included in any inquiry.

Inherent Bias and Targeting

Bias and stereotyping are not explanations that make stakeholders comfortable. However, it is fairly clear that most individuals harbor stereotypes that often unknowingly affect their perceptions of others. Decisions to invoke school discipline, knowing that a significant majority of the infractions are for disobedience, defiance, and other subjective student behaviors, involve the ideology, perceptions, values, and, at times, biases of those making the decisions (Skiba, Michael, Nardo, & Peterson, 2002; Wald, 2014), found in studies of both school (Casteel, 1998) and juvenile court personnel (Graham & Lowry, 2004; Levinson, 2007).

Research continues to show that cultural stereotypes impact perceptions and reactions to minority groups in schools and juvenile courts. For example, the association of African American males and increased perceptions of danger, as well as perceptions of the LGBT student community, can lead to harsher punishments (American Psychological Association Zero Tolerance Task Force, 2008; Hunt & Moodie-Mills, 2012; Kirwan Institute, 2014; Majd, Marksamer, & Reyes, 2009).

Comorbid Difficulties

With the myriad of difficulties experienced by the groups that are disproportionately involved in school discipline and the juvenile courts, explanations often entail a combination of risks both over time and concurrently. Rarely is it a singular experience that leads to students' involvement in the school-to-prison pipeline (Howell, 2003; Mallett, 2013). Although explanatory reasons for this involvement have identified school environments, teachers, and school resource officers, it is important to consider the impact that family functioning, neighborhoods, poverty, trauma, and related difficulties have on the child or adolescent. The cumulative difficulties can be substantial in impairing the child or adolescent (Skiba & Williams, 2014; Equity Project at Indiana University, 2014). In addition, there is disproportionate involvement of students of color within the special education population as well as the families involved with children's service agencies and children who have been placed in foster care, requiring additional investigations to identify pathways, causes, and prevention points (Children's Defense Fund, 2014; Summers, Wood, & Donovan, 2013; U.S. Department of Education, 2012).

Inequitable Distribution of Resources

Not all school districts or school discipline protocols are alike; they are differentiated via location, student population, family income levels, and community resources, among other factors. Inequitable differences across schools and districts are as follows: Low-income students are more likely to be punished within schools (McNulty-Eitle, 2004); large school districts with larger minority populations have greater security measures and discipline outcomes (McCurdy, 2014); the No Child Left Behind Act has a significantly more harmful impact on low-performing, often poorly resourced school districts (Heitzeg, 2014); and more poorly performing schools have trouble in hiring and retaining qualified teachers (Kupchik, 2010). The multifaceted impact of policies and subsequent rules and regulations that accompany school funding decisions at the local, state, and federal level should be taken into account when discerning these complex explanations for the rise of the school-to-prison pipeline, as well as how to appropriately correct these problems in the schools and the juvenile courts.

Segregation by Race and Class

A common narrative for many students caught within the pipeline is that there is subtle, or not so subtle, racial profiling, leading to disproportionate outcomes for students of color, impoverished students, and those with special education disabilities, among others. Although this inherent bias explanation was discussed earlier, it has led to recommendations and concerns about teachers' ethnicity and ability to work across student groups. There is an alternative paradigm that may be important in determining the reasons for disproportionate impacts of school discipline: that many schools are segregated by class and race and that most low-income students and students of color attend different schools compared to most middle-class and Caucasian students, thus taking the primary focus off the teacher or classroom as a causative factor (NAACP, 2005).

Consequently, when administrators and educators at many of these more segregated schools see the potential for greater safety concerns, they may develop school discipline procedures that rely more heavily on out-of-school alternatives for students identified as risky or troublesome. These strong responses to students, primarily low-income and/or of color and concentrated in larger urban school districts (Addington, 2014; Hirschfield, 2010), may emanate from teachers of any ethnic group, showing that the response is related to the race and class differential and less so to teacher perceptions or bias. In other words, it may be less so to cultural insensitivity or ineptness of those working with students who are different (race, disability, and socioeconomic class, among others), and more so to school and district structural explanations that need to be accounted for and analyzed (Ferguson, 2000). However, this narrative is incomplete, and any investigation into race and class segregation must account for the fact that schools with a relatively higher proportion of teachers of color tend to have lower rates of disproportionality in discipline (McLoughlin & Noltemeyer, 2010; Roch, Pitts, & Navarro, 2010; Rocha & Hawes, 2009).

REFERENCES

Abram, K. M., Choe, J. Y., Washburn, J. J., Teplin, L. A., King, D. C., Dulcan, M. K., & Bassett, E. D. (2014). *Suicidal thoughts and behaviors among detained youth.* Washington, DC: Office of Juvenile Justice and Delinquency Prevention, Office of Justice Programs, U.S. Department of Justice.

Abram, K. M., Teplin, L. A., King, D. C., Longworth, S. L., Emanuel, K. M., Romero, E. G., . . . Olson, N. D. (2013). *PTSD, trauma, and comorbid psychiatric disorders in detained youth.* Washington, DC: Office of Juvenile Justice and Delinquency Prevention, Office of Justice Programs, U.S. Department of Justice.

Addington, L. A. (2014). Surveillance and security approaches across public school levels. In G. W. Muschert, S. Henry, N. L. Bracy, & A. A. Peguero (Eds.), *Responding to school violence: Confronting the Columbine effect* (pp. 71–88). Boulder, CO: Lynne Rienner.

Advancement Project. (2005). *Education on lockdown: The schoolhouse to jailhouse track.* Washington, DC: Author.

Advancement Project, Education Law Center–PA, FairTest, The Forum for Education and Democracy, Juvenile Law Center, & NAACP Legal Defense and Educational Fund, Inc. (2011). *Federal policy, ESEA reauthorization, and the school-to-prison pipeline,* Washington, DC: Author.

Altarac, M., & Saroha, E. (2007). Lifetime prevalence of learning disability among US children. *Pediatrics, 119,* 577–584.

American Bar Association. (2014). *ABA policy on trauma-informed advocacy for children and youth.* Washington, DC: Author.

American Psychological Association Zero Tolerance Task Force. (2008). Are zero tolerance policies effective in the schools? An evidentiary review and recommendations. *American Psychologist, 63*(9), 852–862.

Armstrong, K. H., Dedrick, R. F., & Greenbaum, P. E. (2003). Factors associated with community adjustment of young adults with serious emotional disturbances: A longitudinal analysis. *Journal of Emotional and Behavioral Disorders, 11*, 66–76.

Ayassee, R. H. (1995). Addressing the needs of foster children: The foster youth services program. *Social Work in Education, 17*(4), 207–216.

Balfanz, R., Byrnes, V., & Fox, J. (2015). Sent home and put off-track: The antecedents, disproportionalities, and consequences of being suspended in the ninth grade. In D. J. Losen (Ed.), *Closing the school discipline gap: Research for policymakers*. New York, NY: Teachers College.

Bazelon Center for Mental Health Law. (2003). *Teaming up: Using the IDEA and Medicaid to secure comprehensive mental health services for children and youth.* Washington, DC: Author.

Beck, A. J., Cantor, D., Hartge, J., & Smith, T. (2013). *Sexual victimization in juvenile facilities report by youth, 2012.* Washington, DC: U.S. Department of Justice, Office of Justice Programs, Bureau of Justice Statistics.

Bender, K. (2009). Why do some maltreated youth become juvenile offenders? A call for further investigation and adaption of youth services. *Children Youth Services Review, 32*, 466–473.

Boden, J. M., Horwood, L. J., & Fergusson, D. M. (2007). Exposure to childhood sexual and physical abuse and subsequent educational achievement outcomes. *Child Abuse and Neglect, 10*, 1101–1114.

Bracy, N. L. (2010). Circumventing the law: Students' rights in schools with police. *Journal of Contemporary Criminal Justice, 26*, 294–315.

Breda, C. S. (2003). Offender ethnicity and mental health service referrals from juvenile courts. *Criminal Justice and Behavior, 30*(6), 644–667.

Brunelle, N., Brochu, S., & Cousineau, M. (2000). Drug-crime relations among drug-consuming juvenile delinquents: A tripartite model. *Contemporary Drug Problems, 27*(4), 835–867.

Buehler, C., Orme, J. G., Post, J., & Patterson, D. A. (2000). The long-term correlates of family foster care. *Children and Youth Services Review, 22*(8), 595–625.

Buffington, K., Pierkhising, C. B., & Marsh, S. (2010). *Ten things every juvenile court judge should know about trauma and delinquency.* Reno, NV: National Council of Juvenile and Family Court Judges.

Burdge, H., Licona, A. C., & Hyemingway, Z. T. (2014). *Youth of color: Discipline disparities, school push-out, and the school-to-prison pipeline.* San Francisco, CA: Gay-Straight Alliance Network; Tucson, AZ: Crossroads Collaborative at the University of Arizona.

Burley, M., & Halpern, M. (2001). *Educational attainment of foster youth: Achievement and graduation outcomes for children in state care* (Document No. 01-11-3901). Olympia, WA: Washington State Institute for Public Policy.

Burrell, S., & Warboys, L. (2000). *Special education and the juvenile justice system.* Washington, DC: Office of Juvenile Justice and Delinquency Prevention, Office of Justice Programs, U.S. Department of Justice.

Burwick, A., Oddo, V., Durso, L., Friend, D., & Gates, G. (2014). *Identifying and serving LGBTQ youth: Case studies of runaway and homeless youth program grantees.* Washington, DC: Office of Justice Programs, Bureau of Justice Statistics, U.S. Department of Justice.

Carter, P. L., Fine, M., & Russell, S. (2014, March). *Discipline disparities overview.* Discipline disparities series: New Research. Bloomington, IN: The Equity Project at Indiana University. Available at http://rtpcollaborative.indiana.edu/briefing-papers

Caspi, A., McClay, J., Moffitt, T. E., Mill, J., Martin, J., Craig, I. W., . . . Poulton, R. (2002). Role of genotype in the cycle of violence in maltreated children. *Science, 297,* 851–854.

Casteel, C. A. (1998). Teacher-student interactions and race in integrated classrooms. *Journal of Educational Research, 92*(2), 115–120.

Cauffman, E. (2004). A statewide screening of mental health symptoms among juvenile offenders in detention. *Journal of the American Academy of Child & Adolescent Psychiatry, 43*(4), 430–439.

Center for Civil Rights Remedies. (2013). *A summary of new research, closing the school discipline gap: Research to practice.* Washington, DC: Civil Rights Project.

Centers for Disease Control and Prevention. (2009). *Suicide prevention: Youth suicide.* Atlanta, GA: National Center for Injury Prevention and Control, Division of Violence Prevention.

Centers for Disease Control and Prevention. (2013). *2010, US suicide injury deaths and rates per 100,000.* Atlanta, GA: Author.

Chassin, L. (2008). Juvenile justice and substance abuse. *The Future of Children, 18*(2), 165–184.

Child Help. (2014). *National child abuse statistics: Child abuse in America.* Phoenix, AZ: Author.

Children's Defense Fund. (1975). *School suspensions: Are they helping children?* Cambridge, MA: Washington Research Project.

Children's Defense Fund. (2013). *Child poverty in America, 2012: National analysis.* Washington, DC: Author.

Children's Defense Fund. (2014). *The state of America's children*. Washington, DC: Author.

Children's Law Center. (2003). *Education summit*. Symposium Report, May 16, 2003. Washington, DC: Author.

Cocozza, J., & Skowyra, K. (2000). Youth with mental health disorders: Issues and emerging responses. *Juvenile Justice Journal, 7*(1), 3–13.

Coleman, M. S. (2004). *Children left behind: The educational status and needs of youth living in foster care in Ohio*. Washington, DC: National Center for Research and Data, Child Welfare League of America.

Collishaw, S., Pickles, A., Messer, J., Rutter, M., Shearer, C., & Maughan, B. (2007). Resilience to adult psychopathology following childhood maltreatment: Evidence from a community sample. *Child Abuse & Neglect, 31*, 211–229.

Conger, D., & Rebeck, A. (2001). *How children's foster care experiences affect their education*. New York, NY: Vera Institute for Justice.

Cooley, S. (1995). *Suspension/expulsion of regular and special education students in Kansas: A report to the Kansas State Board of Education*. Topeka, KS: Kansas State Board of Education.

Courtney, M. E., Roderick, M., Smithgall, C., Gladden, R. M., & Nagaoka, J. (2004). *The educational status of foster children*. Chicago, IL: Chapin Hall Center for Children.

Courtney, M. E., Terao, S., & Bost, N. (2004). *Midwest evaluation of the adult functioning of former foster youth: Conditions of youth preparing to leave state care*. Chicago, IL: Chapin Hall Center for Children.

Croysdale, A., Drerup, A., Bewsey, K., & Hoffman, N. (2008). Correlates of victimization in a juvenile justice population. *Journal of Aggression, Maltreatment & Trauma, 17*(1), 103–117.

Cuevas, C. A., Finkelhor, D., Shattuck, A., Turner, H., & Hamby, S. (2013). *Children's exposure to violence and the intersection between delinquency and victimization*. Washington, DC: Office of Juvenile Justice and Delinquency Promotion, Office of Justice Programs, U.S. Department of Justice.

Currie, J., & Tekin, E. (2006). *Does child abuse cause crime?* Andrew Young School of Public Policy, Research Paper Studies, Georgia State University.

Darensbourg, A., Perez, E., & Blake, J. J. (2010). Overrepresentation of African American males in exclusionary discipline: The role of school-based mental health professionals in dismantling the school to prison pipeline. *Journal of African American Males in Education, 1*(3), 196–211.

DeMatteo, D., & Marczyk, G. (2005). Risk factors, protective factors, and the prevention of antisocial behavior among juveniles. In K. Heilbrun,

N. E. Seven Goldstein, & R. E. Redding (Eds.), *Juvenile delinquency: Prevention, assessment, and intervention* (pp. 19–44). New York, NY: Oxford University Press.

Dembo, R., Wothky, W., Shemwell, M., Pacheco, K., Seeberger, W, Rollie, M., . . . Livingston, S. (2000). A structural model of the influence of family problems and child abuse factors on serious delinquency among youths processed at a juvenile assessment center. *Journal of Child and Adolescent Substance Abuse, 10,* 17–31.

Devine, John. (1996). *Maximum security: The culture of violence in inner-city schools.* Chicago: University of Chicago Press.

Dong, M., Anda, R. F., Felitti, V. J., Dube, S. R., Williamson, D. F., Thompson, T. J., . . . Giles, W. H. (2004). The interrelatedness of multiple forms of childhood abuse, neglect, and household dysfunction. *Child Abuse and Neglect, 28*(7), 771–784.

Douglas, K. S., Herbozo, S., Poythress, N. G., Belfrage, H., & Edens, J. F. (2006). Psychopathy and suicide: A multisample investigation. *Psychological Services, 3*(2), 97–116.

Drake, B., & Zuravin, S. (1998). Bias in child maltreatment reporting. *American Journal of Orthopsychiatry, 68*(2), 295–304.

Egeland, B. (1997). Mediators of the effects of child maltreatment on developmental adaptation in adolescence. In D. Cicchetti & S. L. Toth (Eds.), *Rochester symposium on developmental psychopathology, volume 8, developmental perspectives on trauma: Theory, research, and intervention* (pp. 403–434). Rochester, NY: University of Rochester Press.

Equity Project at Indiana University. (2014, March). *Discipline disparities series: Key findings.* Discipline disparities series: New Research. Bloomington, IN: The Equity Project at Indiana University. Available at http://rtpcollaborative .indiana.edu/briefing-papers

Estrada, R., & Marksamer, J. (2006). Lesbian, gay, bisexual and transgender young people in state custody: Making the child welfare and juvenile justice systems safe for youth through litigation, advocacy and education. *Temple Law Review, 79*(2), 415–438.

Evans, E., Hawton, K., & Rodham, K. (2004). Factors associated with suicidal phenomena in adolescents: A systematic review of population-based studies. *Clinical Psychology Review, 24,* 957–979.

Fabelo, T., Thompson, M. D., Plotkin, M., Carmichael, D., Marchbanks, M. P. III, & Booth, E. A. (2011). *Breaking schools' rules: A statewide study of how school discipline relates to students' success and juvenile justice involvement.* New York, NY; College Station, TX: Council of State Governments Justice Center; Public Research Policy Research Institute of Texas A & M University.

Farrington, D. P. (1997). Early prediction of violent and nonviolent youthful offending. *European Journal on Criminal Policy and Research, 5,* 51–66.

Fedders, B. (2006). Coming out for kids: Recognizing, respecting, and representing LGBTQ youth. *Nevada Law Journal, 6,* 774–792.

Felitta, V. J., Anda, R. F., Nordenberg, D., Williamson, D. F., Spitz, A. M., Edwards, V., . . . Marks, J. S. (2008). The relationships of adult health status to childhood abuse and household dysfunction. *American Journal of Preventive Medicine, 14,* 245–258.

Fergus, S., & Zimmerman, M. A. (2004). Adolescent resilience: A framework for understanding healthy development in the face of risk. *Annual Review of Public Health, 26,* 399–419.

Ferguson, A. A. (2000). *Bad boys: Public schools in the making of black masculinity.* Ann Arbor, MI: The University of Michigan Press.

Ford, J. D., Chapman, J. F., Hawke, J., & Albert, D. (2007). *Trauma among youth in the juvenile justice system: Critical issues and new directions.* Delmar, NY: National Center for Mental Health and Juvenile Justice.

Fraser, M. W. (Ed.). (2004). *Risk and resilience in childhood: An ecological perspective,* 2nd edition. Washington, DC: NASW Press.

Freidman, M. S., Marshal, M. P., Guadamuz, T. E., Wei, C., Wong, C. F., Saewyc, E., & Stall, R. (2011). A meta-analysis of disparities in childhood sexual abuse, parental physical abuse, and peer victimization among sexual minority and sexual nonminority individuals. *American Journal of Public Health, 101*(8), 1481–1494.

Freidman, R. M., Katz-Leavy, J. W., Mandersched, R., & Sondheimer, D. (1996). Prevalence of serious emotional disturbance in children and adolescents. In R. Mandersched & M.Sonnenschein (Eds.), *Mental health, United States: 1996* (pp. 71–89). Washington, DC: U.S. Department of Health and Human Services.

Gallagher, C., & Dobrin, A. (2005). The association between suicide screening practices and attempts requiring emergency care in juvenile justice facilities. *Journal of the American Academy of Child & Adolescent Psychiatry, 44*(5), 485–493.

Gallagher, C., & Dobrin, A. (2006). Facility-level characteristics associated with serious suicide attempts and deaths from suicide in juvenile justice residential facilities. *Suicide and Life Threatening Behavior, 36*(3), 363–375.

Goldstein, N., Olubadewo, O., Redding, R., & Lexcen, F. (2005). Mental health disorders: The neglected risk factor in juvenile delinquency. In K. Heilbrum (Ed.), *Juvenile delinquency: Prevention, assessment and intervention* (pp. 85–110). New York, NY: Oxford University Press.

Gorman-Smith, D., & Tolan, P. H. (1998). The role of exposure to violence and developmental problems among inner-city youth. *Development and Psychopathology, 10,* 101–116.

Gould, M. S., Greenberg, T., Velting, D. M., & Shaffer, D. (2003). Youth suicide risk and preventive interventions: A review of the past 10 years. *Journal of the American Academy of Child and Adolescent Psychiatry, 42,* 386–405.

Graham, S., & Lowry, B. S. (2004). Priming unconscious racial stereotypes about adolescent offenders. *Law and Human Behavior, 28*(5), 483–504.

Graham, T., & Corcoran, K. (2003). Mental health screening results for Native American and Euro-American youth in Oregon juvenile justice settings. *Psychological Reports, 92*(3, Pt. 2), 1053–1060.

Gray, D., Achilles, J., Keller, T., Tate, D., Haggard, L., Rolfs, R., . . . McMahon, W. (2002). Utah youth suicide study, phase 1: Government agency contact before death. *Journal of the American Academy of Child and Adolescent Psychiatry, 41*(4), 427–434.

Gregory, A., Skiba, R. J., & Noguera, P. A. (2010). The achievement gap and the discipline gap: Two sides of the same coin? *Education Researcher, 59,* 59–68.

Grisso, T. (2008). Adolescent offenders with mental disorders. *The Future of Children, 18*(2), 143–162.

Guterman, N. B. (2001). *Stopping child maltreatment before it starts: Emerging horizons in early home visitation services.* Thousand Oaks, CA: Sage.

Harry, B., & Klinger, J. (2006). *Why are so many minority students in special education: Understanding race and disability in schools.* New York, NY: Teachers College.

Hawkens, J. D., Herrenkohl, T. L., Farrington, D. P., Brewer, D., Catalano, R. F., & Harachi, T. W. (1998). A review of predictors of youth violence. In R. Loeber & T. P. Farrington (Eds.), *Serious and violent juvenile offenders: Risk factors and successful interventions* (pp. 106–146). Thousand Oaks, CA: Sage.

Hawkens, J. D., Herrenkohl, T. I., Farrington, D. P., Brewer, D., Catalano, R. F., Harachi, T. W., & Cothern, L. (2000). *Predictors of youth violence.* Washington, DC: Office of Juvenile Justice and Delinquency Prevention, Office of Justice Programs, U.S. Department of Justice.

Hayes, L. (2009). *Characteristics of juvenile suicide in confinement.* Washington, DC: Office of Juvenile Justice and Delinquency Prevention, Office of Justice Programs, U.S. Department of Justice.

Heilbrun, K. (1997). Prediction versus management models relevant to risk assessment: The importance of legal decision-making context. *Law and Human Behavior, 21,* 347–359.

Heitzeg, N. A. (2014). Criminalizing education: Zero tolerance policies, police in the hallways, and the school to prison pipeline. In A. J. Nocella II, P. Parmar, & D. Stovall (Eds.), *From education to incarceration: Dismantling the school-to-prison pipeline* (pp. 11–46). New York, NY: Peter Lang.

Heller, S. S., Larrieu, J. A., D'Imperio, R., & Boris, N. W. (1999). Research on resilience to child maltreatment: Empirical considerations. *Child Abuse & Neglect, 23*(4), 321–338.

Hennessey, M., Ford, J. D., Mahoney, K., Ko, S. J., & Siegfried, C. B. (2004). *Trauma among girls in the juvenile justice system.* Los Angeles, CA: National Child Traumatic Stress Network.

Hill, R. B. (2005). The role of race in parental reunification. In D. Derezotes, J. Poertner, & M. F. Testa (Eds.), *Race matters in child welfare: The overrepresentation of African American children in the system* (pp. 187–200). Washington, DC: Child Welfare League of America.

Himmelstein, K. E. W., & Bruckner, H. (2011). Criminal-justice and school sanctions against nonheterosexual youth: A national longitudinal study. *Pediatrics, 127*(1), 49–57.

Hirschfield, P. J. (2010). School surveillance in America: Disparate and unequal. In T. Monahan & R. D. Torres (Eds.), *Schools under surveillance: Cultures of control in public education* (pp. 38–54). New Brunswick, NJ: Rutgers University.

Hockenberry, S., & Puzzanchera, C. (2014). *Juvenile court statistics, 2011.* Washington, DC: Office of Juvenile Justice and Delinquency Prevention, Office of Justice Programs, U.S. Department of Justice.

Holman, B., & Ziedenberg, J. (2014). *The dangers of detention: The impact of incarcerating youth in detention and other secure facilities.* Washington, DC: Justice Policy Institute.

Holsinger, K., & Holsinger, A. (2005). Differential pathways to violence and self-injurious behavior: African American and white girls in the juvenile justice system. *Journal of Research in Crime and Delinquency, 42,* 211–242.

Holzer, H., Schanzenbach, D. W., Duncan, G. G., & Ludwig, J. (2007). *The economic costs of poverty: Subsequent effects of children growing up poor.* Washington, DC: Center for American Progress.

Hooks, J. (2012). *Mental health and the juvenile justices system.* Columbus, OH: Correctional Institution Inspection Committee.

Howell, J. C. (2003). *Preventing & reducing juvenile delinquency: A comprehensive framework.* Thousand Oaks, CA: Sage.

Human Rights Watch. (2009). *Hatred in the hallways: Violence and discrimination against lesbian, gay, bisexual, and transgender students in U.S. schools.* New York, NY: Author.

Hunt, J., & Moodie-Mills, A. C. (2012). *The unfair criminalization of gay and transgender youth: An overview of the experiences of LGBT youth in the juvenile justice system.* Washington, DC: Center for American Progress.

Hyames, S., & de Hames, M. V. (2000). *Educational experiences and achievement of children and youth in the care of the department receiving services from Chicago public schools.* Urbana-Champaign, IL: Children and Family Resource Center, University of Illinois.

Irvine, A. (2010). "We've had three of them": Addressing the invisibility of lesbian, gay, bisexual, and gender nonconforming youths in the juvenile justice system. *Columbia Journal of Gender and Law, 18*(3), 675–701.

Kansas Department of Education. (2004). *Biennial performance report: Performance goals and indicators.* Topeka, KS: Author.

Kelly, B. T., Thornberry, T. P., & Smith, C. A. (1997). *In the wake of childhood maltreatment.* Washington, DC: Office of Juvenile Justice and Delinquency Prevention, U.S. Department of Justice.

Kempf-Leonard, K. (2007). Minority youths and juvenile justice: Disproportionate minority contact after nearly 20 years of reform efforts. *Youth Violence and Juvenile Justice, 5,* 71–87.

Kilpatrick, D. G., Ruggiero, K. J., Acierno, R., Saunders, B. E., Resnick, H. S., & Best, C. L. (2003). Violence and risk of PTSD, major depression, substance abuse/dependence, and comorbidity: Results from the national survey of adolescents. *Journal of Consulting and Clinical Psychiatry, 71,* 692–700.

Kinscherff, R. (2012). *A primer for mental health practitioners working with youth involved in the juvenile justice system.* Washington, DC: Technical Assistance Partnership for Child and Family Mental Health.

Kirwan Institute. (2014). *State of the science: Implicit bias review 2014.* Columbus, OH: Kirwan Institute for the Study of Race and Ethnicity, Ohio State University.

Koenig, A. L., Cichetti, D., & Rogosch, F. A. (2000). Child compliance/noncompliance and maternal contributors to internalization in maltreating and nonmaltreating dyads. *Child Development, 71,* 1018–1032.

Kosciw, J. G., Greytak, E. A., Bartkiewicz, M. J., Boesen, M. J., & Palmer, N. A. (2012). *The 2009 national school climate survey: The experience of lesbian, gay, bisexual, and transgender youth in our nation's schools.* New York, NY: Gay, Lesbian, and Straight Education Network.

Kosciw, J. G., Greytak, E. A., Diaz, E. M., & Bartkiewicz, M. J. (2010). *The 2009 national school climate survey: The experience of lesbian, gay, bisexual, and transgender youth in our nation's schools.* New York, NY: Gay, Lesbian, and Straight Education Network.

Kosciw, J. G., Palmer, N. A., Kull, R. M., & Greytak, E. A. (2013). The effect of negative school climate on academic outcomes for LGBT youth and the role of in-school supports. *Journal of School Violence, 12*(1), 45–63.

Kracke, D., & Hahn, H. (2008). The nature and extent of childhood exposure to violence: What we know, why we don't know more, and why it matters. *Journal of Emotional Abuse, 8*(1–2), 24–49.

Kupchik, A. (2010). *Homeroom security: School discipline in an age of fear.* New York, NY: New York University Press.

Kurtz, P. D., Gaudin, J. M., Wodarski, J. S., & Howing, P. T. (1993). Maltreatment and the school-aged child: School performance consequences. *Child Abuse and Neglect, 17*(5), 581–589.

Kvarfordt, C. L., Purcell, P., & Shannon, P. (2005). Youth with learning disabilities in the juvenile justice system: A training needs assessment of detention and court services personnel. *Child & Youth Care Forum, 34*(1), 27–42.

Langrehr, K. J. (2011). Racial distinctions in the psychosocial histories of incarcerated youth. *Psychological Services, 8*(1), 23–35.

Lansford, J., Dodge, K. A., Pettit, G. S., Bates, J. E., Crozier, J., & Kaplow, J. (2002). Maltreatment on psychological, behavioral, and academic problems in adolescence. *Archives of Pediatric and Adolescent Medicine, 156,* 824–830.

Lawrence, R. G. (2007). *School crime and juvenile justice* (2nd ed). New York, NY: Oxford University Press.

Leiter, J. (2007). School performance trajectories after the advent of reported maltreatment. *Children and Youth Services Review, 29,* 363–382.

Leiter, J., & Johnsen, M. C. (1997). Child maltreatment and school performance declines: An event-history analysis. *American Educational Research Journal, 34*(3), 563–589.

Lemmon, J. H. (1999). How child maltreatment affects dimensions of juvenile delinquency in a cohort of low-income urban males. *Justice Quarterly, 16,* 357–376.

Lemmon, J. H. (2006). The effects of maltreatment recurrence and child welfare services on dimensions of delinquency. *Criminal Justice Review, 31*(1), 5–32.

Leone, P., & Weinberg, L. (2010). *Addressing the unmet educational needs of children and youth in the juvenile justice and child welfare systems.* Washington, DC: Center for Juvenile Justice Reform, Georgetown University.

Levinson, J. (2007). Forgotten racial equality: Implicit bias, decision making, and misremembering. *Duke Law Review, 12,* 307–350.

Loeber, R., & Farrington, D. P. (Eds.). (1998). *Serious and violent juvenile offenders: Risk factors and successful interventions.* Thousand Oaks, CA: Sage.

Losen, D. L., & Gillespie, J. (2012). *Opportunities suspended: The disparate impact of disciplinary exclusion from school.* Los Angeles, CA: Civil Rights Project at UCLA.

Losen, D. L., Hewitt, D., & Toldson, I. (2014, March). *Eliminating excessive and unfair discipline in schools: Policy recommendations for reducing disparities.* Discipline disparities series: New Research. Bloomington, IN: The Equity Project at Indiana University. Available at http://rtpcollaborative.indiana .edu/briefing-papers

Losen, D. L., & Martinez, T. (2013). *Out of school & off track: The overuse of suspensions in American middle and high schools.* Los Angeles, CA: Civil Rights Project at UCLA.

Lu, Y. E., Landsverk, J., Ellis-MacLeod, E., Newton, R., Ganger, W., & Johnson, E. (2004). Race, ethnicity and case outcomes in child protective services. *Children and Youth Services Review, 26*(5), 447–461.

Luthar, S. S. (2003). *Resilience and vulnerability: Adaptation in the context of childhood adversities.* Cambridge, UK: Cambridge University Press.

Majd, K. (2011). Students of the mass incarceration nation. *Howard Law Journal, 54*(2), 343–394.

Majd, K., Marksamer, J., & Reyes, C. (2009). *Hidden justice: Lesbian, gay, bisexual and transgender youth in juvenile courts.* San Francisco, CA: National Center for Lesbian Rights.

Mallett, C. (2008). The disconnect between delinquent youths with mental health and special education disabilities and juvenile court outcomes. *Corrections Compendium, 33*(5), 1–23.

Mallett, C. (2011). *Seven things juvenile courts should know about learning disabilities.* Reno, NV: National Council of Juvenile and Family Court Judges.

Mallett, C. (2012). The School Success Program: Improving maltreated children's academic and school-related outcomes. *Children & Schools, 34*(1), 13–26.

Mallett, C. (2013). *Linking disorders to delinquency: Treating high risk youth in the juvenile justice system.* Boulder, CO: Lynne Rienner.

Mallett, C., Stoddard-Dare, P., & Seck, M. (2009). Predicting juvenile delinquency: The nexus of child maltreatment, depression, and bipolar disorder. *Criminal Behaviour and Mental Health, 19*(4), 235–246.

Margolin, G., & Gordis, E. B. (2000). The effect of family and community violence on children. *Annual Review of Psychology, 51*, 445–479.

Massachusetts Advocacy Center. (1986). *The way out: Student exclusion practices in Boston Middle Schools.* Boston, MA: Author.

Masten, A. S., Best, K. M., & Garmezy, N. (1990). Resilience and development: Contributions from the study of children who overcome adversity. *Development and Psychopathology, 2*, 425–444.

Matta-Oshima, K. M., Huang, J., Jonson-Reid, M., & Drake, B. (2010). Children with disabilities in poor households: Association with juvenile and adult offending. *Social Work Research, 34*(2), 102–113.

Maxfield, M. G., Weiler, B. L., & Widom, C. S. (2000). Comparing self-reports and official records of arrest. *Journal of Quantitative Criminology, 16*(1), 87–110.

Maxfield, M. G., & Widom, C. S. (1996). The cycle of violence: Revisited six years later. *Archives of Pediatric and Adolescent Medicine, 150*, 390–395.

McCarthy, J. D., & Hoge, D. R. (1987). The social construction of school punishment: Racial disadvantage out of universalistic process. *Social Forces, 65*, 1101–1120.

McCurdy, J. (2014). Targets for arrest. In A. J. Nocella II, P. Parmar, & D. Stovall (Eds.), *From education to incarceration: Dismantling the school-to-prison pipeline* (pp. 86–101). New York, NY: Peter Lang.

McGee, R., Wolfe, D., & Olson, J. (2001). Multiple maltreatment, attribution of blame, and adjustment among adolescents. *Development and Psychopathology, 13*, 827–846.

McGloin, J. M., & Widom, C. S. (2001). Resilience among abused and neglected children grown up. *Development and Psychopathology, 13*(4), 1021–1038.

McLoughlin, C. S., & Noltemeyer, A. L. (2010). Research into factors contributing to discipline use and disproportionality in major urban schools. *Current Issues in Education, 13*(2), 1–20.

McNulty-Eitle, T., & Eitle, D. J. (2004). Inequality, segregation, and the overrepresentation of African Americans in school suspension. *Sociological Perspectives, 47*, 269–287.

Mears, D. P., & Aron, L. Y. (2003). *Addressing the needs of youth with disabilities in the juvenile justice system: The current state of knowledge*. Washington, DC: Urban Institute, Justice Policy Center.

Melton, G. B., & Pagliocca, P. M. (1992). Treatment in the juvenile justice system: Directions for policy and practice. In J. J. Cocozza (Ed.), *Responding to the mental health needs of youth in the juvenile justice system* (pp. 107–139). Seattle, WA: The National Coalition for the Mentally Ill in the Criminal Justice System.

Memory, J. (1989). Juvenile suicides in secure detention facilities: Correction of published rates. *Death Studies, 13*, 455–463.

Merrell, K. W., & Walker, H. M. (2004). Deconstructing a definition: Social maladjustment versus emotional disturbance and moving the EBD field forward. *Psychology in the Schools, 41*(8), 899–910.

Mitchum, P., & Moodie-Mills, A. C. (2014). *Beyond bullying: How hostile school climate perpetuates the school-to-prison pipeline for LBGT youth.* Washington, DC: Center for American Progress.

Monahan, J., Steadman, H. J., Silver, E., Appelbaum, P. S., Robbins, P. C., Mulvey, E. P., . . . Silver, E. (2001). *Rethinking risk assessment: The MacArthur study of mental disorder and violence.* New York, NY: Oxford University Press.

Morgan, E., Salomon, N., Plotkin, M., & Cohen, R. (2014). *The school discipline consensus report: Strategies from the field to keep students engaged in school and out of the juvenile justice system.* Washington, DC: The Council of State Governments Justice Center.

Murdoch, T. B., & Bolch, M. B. (2005). Risk and protective factors for poor school adjustment in lesbian, gay, and bisexual (LBG) high school youth: Variable and person-centered analyses. *Psychology in the Schools, 42,* 159–172.

NAACP. (2005). *Interrupting the school to prison pipeline.* Washington, DC: Author.

National Center for Child Traumatic Stress. (2009). *Child sexual abuse: Coping with the emotional stress of the legal system.* Los Angeles, CA: UCLA.

National Center for Children in Poverty. (2000). *Promoting resilience: Helping young children and parents affected by substance abuse, domestic violence, and depression in the context of welfare reform.* New York, NY: Author.

National Council on Crime and Delinquency. (2007). *And justice for some: Differential treatment of youth of color in the justice system.* Oakland, CA: Author.

National Low Income Housing Coalition. (2013). *Out of reach, 2013.* Washington, DC: Author.

National Youth in Care Network. (2001). *Who will teach me to learn: Creating positive experiences for youth in care.* Ottawa: National Youth in Care Network.

Neiman, S., & DeVoe, J. F. (2009). *Crime, violence, discipline, and safety in US public schools: Findings from the school survey on crime and safety.* Washington, DC: U.S. Department of Education.

Nicholson-Crotty, S., Birchmeier, Z., & Valentine, D. (2009). Exploring the impact of school discipline on racial disproportion in the juvenile justice system. *Social Science Quarterly, 90*(4), 1003–1018.

Noltmeyer, A., & McLoughlin, C. S. (2010). Patterns of exclusionary discipline by school typology, ethnicity, and their interactions. *Perspectives on Urban Education, 7,* 27–40.

Office of Juvenile Justice and Delinquency Prevention. (2014). *OJJDP statistical briefing book*. Washington, DC: Office of Justice Programs, U.S. Department of Justice.

Payne, A. A. (2012). Communal school organization effects on school disorder: Interactions with school structure. *Deviant Behavior, 33,* 507–524.

Payne, A. A., Gottfredson, D. C., & Gottfredson, G. D. (2008). Schools as communities: The relationships among communal school organization, students bonding, and school disorder. *Criminology, 41,* 749–777.

Penn, J., Esposito, C., Schaeffer, L., Fritz, G., & Spirito, A. (2003). Suicide attempts and self-multivariate behavior in a juvenile correctional facility. *Journal of the American Academy of Child and Adolescent Psychiatry, 42*(7), 121–135.

Perez, C., & Widom, C. S. (1994). Childhood victimization and long-term intellectual and academic outcomes. *Child Abuse & Neglect, 18,* 617–633.

Piquero, A. R. (2008). Disproportionate minority contact. *The Future of Children, 18*(2), 59–79.

Putnins, A. L. (2005). Correlates and predictors of self-reported suicide attempts among incarcerated youths. *International Journal of Offender Therapy and Comparative Criminology, 49,* 143–157.

Puzzanchera, C., & Robson, C. (2014). *Delinquency cases in juvenile court, 2010.* Washington, DC: Office of Juvenile Justice and Delinquency Prevention, Office of Justice Programs, U.S. Department of Justice.

Quinn, M. M., Rutherford, R. B., Leone, P. E., Osher, D. M., & Poirier, J. M. (2005). Youth with disabilities in juvenile corrections: A national survey. *Exceptional Children, 71*(3), 339–345.

Rausch, M. K., & Skiba, R. J. (2004). *Unplanned outcomes: Suspensions and expulsions in Indiana.* Bloomington, IN: Center for Evaluation and Education Policy.

Roch, C. H., Pitts, D. W., & Navarro, I. (2010). Representative bureaucracy and policy tools: Ethnicity, student discipline, and representation in public schools. *Administration & Society, 42*(1), 38–65.

Rocha, R. R., & Hawes, D. P. (2009). Racial diversity, representative bureaucracy, and equity in multiracial school districts. *Social Science Quarterly, 90*(2), 326–344.

Rosenblatt, J. A., Rosenblatt, A. R., & Biggs, E. E. (2000). Criminal behavior and emotional disorder: Comparing youth served by the mental health and juvenile justice systems. *Journal of Behavioral Health Services & Research, 27*(2), 227–237.

Rowe, E., & Eckenrode, J. (1999). The timing of academic difficulties among maltreated and nonmaltreated children. *Child Abuse & Neglect, 23,* 813–818.

Rozalski, M., Deignan, M., & Engel, S. (2008). The world of juvenile justice according to the numbers. *Reading and Writing Quarterly: Overcoming Learning difficulties, 24*, 143–147.

Ruddy, S. A., Bauer, L., Neiman, S., Hryczaniuk, C. A., Thomas, T. L., & Parmer, R. J. (2010). *2007–08 school survey on crime and safety (SSOCS): Survey documentation for restricted-use data file uses.* Washington, DC: U.S. Department of Education.

Russell, S. T., Kostroski, O., Horn, S., & Saewyc, E. (2010). Social policy report: Safe schools policy for LGBTQ students. *Center for Research in Child Development, 24*(2), 1–24.

Rutter, M. (2006). The promotion of resilience in the face of adversity. In S. S. Luthar (Ed.), *Resilience and vulnerability: Adaptation in the context of childhood adversities* (pp. 489–509). Cambridge, UK: Cambridge University Press.

Ryan, C., Huebner, D., Diaz, R. M., & Sanchez, J. (2009). Family rejection as a predictor of negative health outcomes in white and Latino lesbian, gay, and bisexual young adults. *Pediatrics, 123*, 346–352.

Savage, T. A., & Schanding, G. T. (2013). Creating and maintaining safe and responsive schools for lesbian, gay, transgender, and queer youths: Introduction to the special issue. *Journal of School Violence, 12*(1), 1–6.

Scarborough, A., & McCrae, J. (2009). School-age special education outcomes of infants and toddlers investigated for maltreatment. *Children and Youth Services Review, 32*(1), 80–88.

Schwartz, D., & Gorman, A. (2003). Community violence exposure and children's academic performance. *Journal of Educational Psychology, 95*, 163–173.

Scott, M., Snowden, L., & Libby, A. M. (2002). From mental health to juvenile justice: What factors predict this transition? *Journal of Child and Family Studies, 11*(3), 299–311.

Sedlak, A. J., & McPherson, K. (2010). *Survey of youth in residential placement: Youth's needs and services.* SYRP Report. Rockville, MD: Westat.

Shader, M. (2001). *Risk factors for delinquency: An overview.* Washington, DC: Office of Justice Programs, Office of Juvenile Justice and Delinquency Prevention, U.S. Department of Justice.

Shonk, S. M., & Cicchetti, D. (2001). Maltreatment, competency deficits, and risk for academic and behavioral maladjustment. *Developmental Psychology, 37*(1), 3–17.

Shufelt, J. L., & Cocozza, J. J. (2006). *Youth with mental health disorders in the juvenile justice system: Results from a multi-state prevalence study.* Delmar, NY: National Center for Mental Health and Juvenile Justice.

Skiba, R. J., Arrendonda, M. I., & Rausch, M. K. (2014, March). *New and developing research on disparities in discipline.* Discipline disparities series: New Research. Bloomington, IN: The Equity Project at Indiana University. Available at http://rtpcollaborative.indiana.edu/briefing-papers

Skiba, R. J., Horner, R. H., Chung, C. G., Rausch, M. K., May, S. L., & Tobin, T. (2011). Race is not neutral: A national investigation of African American and Latino disproportionality in school discipline. *School Psychology Review, 40*(1), 85–107.

Skiba, R. J., Michael, R. S., Nardo, A. C., & Peterson, R. (2000). *The color of discipline: Sources of racial and gender disproportionality in school punishment.* Indiana Education Policy Center, Research Report SRS1. Bloomington, IN: Indiana University.

Skiba, R. J., Michael, R. S., Nardo, A. C., & Peterson, R. (2002). The color of discipline: Sources of racial and gender disproportionality in school punishment. *Urban Review, 34,* 317–342.

Skiba, R. J., Shure, L., & Williams, N. (2012). Racial and ethnic disproportionality in suspension and expulsion. In A. L. Noltemeyer & C. S. Mcloughlin (Eds.), *Disproportionality in education and special education* (pp. 89–118). Springfield, IL: Charles C Thomas.

Skiba, R. J., & Williams, N. T. (2014, March). *Are black kids worse? Myths and facts about racial differences in behavior.* Discipline disparities series: New Research. Bloomington, IN: The Equity Project at Indiana University. Available at http://rtpcollaborative.indiana.edu/briefing-papers

Slade, E. P., & Wissow, L. S. (2007). The influence of childhood maltreatment on adolescents' academic performance. *Economics of Education Review, 26,* 604–614.

Smith, C. A., Ireland, T. O., & Thornberry, T. P. (2005). Adolescent maltreatment and adolescent involvement in delinquency. *Child Abuse and Neglect, 29,* 1099–1119.

Smith, C. A., & Thornberry, T. O. (1995). The relationship between childhood maltreatment and adolescent involvement in delinquency. *Criminology, 33*(4), 451–481.

Smithgall, C., Gladden, R. M., Howard, E., Goerge, R., & Courtney, M. E. (2004). *Education experiences of children in out-of-home care.* Chicago, IL: Chapin Hall Center for Children.

Staudt, M. (2001). Psychopathology, peer relations, and school functioning of maltreated children: A literature review. *Children & Schools, 23*(2), 85–100.

Stewart, A., Livingston, M., & Dennison, S. (2008). Transitions and turning points: Examining the links between child maltreatment and juvenile offending. *Child Abuse and Neglect, 32,* 51–66.

Stouthamer-Loeber, M., Wei, E. H., Homish, D. L., & Loeber, R. (2002). Which family and demographic factors are related to both maltreatment and persistent serious juvenile delinquency? *Children's Services: Social Policy, Research, and Practice, 5*(4), 261–272.

Substance Abuse and Mental Health Services Administration. (2013). *National survey on drug use and health.* Washington, DC: Center for Mental Health Services, U.S. Department of Health and Human Services.

Sum, A., Khatiwada, I., McLaughlin, J., & Palma, S. (2009). *The consequences of dropping out of high school: Joblessness and jailing for high school dropouts and the high cost to taxpayers.* Boston, MA: Center for Labor Market Studies, Northeastern University.

Summers, A., Wood, S., & Donovan, J. (2013). *Disproportionality rates for children of color in foster care.* Technical Assistance Bulletin. Reno, NV: National Council of Juvenile and Families Court Judges.

Teplin, L., Abram, K., McClelland, G., Mericle, A., Dulcan, M., & Washburn, D. (2006). *Psychiatric disorders of youth in detention.* Washington, DC: Office of Justice Programs, Office of Juvenile Justice and Delinquency Prevention, U.S. Department of Justice.

Thompson, M., Ho, C., & Kingree, J. (2007). Prospective associations between delinquency and suicidal behaviors in a nationally representative sample. *Journal of Adolescent Health, 40*, 232–237.

Thornberry, T. P., Ireland, T. O., & Smith, C. A. (2001). The importance of timing: The varying impact of childhood and adolescent maltreatment on multiple problem outcomes. *Development and Psychopathology, 13*(4), 957–979.

Tolou-Shams, M., Brown, L., Gordon, G., & Fernandez, I. (2007). Arrest history as an indicator of adolescent/young adult substance use and HIV risk. *Drug and Alcohol Dependence, 88*, 87–90.

Tooney, R. B., Ryan, C., Diaz, R. M., & Russell, S. T. (2011). High school gay-straight alliances (GSAs) and young adult well-being: An examination of GSA presence, participation, and perceived effectiveness. *Applied Developmental Science, 15*, 175–185.

Turner, H. A., Finkelhor, D., & Ormrod, R. (2006). The effect of lifetime victimization on the mental health of children and adolescents. *Social Science & Medicine, 62*, 13–27.

U.S. Department of Commerce. (2013). *Current population survey, 2013: Annual social and economic survey.* Washington, DC: Bureau of the Census.

U.S. Department of Education. (2000). *21st annual report to Congress on the implementation of the Individuals with Disabilities Education Act.* Washington, DC: Author.

U.S. Department of Education. (2012). *31st annual report to Congress on the implementation of the Individuals with Disabilities Education Act, 2009.* Washington, DC: Office of Special Education and Rehabilitative Services, Office of Special Education Programs.

U.S. Department of Education. (2014a). *Indicators of school crime and safety, 2014.* Washington, DC: National Center for Education Statistics, Institute of Education Services.

U.S. Department of Education. (2014b). *Guiding principles: A resource guide for improving school climate and discipline.* Washington, DC: Author.

U.S. Department of Health and Human Services. (2001). *Youth violence: A report of the surgeon general.* Washington, DC: U.S. Government Printing Office.

U.S. Department of Health and Human Services. (2013a). *Information on poverty and income statistics: A summary of current 2013 current population survey data.* Washington, DC: U.S. Government Printing Office.

U.S. Department of Health and Human Services. (2013b). *Child maltreatment 2012.* Washington, DC: U.S. Government Printing Office.

U.S. Department of Justice. (2012). *Disproportionate minority contact technical assistance manual* (4th ed.). Washington, DC: Office of Juvenile Justice and Delinquency Prevention, Office of Justice Programs, U.S. Department of Justice.

U.S. Government Accountability Office. (2007). *African American children in foster care: Additional HHS assistance needed to help states reduce the proportion in care.* Washington, DC: Author.

Vander-Stoep, A., Evans, C., & Taub, J. (1997). Risk of juvenile justice system referral among children in a public mental health system. *Journal of Mental Health Administration, 24,* 428–421.

Wagner, M., Kutash, K., Duchnowski, A. J., Epstein, M. H., & Sumi, W. C. (2005). The children and youth we serve: A national picture of the characteristics of students with emotional disturbances receiving special education. *Journal of Emotional and Behavioral Disorders, 13,* 79–96.

Wald, J. W. (2014). *Can "de-biasing" strategies help to reduce racial disparities in school discipline?* Cambridge, MA: Institute for Race & Justice, Harvard Law School.

Wang, X., Blomberg, T. G., & Li, S. D. (2005). Comparison of the educational deficiencies of delinquent and nondelinquent students. *Evaluation Review: A Journal of Applied Social Research, 29*(4), 291–312.

Watts, D., & Wright, L. (1990). The relationships of alcohol, tobacco, marijuana, and other illegal drug use to delinquency among Mexican-American, black, and white adolescent males. *Adolescence, 25*(97), 171–181.

Welch, K., & Payne, A. A. (2010). Racial threat and punitive school discipline. *Social Problems, 47*, 25–48.

White, N. A., & Loeber, R. (2008). Bullying and special education as predictors of serious delinquency. *Journal of Research in Crime and Delinquency, 45*(4), 380–397.

Widom, C. S. (2003). Understanding child maltreatment and juvenile delinquency: The research. In J. Wiig, C. S. Widom, & J. A. Tuell (Eds.), *Understanding child maltreatment & juvenile delinquency* (pp. 1–10). Washington, DC: Child Welfare League of America.

Wiebush, R., Freitag, R., & Baird, C. (2001). *Preventing delinquency through improved child protection services.* Washington, DC: Office of Juvenile Justice and Delinquency Prevention, Office of Justice Programs, U.S. Department of Justice.

Wiggins, C., Fenichel, E., & Mann, T. (2007). *Developmental problems of maltreated children and early intervention options for maltreated children.* Washington, DC: U.S. Department of Health and Human Services, Child Protective Services Project.

Wodarski, J., Kurtz, D., Gaudin, J., & Howing, P. (1990). Maltreatment and the school-age child: Major academic, socioemotional, and adaptive outcomes. *Social Work, 35*(6), 506–513.

Wu, S. C., Pink, W. T., Crain, R. L., & Moles, O. (1982). Student suspension: A critical reappraisal. *The Urban Review, 14*, 245–303.

Yun, I., Ball, J. D., & Lim, H. (2011). Disentangling the relationship between child maltreatment and violent delinquency: Using a nationally representative sample. *Journal of Interpersonal Violence, 26*(1), 88–110.

Zolotor, A., Kotch, J., Dufort, V., Winsor, J., Catellier, C., & Bou-Saada, I. (1999). School performance in a longitudinal cohort of children at risk of maltreatment. *Maternal and Child Health Journal, 3*(1), 19–27.

Chapter 5: School Safety and Effective Discipline

Schools must prioritize the provision of safe learning environments for all students, for without such safety measures there can be little effective education. Stakeholders agree that teaching and learning must occur without disruptions, chaos, and fears, though not all agree on how to provide such environments for teachers, administrators, and students. Significant evidence has emerged over the past 2 decades regarding school safety, discipline measures, and the utilization of zero-tolerance policies. Research on these policies has focused on both the removal of the most difficult and persistently disruptive students to improve the learning environment and the communication of the deterrence message to students that violence and misbehaviors will not be tolerated in the learning environment (American Psychological Association Zero Tolerance Task Force, 2008). In many of these policy and practice areas, sufficient knowledge, by utilizing well-designed methods and representative samples, has been generated to assess current practice and to direct ongoing and future decisions around school discipline and safety concerns. It is important to continue to evaluate policy decisions, practice guidelines, and interventions utilized within schools (and elsewhere), and to change policies and practice based on cumulative evidence.

However, research-based policy and subsequent practice has not been the norm for schools, school districts, and other decision makers in today's punitive paradigm. Many decisions across education systems have been made based on nonempirically driven agendas. Though some of the explanations for this are understandable—emotive and fearful reactions to school shootings, worries regarding youthful offender crime, the desire for accountability, expanding police presence in schools, and disruptive student removal and deterrence—the outcomes have often times been counterintuitively harmful for students and the school learning environments. Thus, most of the outcomes of interest—improved safety in schools, student accountability, and efficient school management—have not been achieved across school districts, and in many areas these discipline and zero-tolerance measures have caused regression or worsening of the problems. The policies and reasons for doing so were neither well investigated nor explored prior to embracing the zero-tolerance philosophy and subsequent discipline codes, strict school safety measures, expanded use of safety personnel, and other school security changes.

Fortunately, moving forward, the evidence in many of these areas can now guide policy and practice decisions. The movement today needs to be decidedly against the harsh discipline routines that have enveloped so many schools and so many students. The pendulum has swung too far in the direction of control, discipline, and punishment, actions that are simply not working across the nation's school districts.

ENDING THE CRIMINALIZATION OF EDUCATION

Moving Away From Zero-Tolerance Policies

Moving away from current, and often entrenched and far-reaching, zero-tolerance policies is not simple or easy. It took years for these school policies and practices to develop; it will take time to turn back what is ineffective or harmful. Important stakeholders, including the United States Attorney General's Office, the American Academy of Pediatrics, and the American Psychological Association, among others, have condemned these harsh policies and recommend that student discipline dispensation be determined on a case-by-case basis, looking at the mitigating circumstances around the problems, and utilizing developmentally appropriate interventions and decision making (American Academy of Pediatrics, 2013; American Psychological Association Zero Tolerance Task Force, 2008; Kang-Brown, Trone, Fratello, & Daftary-Kapur, 2013). Most school districts' student codes of conduct do not allow individualized responses to student infractions. Many times, the problem starts with these discipline codes.

Student Codes of Conduct

Student codes of conduct outline behaviors that are expected of students, as well as behaviors that the school district has determined are not permitted. They are often a result of state mandates, district rules, and school-based administration decisions—often parents or parent groups are also involved in their creation, though students are rarely involved (Kupchik, 2010). Violations of the code of conduct often include minor or less serious violations such as tardiness, cell phone and other technology use, foul language, dress code violations, and school disruptions. In addition, the code of conduct may include minor or more serious violations that may also be crimes—truancy, assault, fighting, drug activity, and weapon possession, among others. The code typically indicates the disciplinary action that is to be taken by school personnel for certain violations and is provided in writing to students and families (Morgan, Salomon, Plotkin, & Cohen, 2014). Most codes focus on punishments for students' infractions, misbehaviors, or related problems, with little to no discussion of the school learning environment or roles that students, teachers, and staff have in building a positive and safe school (Morgan et al., 2014).

A school district's code of conduct is important in directing and conveying the important priorities in schools that are necessary for conducive learning: the imposition of firm, clear, and consistent rules; punishments for misbehaving and rule breaking; punishments to be equitable; punishments to be of consequence to the importance of the rule; and effectively communicating these rules to students and school staff with consistent application when necessary (Arum, 2003; Gottfredson, Gottfredson, Payne, & Gottfredson, 2005). It is important that a student code of conduct be focused on rehabilitation of the student, have available graduated responses and not automatic discipline measures for the school administrators in determining appropriate decisions, and not utilize suspension or out-of-school punishment for minor misbehaviors, attendance problems, or disruptions. Unfortunately, minor misbehaviors and disruptions account for a large majority of school suspensions (Center for Civil Rights Remedies, 2014; Fabelo, Thompson, Plotkin, Carmichael, Marchbanks, & Booth, 2011). Two case studies—Buffalo and Denver Public School Districts—can illuminate how to implement student codes of conduct that balance safety, accountability, and rehabilitative discipline.

The Buffalo, New York, Public School District has recently amended its policies and student code of conduct, thus renaming the document the Standards for Community-wide Conduct and Intervention Supports (Buffalo Public Schools, 2013). These standards show a commitment to school safety and student accountability within an environment where teaching and learning can occur (see Table 5.1). The school district implemented a three-tiered positive behavioral support

TABLE 5.1 Buffalo, New York, Public Schools' Graduated Responses

Level 1: Classroom and Social Skills Interventions and Responses
• Aimed at teaching correct and alternative behavior so students can learn and demonstrate respectful behavior • May be appropriate when the student has no prior incidents and interventions have not been put in place

Level 2: Administrative Interventions and Responses
• May involve the school administration and aim at correcting behavior by emphasizing the seriousness of the behavior while keeping the student in school • May be appropriate when supports have been put in place in the classroom to address behavior but the behavior has continued to negatively affect the learning of the student and others

Level 3: Suspension and Referral Responses
• May involve the short-term removal of a student from the school because of the severity of the behavior • May be appropriate when interventions and supports have been put in place but the behavior is escalating (repeated offenses)

Level 4: Extended Suspension and Referral Responses
• Involves the removal of a student from the school because of the severity of the behavior • May involve placement of the student in a safe environment that provides additional structure to address the behavior • Focus is on monitoring the safety of the school community and on ending self-destructive and dangerous behavior • May be appropriate when a student's behavior seriously affects the safety of others in the school

system across the schools that provides universal (all students), secondary (some at-risk students), and tertiary (individual students) interventions. These positive engagement strategies are supplemented with a variety of additional programs or interventions, when needed, across peer mediation, parent involvement, mentoring, conflict resolution, community-provider involvement, restorative justice, and mental health services, among others. When these do not prevent or redirect a student and a problem, a series of graduated responses are available to school teachers and administrators (Buffalo Public Schools, 2013).

These graduated response levels are then matched to a detailed list of inappropriate and disruptive behaviors (ranging from minor disruptions to criminal activities), providing all stakeholders the framework with which to minimize punitive responses and maximize rehabilitative alternatives. This district-wide policy provides administrators and teachers discipline response flexibility and the ability to assess each situation within its own context, reviewing mitigating information, history, and possible explanations for the code violations. These are important components of rehabilitative discipline (American Academy of Pediatrics, 2013).

A similar overhaul of discipline procedures was completed by the Denver Public Schools in the past 5 years (Denver Public Schools, 2014). In Table 5.2, a list of infractions in violation of the code of conduct as well as the range consequences and rehabilitative alternatives is provided. Types One to Four offenses minimize or restrict out-of-school discipline decisions under almost all circumstances; Type Five offenses are mandated by federal law for out-of-school discipline.

These offenses are handled through graduated sanctions. Infractions, except for those mandated by law, are addressed within the classroom with the teachers, students, and when necessary, parents from Levels A through C. Only after these interventions and

TABLE 5.2 Denver Public Schools' Rehabilitative Alternatives

Disciplinary Offense	Consequences
Type One Offenses • Classroom disruption • Excessive tardiness • Picking on, bothering, or distracting other students • Use of profanity or vulgarity • Dress code violation • Minor disruption of school activity • Minor defiance of authority/disobedience (e.g., purposefully not following directions) • Verbal insults or put-downs • Use of cell phones, gameboys, and similar electronic devices at unauthorized times • Minor damage or defacement of school property • Tobacco offenses • Unauthorized use of school equipment • Gambling • Minor physical aggression with another student (e.g., pushing, shoving) • Scholastic dishonesty • Other minor school-based misconduct	For Type One offenses, school officials should refer to Level A of the Discipline Ladder. If similar violations occur during the same school year, the intervention moves to the next level on the ladder (e.g., from Level A to Level B, and so on). Students should not be recommended for expulsion for Type One offenses. The only exception to this is that persistent misconduct resulting in suspensions can lead to the student being declared "habitually disruptive," for which the student will be recommended for expulsion.

(continued)

TABLE 5.2 Denver Public Schools' Rehabilitative Alternatives *(continued)*

Disciplinary Offense	Consequences
Type Two Offenses • False activation of a fire alarm • Possession of fireworks/firecrackers • Bullying: Level I (e.g., verbal and written aggression or intimidation) • Harassment based on race, ethnicity, sexual orientation, gender identity, disability, or religion: Level I (e.g., verbal and written harassment) • Sexual harassment: Level I (e.g., verbal and written harassment) • Consensual but inappropriate physical contact • Destruction or theft of school property, including graffiti (less than $500) • Severe defiance of authority/disobedience (e.g., demonstrating gross disrespect for school personnel) • Trespassing • Theft from an individual (less than $500) • Other school-based misconduct that disrupts the school environment • Recurring Type One offenses (after going through Levels A to C of the Discipline Ladder)	For Type Two offenses, school officials should refer to Level D of the Discipline Ladder. If similar violations occur during the same school year, the intervention moves to a higher level on the ladder (e.g., from Level D to Level E, and so on). Students should not be recommended for expulsion for Type Two offenses. The only exception to this is that persistent misconduct resulting in suspensions can lead to the student being declared "habitually disruptive," for which the student will be recommended for expulsion. A student may be referred to law enforcement for the offense of "trespassing" but only if, after being asked to leave the school campus, the trespassing student refuses.
Type Three Offenses • Bullying: Level II (e.g., physical acts of aggression or intimidation and repeat Level I behavior) • Harassment based on race, ethnicity, sexual orientation, gender identity, disability, or religion: Level II (e.g., acts of physical harassment and repeat Level I behavior) • Sexual harassment: Level II (e.g., acts of physical harassment and repeat Level I behavior) (Policies JBB and JLF should be referenced to determine whether the student's behavior rises to the level of an offense that must be reported to law enforcement or the Denver Department of Human Services.) • Fighting: Level I (may include incidents that result in minor injuries such as cuts, scrapes, and bloody noses) • Being under the influence of drugs or alcohol • Possession of alcohol or unauthorized (but legal) drugs • Possession of illegal drugs • Destruction or theft of school property, including graffiti ($500–$5000) • Theft from an individual ($500–$5000) • Other school-based misconduct that substantially disrupts the school environment • Recurring Type Two offenses	For Type Three offenses, school officials should refer to Level E of the Discipline Ladder. If similar violations occur during the same school year, the intervention moves to a higher level on the ladder (e.g., from Level E to Level F). Students should not be recommended for expulsion for Type Three offenses. The only exception to this is that persistent misconduct resulting in suspensions can lead to the student being declared "habitually disruptive," for which the student will be recommended for expulsion.

(continued)

TABLE 5.2 *continued*

Type Four Offenses • Arson • Fighting: Level II (including incidents with significant injuries, but that do not rise to the level of the Type Five offense "1st- or 2nd-degree assault") (Note: will be classified as 3rd-degree assault for reporting purposes) • Destruction or theft of school property, including graffiti (more than $5000) • Theft from an individual (more than $5000) • Possession of an explosive (nonfireworks firecrackers) that seriously endangers the welfare or safety of other students or school personnel. • Willfully causing damage to the property of a school employee • Assault, harassment, or false allegation of abuse against a school employee • Hazing activities (e.g., forcing prolonged physical activity, forcing excessive consumption of any substance, forcing prolonged deprivation of sleep, food, drink, or any other behavior that recklessly endangers the health or safety of an individual for purposes of initiation into any student group) • Child abuse • Unlawful sexual behavior and/or unlawful sexual contact, and/or indecent exposure • Witness intimidation or retaliation • Other student behavior presenting an active or ongoing danger to the welfare or safety of school occupants • Recurring Type Three offenses: Habitual disruption (habitually disruptive students are eligible for expulsion, though not for referral to law enforcement)	For Type Four offenses, school officials should refer to Level F of the Discipline Ladder. If the misconduct has seriously endangered the welfare or safety of other students or school personnel, and the student's continued presence in the school constitutes a significant safety risk, the student may be recommended for expulsion. Persistent misconduct resulting in suspensions can lead to the student being declared "habitually disruptive." "Habitual disruption" is not an independent offense but rather refers to a classification under state law in which persistent misconduct at any level can result in the student being declared "habitually disruptive," for which the student may be recommended for expulsion.
Type Five Offenses • Robbery • First- or second-degree assault, and sexual assault • Sale or distribution of, or intent to sell or distribute, unauthorized drugs or controlled substances • Carrying, bringing, using, or possessing a knife or dangerous weapon without the authorization of the school or district (including any firearm or firearm facsimile that could reasonably be mistaken for an actual firearm, spring action or compressed air device such as BB guns, fixed-blade knives with blades longer than 3", pocket knives with blades longer than 3.5", spring-loaded knives, and any other objects used or intended to inflict death or serious bodily injury)	The Discipline Ladder does not apply to Type Five Offenses. Students who commit these offenses are to be given a 3–10-day out-of-school suspension and, as required by state law, there will be a recommendation for expulsion and notification of law enforcement.

coordination efforts have been unsuccessful through rehabilitative discipline are school administrators brought into the team at Level D. Out-of-school discipline—suspension or expulsion—is not available as a discipline option until the Levels E and F are reached (see Table 5.3).

These codes of conduct examples highlight a number of important components for the students, families, and school personnel, as well as explicate a rehabilitative school discipline philosophy. These components are as follows: outlining and effectively communicating a process to establish and reinforce positive student behaviors and expectations; describing supportive student strategies; explaining the match between student misbehavior and misconduct severity; trying out a tiered range of increasingly strong interventions before suspension or expulsion for minor offenses; limiting expulsions to extreme cases; and providing due process protection for students. In other words, codes of conduct should meet the three important principles necessary

TABLE 5.3 Denver Public Schools' Discipline Ladder

Level A: Teacher/Student
- The student is provided an opportunity to tell his/her version of the incident.
- The teacher or designated staff counsels the student.
- One or more interventions are initiated as appropriate.
- Any intervention will be documented.

Level B: Teacher/Student/Parent
- The student is provided an opportunity to tell his/her version of the incident.
- The teacher or designated staff notifies the student's parent/guardian.
- The teacher counsels the student and, if possible, the parent/guardian.
- One or more interventions are initiated as appropriate.
- Any intervention will be documented.

Level C: Teacher/Support Staff/Student/Parent
- If intervention at Level B has not been successful, the teacher or designated staff can determine whether to involve a social worker, nurse, guidance counselor, psychologist, or any other member of the school's support staff.
- The student is provided an opportunity to tell his/her version of the incident.
- The parent/guardian is notified.
- The teacher and any member of the support staff who has been involved will conference with the student and, if possible, the parent/guardian to provide support for correcting the misbehavior. If possible, all of the student's teachers will be included in the conference.
- One or more interventions are initiated as appropriate.
- Any referral or intervention will be documented.

(continued)

TABLE 5.3 *continued*

Level D: Administrative-Level Referral
- The student is referred to the appropriate administrator or designated staff person.
- Documentation of the steps taken to intervene and change the student's behavior is provided.
- The student is provided an opportunity to tell his/her version of the incident.
- The administrator or designated staff person schedules a conference with the parent/guardian and determines whether further consultation with support personnel is necessary.
- One or more interventions are initiated as appropriate.
- If necessary, in-school suspension till 3 days may be utilized.
- School officials should consider developing a behavior intervention plan for the student (in some cases, such a plan might be mandatory).
- Referrals and interventions will be documented.

Level E: Suspension Options
- The student is referred to the appropriate administrator or designated staff person.
- Documentation of the steps taken to intervene and change the student's behavior is provided.
- The student is provided an opportunity to tell his/her version of the incident.
- The administrator or designated staff person schedules a conference with the parent/guardian and determines whether further consultation with support personnel is necessary.
- One or more interventions are initiated as appropriate.
- If previous interventions have not been successful, the principal or principal's designee may consider the use of an in-school suspension of 1–3 days or a one-day out-of-school suspension.
- Elementary school students should not receive out-of-school suspensions for Type One offenses.
- School officials should consider developing a behavior intervention plan for the student (in some cases, such a plan might be mandatory).
- On return to school after suspension, further steps to encourage positive behavior are to be considered.

Level F: Additional Suspension Options
- The student is referred to the appropriate administrator or designated staff person.
- Documentation of the steps taken to intervene and change the student's behavior is provided.
- The student is provided an opportunity to tell his/her version of the incident.
- The administrator or designated staff person schedules a conference with the parent/guardian and determines whether further consultation with support personnel is necessary.
- One or more interventions are initiated as appropriate.
- If previous interventions have not been successful, the principal or principal's designee may issue an additional 1–3-day in-school suspension and/or a 1–3-day out-of-school suspension.
- Elementary school students should not receive out-of-school suspensions for Type One offenses.
- School officials should consider developing a behavior intervention plan for the student (in some cases, such a plan might be mandatory).
- Persistent misconduct can result in the student being declared "habitually disruptive," for which the student will be recommended for expulsion.
- On return to school after suspension, further steps to encourage positive behavior are to be considered.

for effective codes of conduct: defining expectations for appropriate behavior for the entire school community; responding to misbehavior in a tailored way to the offense severity, as well as the students' and victims' needs, with the goal of keeping the offending student in school; and ensuring that disciplinary measures are consistently and properly implemented (American Academy of Pediatrics, 2013; Morgan, Salomon, Plotkin, & Cohen, 2014).

The school's student code of conduct is an important document from which to build a rehabilitative discipline system, and it should, as noted, set the framework for appropriate, reasoned, and graduated responses. This document and its implementation can set the foundation for the safety paradigm of the school, one that is primarily democratic, inclusive, and has a positive psychosocial design (Kupchik, 2010). These positive environments decrease student misbehavior across many measures because they often allow the student to believe they have input into school policies, the rules and codes are fair, positive behavior is rewarded, behavioral problem-solving skills and interventions are provided, and communal support and values are shared across students, teachers, and staff. Rules are vital but insufficient on their own and often alienate students from school personnel. It is important how they are enforced, implemented, and integrated with rehabilitative interventions that build a sense of school community and cooperation (Gottfredson et al., 2005; Gregory, Bell, & Pollock, 2014; U.S. Department of Education, 2000; Welsh, 2003).

Within this communal framework, a number of preventative and interventive programs have been developed—restorative practices, socio-emotional learning, and positive behavioral protocols—that are often effective in improving student behaviors, classroom environments, and overall school climate and safety. These practices should be considered part of any redesigned code of conduct and discipline system. Themes across these interventions and programs include a focus on increasing student engagement and relationship building among teachers, students, and families, and on utilizing problem-solving and prevention work to improve the school climate and community (Losen, Hewitt, & Toldson, 2014).

Restorative Practices

Restorative practices are student-focused interventions that try to change the perspective of students with behavioral difficulties and other related problems. These practices are appropriate for those situations when the student is primarily responsible for the disruptions or unsafe school behaviors, with a focus on accountability. This collaborative approach includes all willing stakeholders in the incident or problem, uses a constructive collaborative approach with a focus on repairing the harm to victims and making the school community whole, and also helps the young person decrease future problems and recidivism. These practices help build and improve school climate by increasing student understanding of the rules and trust in the rule enforcement, thus requiring a school philosophy to shift and embrace this foundation at all implementation levels (Bazemore, 2001; Bilchik, 1997; Dohrn, 2000; Macready, 2009). In other words, restorative practice is not just the utilization of behavior modification techniques or a focus on conflict resolution but also a school community-wide effort (Calhoun & Daniels, 2008).

Restorative practices take numerous forms, including peer juries that bring together a student who has broken a code violation with trained student jurors, peer mediation that brings two or more students together for conflict resolution with trained student mediators, and peace circles that allow student dialogue, process, and collective decision making (Hereth, Kaba, Meiners, & Wallace, 2012). There are also broader school-wide applications of these restorative practices, which typically incorporate four foundation values: (1) opportunities for involved parties to meet and discuss the problem and harm; (2) offenders attempting to repair the harm caused; (3) restoring the victims and offenders to be whole and return to contributing school community members; and (4) including those with a stake in the problem to participate in its resolution (American Psychological Association Zero Tolerance Task Force, 2008).

There is increasing empirical support for implementing these approaches, particularly when compared to current restrictive and harsh penalties for student infractions and misbehaviors (Latimer, Dowden, & Muise, 2005; Schiff, 2013). And encouragingly, over the past few years, studies have used improved research designs and found continued positive outcomes for restorative justice programming. Over the course of two academic school years, four high schools in the Chicago Public School system that had implemented varying degrees of restorative programming, including mediation, peer juries, conferences, and peace circles, found till 80% reductions in student misconduct and arrests and improvements in attendance (Hereth et al., 2012). Recent national reviews and numerous school district studies of restorative justice practices found reduced suspension and expulsion rates, decreased referrals for discipline measures, improved academic achievement, and stronger relationship building across stakeholders (Losen, Hewitt, & Toldson, 2014; Skiba, Arrendonda, & Rausch, 2014), with particular improvements in some reviews for African American students (Gonzalez, 2015).

Socio-Emotional Learning

Socio-emotional learning is primarily a classroom-focused paradigm, though it can be a stand-alone program component, as well as a school-wide curriculum for learning, teaching, and building the social environment. This ecological management approach includes not only quality instruction planning but also a focus on the behavioral needs of the students, monitoring of student engagement, and skills application to avoid escalating conflicts (Osher, Bear, Sprague, & Doyle, 2010). These programming efforts often incorporate character education and emotional development interventions that are aimed at aiding in children's and adolescents' acquisition of knowledge, improved attitudes, and skill building to recognize and manage their emotions, establish positive relationships, and make responsible decisions (Durlack & Weissberg, 2007).

In general, these programs have had a significant impact on building social and emotional skills, reducing aggression and behavior problems, improving academic performance for all grade levels and student ethnic groups, improving tolerance, and decreasing out-of-school suspensions (Berkowitz & Bier, 2005; Payton et al., 2008). Components of many of these programs that were found to be effective include interactive teaching strategies, mentoring, role-playing, group discussion, and family involvement through extracurricular activities or parent training (Person, Moiduddin, Hgue-Angus, & Malone, 2009). Three of the programs with significantly strong empirical support include Positive Action, Too Good for Violence, and Connect with Kids (Social and Character Development Research Consortium, 2010; What Works Clearninghouse, 2006a, 2006b). When used more broadly in schools, this learning-centered approach may include support teams and planning centers, and it has been found to decrease school incidents by more than half, improve attendance rates, and lower district-wide out-of-school suspensions by 60% (Losen, Hewitt, & Toldson, 2014; Skiba, Arrendonda, & Rausch, 2014).

Positive Behavioral Protocols

These programs are utilized as targeted interventions for students with behavioral, control, or related difficulties within the classroom or school. Typically, these programs use student or other leaders to engage students in daily or weekly social skill-building exercises—interactive activities designed for improving anger management, conflict resolution, and social skills. Alternative formats include small-group and one-on-one intervention sessions, and often family members are involved for education and learning purposes, because the young person may have similar or related difficulties at home (Child Trends, 2007a).

Two of the more rigorously evaluated programs with significant preventative and intervention impact are Reconnecting Youth and Cognitive-Behavioral Training Program for Behaviorally Disordered Adolescents. Reconnecting Youth is for high school students dealing with aggression, depression, or substance abuse problems and is a daily, semester-long class that promotes school relationships, involves parents in necessary planning, and helps with crisis management. Cognitive-Behavioral Training Program is for young people with self-control problems that lead to aggression or violence and consists of 12 individual sessions that help students develop problem-solving strategies to minimize harmful outcomes (Child Trends, 2007b; Eggert, Thompson, Herting, & Nicholas, 1994, 1995).

DISMANTLING THE SCHOOL-TO-PRISON PIPELINE

Dismantling the pipeline poses significant challenges for schools. Shifting from a punitive paradigm toward a school framework and code of conduct that builds relationships among students, teachers, and administrators as well as promoting safe and effective learning throughout the campus requires commitment from all parties. These changes need to occur within the classroom, throughout the school, and across the district. A multipronged approach is the only way to ensure a successful transition toward making schools, classrooms, and students safer, while keeping students in school.

Classroom and School

The evidence on improving classroom safety and student behavioral outcomes continues to revolve around creating school climates in which positive school staff and student relationships are emphasized through increased engagement and preventative efforts (Hawkins, Catalano, Kosterman, Abbott, & Hill, 1999; Muschert & Peguero, 2010). These important classroom and school environmental themes are core elements for many effective programs and interventions.

School-Wide Positive Behavior Interventions and Supports

One of the stronger empirically supported school-based programs that utilizes relationship-based foundations is the School-Wide Positive Behavior Interventions and Supports (SWPBIS), which is used in more than 16,000 schools nationwide (U.S. Department of Education, 2015). The SWPBIS incorporates a three-tiered approach across the classroom and school: (1) The primary tier addresses prevention by teaching behavioral expectations, rewarding positive behavior, providing a continuum of consequences, and using data collection for decision making; (2) the secondary tier is for at-risk students and targets these young people for interventions to help with behavioral problems; and (3) the tertiary tier is for students with more serious behavior problems and often includes more intense individualized interventions with family and community partners (Sugai & Horner, 2010). This comprehensive and proactive approach assumes that actively teaching these expectations changes students' behaviors, while requiring the school personnel to define and teach a set of positive expectations for students, acknowledge and reward behaviors, systematically supervise students throughout the day, and implement a fair and consistent continuum of corrective consequences (U.S. Department of Education, 2015).

Reviews have found reductions in problem student behavior and out-of-class referrals and improved academic outcomes, including school safety perceptions (Bradshaw, Mitchell, & Leaf, 2010; Horner et al., 2009; Osher et al., 2010; Vincent, Sprague, & Gau, 2013). In addition, these interventions and supports are applicable and effective across grade levels and are sustainable over time (Bradshaw, Koth, Thornton, & Leaf, 2008; Lohrmann-O'Rourke et al., 2000; Luiselli, Putnam, & Sunderland, 2002; Muscott et al., 2004). However, additional research is necessary to determine whether this program model can have long-term effects in addressing the disproportionate impact of school disciplinary measures on students of color, though realigning student codes of conduct with the SWPBIS protocols may prove particularly efficacious (Fenning et al., 2013; Sprague, Vincent, Tobin, & CHiXapkaid, 2013). In addition, using SWPBIS in conjunction with other effective classroom management techniques such as social-emotional learning and/or the ecological management approach has been found effective (Osher et al., 2010).

Professional Development

Many researchers have found that the school-to-prison pipeline begins in the classroom, with teachers and administrators challenged with balancing education, skills-based standardized testing, and student social skills development, and doing so with limited resources and time (Ferguson, 2000). In many school districts, these pose challenges because of classroom size, disparate student abilities, and students who act out, misbehave, or disrupt the learning environment. With the disproportionate impact of school discipline systems on certain student groups—minorities, special education disabilities, lesbian, gay, bisexual, and transgender (LGBT), lower-income, and maltreated—it may be important to improve teachers' abilities to work across these student groups, and in particular in a preventative manner.

In fact, effective professional development for teachers and administrators on improving classroom management and school climate has improved staff retention, student instructional time, and student engagement in learning (Browers & Tornic, 2000). Unfortunately, when school personnel lack training and resources, student academic achievement is lowered, inappropriate special education referrals are increased, and referrals for student disciplinary sanctions become significantly greater (Donavan & Cross, 2002). Professional development is best when it provides opportunities to increase collaboration among school staff and leaders through professional learning communities, with the consideration for restructuring these forums and reallocating resources (Morgan et al., 2014).

Conflict Resolution/Cultural Competency

Conflict resolution is an important in-classroom starting point to improve safety (Osher, Dwyer, & Jackson, 2004), and it revolves around a number of principles: supportive teacher/student relationships, academic rigor, and culturally responsive teaching. These principles, and subsequent interventions and programs, incorporate key approaches: identifying the cause of the conflicts and difficulties, using problem-solving approaches to discipline decisions, incorporating students and their families into the decisions and resolutions, and reintegration of students into the classroom after conflict resolution (Gregory, Bell, & Pollock, 2014).

Supportive relationships are ones that entail trust and can be preventative in times of conflict (Osher et al., 2012); trust can be built through various "getting to know you" instructional activities, working from a student's strengths perspective, and professional development programs. One of the more effective programs includes "My Teaching Partner," a program that pairs a coach and teacher for an academic year and focuses on restorative practices, cultural competency trainings, and understanding and working with the actual experiences of students (Gregory, Bell, & Pollock, 2014; Schiff, 2013; Singleton & Linton, 2006).

Academic rigor is not equitable across schools or classrooms, and this inequity is often because schools have fewer resources and local funding revenue. These are more often communities and students of color (NAACP, 2005). Though resources may limit the ability for schools and classrooms to offer a wider array of rigorous academic options such as honors levels classes and other enriched course work, teachers and administrators can have positive impacts on all students. Positive outcomes can be accomplished through sending messages to students that high academic expectations are for everyone, avoiding direct or inadvertent messages to some students that they are at risk for failure or may not be successful, offering remediation programming and flexible supports, and offering motivating and relevant classroom instruction (Gregory, Bell, & Pollock, 2014; Mehan, 2012; Pas, Bradshaw, Hershfeldt, & Leaf, 2010).

Culturally responsive teaching entails reflecting back to the student their identities and cultures and improving school connections, thus enhancing academic outcomes (Sleeter, 2011; Toomey & Russell, 2011). Effective strategies are as follows: the incorporation of classroom and library material and school-wide events across the range of ethnic, cultural, gender, and sexual identities of the students; the use of self-reflection by teachers to identify any implicit or unfair biases; the use of discussion and book groups across diversity topics; and professional development programs to help teachers self-assess, including the Double-Check Program, Effective Communication, and Connection to Curriculum (Gregory, Bell, & Pollock, 2014; Kang & Banaji, 2006; Schultz, 2008; Sharma, 2008).

Although it is clear that values and possible bias play a role in school discipline disproportionate outcomes, it is increasingly recognized that values or implicit biases can be addressed and interventions can reduce this explanation for why some students are involved with the pipeline—in particular, students of color and those who identify as LGBT (Wald, 2014). Although more definitive research within the schools is necessary to determine the specific steps to be taken in addressing implicit bias and its potential impact, increasing teachers' and administrators' knowledge of another culture's behavioral norms and employing appropriate behavior management strategies that are culturally resonant have proved effective (Majd, Marksamer, & Reyes, 2009; Monroe, 2005; Rudd, 2014; Staats, 2014).

One of the more effective professional development programs is My Teaching Partner, designed to improve teacher–student interactions through reflection and feedback. This program entails ongoing and regular instruction videotape and My Teaching Partner coaching feedback, looking for positive learning environments, effective behavioral expectation settings, and engagement of all students. Program evaluations have found significant reductions in student office referrals and an elimination of racially disproportionate discipline in the classroom (Gregory, Bell, & Pollock, 2014).

Professional development evidence continues to find that improving the school climate, which, in turn, improves outcomes across most measures and, in particular, those disproportionately impacted by school discipline procedures, requires ongoing training and reinforcement of behavior management and skill development of teachers and administrators. In particular, key topics should include building strong learning communities in the classroom, establishing behavior norms and expectations and reinforcing these throughout the classroom and school, understanding the impact of trauma on learning and utilizing trauma-informed care approaches, understanding child and adolescent development, using early warning and screening assessments, collaborating with families, and using data to drive decision making related to intervention strategies (Buffington, Pierkhising, & Marsh, 2010; Grisso, 2008; Morgan et al., 2014).

Student and Family Engagement

Most of the programs noted—SWPBIS, socio-emotional learning, restorative justice, and Reconnecting Youth—prioritize improving student and/or family engagement. Recognizing and then integrating the student's perspective, giving value to the student's difficulties or challenges, and understanding what other mitigating impacts may be causing the problems can often provide both more informed decision making by school personnel and more effective problem solving. When students have input and involvement and are provided autonomy, engagement with the school is often the outcome (Gregory, Bell, & Pollock, 2014; Hafen et al., 2010). When students and families are more connected and engaged with the school, discipline problems decrease and, correspondingly, safety outcomes increase (American Psychological Association Zero Tolerance Task Force, 2008; Kohli, 2012; Steinberg, Allensworth, & Johnson, 2013).

For example, through engaging a student who has made threats against school personnel or students, a more recent shift in school safety assessment is to move away from most schools' current policies and codes of conduct and automatic school-removal provisions. Because strict discipline code decisions have many unintended consequences, this has led to the development of alternative responses (American Psychological Association Zero Tolerance Task Force, 2008). One of the empirically supported options is the Virginia Threat Assessment Guidelines, which is used across schools in Virginia. Threat assessment is a process of evaluating the threat and the circumstances surrounding the threat to uncover any facts or evidence that indicate the threat is likely to be carried out; it is most concerned about students who pose a threat and not about those who make a threat (O'Toole, 2000). In Virginia, threat assessment teams are trained in each school, led by the school administrator, and follow a seven-step process: evaluate the threat; determine whether the threat is transient or substantive; if transient, respond within current rehabilitative alternatives; if substantive, determine whether the threat is serious or very serious; if serious, respond to protect; if very serious, take immediate precautions, consult with law enforcement; and implement a safety plan (Cornell, 2007). The use of this system was associated with a 19% reduction in long-term suspensions and an 8% reduction in expulsions of students in Virginia schools, with greater reductions in schools that had used the guidelines for longer periods of time (Cornell, Shin, Ciolfi, & Sanncken, 2013).

Increased Screening for Student Risk

Because so many of the students caught within the school-to-prison pipeline have maltreatment and trauma histories, as well as mental health disorders that include substance use and abuse problems, it is imperative for schools to improve identification of these problems, allowing prevention and treatment coordination efforts to ensue. Although schools are not expected to expand treatment or programming, for these children and adolescents can be linked with community partners, it would be important for schools to improve screening for some of these problems. Early identification and subsequent treatment of risks and difficulties surrounding trauma and mental health can significantly improve outcomes and save costs by minimizing severe school problems, school dropouts, and justice system involvement (Mulvey & Iselin, 2008; Vincent, Guy, & Grisso, 2012). Table 5.4 includes some of the more reliable and valid measurement screenings for these child and adolescent problem areas (Chestnut Health Systems, 2014; Kamphaus & Reynolds, 2007; National Child Traumatic Stress Network, 2008; Psychological Assessment Resources, 2014; SASSI Institute, 2014).

Mental health, substance abuse, and trauma screenings are brief processes that can be administered by nonprofessional staff as a triage assessment to identify a potentially more serious problem. Traumatic Events Screening Inventory (TESI) is a structured clinical interview that assesses the adolescents' and parents' reports of past or current traumatic events, including maltreatment; Child Welfare Trauma Referral Tool (CWTRT) assesses trauma and mental health needs of children and adolescents; and Trauma Symptom Checklist for Children (TSCC) is a self-report symptom inventory that identifies behavioral and mental health disorders that are often the outcome of maltreatment, and it includes measures that directly assess chronic traumatic stress. The SASSI-3 is a psychological screening measure that can identify adolescents with chemical dependency, substance abuse, and substance use disorder (SASSI Institute, 2014). The GAIN-SS can be used to quickly and accurately identify adolescents who may need a more thorough

TABLE 5.4 Screening Tools: Behavioral Problems, Emotional Disorders, Substance Abuse, and Trauma

Behavioral and Emotional Screening System (BESS): screening for behavioral and emotional problems
Adolescent Substance Abuse Subtle Screening Instrument (SASSI-3): screening for substance abuse
Global Appraisal of Individual Need–Short Screen (GAIN-SS): screening for substance abuse
Traumatic Events Screening Inventory (TESI): screening for trauma history
Child Welfare Trauma Referral Tool (CWTRT): screening for trauma history
Trauma Symptom Checklist for Children (TSCC): screening for behavioral and mental health problems due to trauma

assessment for substance use disorders, as well as for internalizing or externalizing psychiatric disorders (Dennis, Feeney, Stevens, & Bedoya, 2006). The MAST is a 25-item structured screening tool that can be used to detect an alcohol problem, though it may under-identify adolescents who are unaware of this potential problem. These screenings can identify children and adolescents who are in need for further diagnostic assessments by professionals (National Center for Mental Health and Juvenile Justice, 2007).

Thus, prevention and diversion efforts, which can naturally flow from appropriate screenings, assessments, and coordination of services, are always less costly than efforts invested on students who continue through the school discipline pipeline and become formally involved with the juvenile courts. For example, diversion services for first-time referrals to the juvenile courts, from schools and other sources, save more than nine dollars for every one dollar invested; Functional Family Therapy, a delinquency prevention program that helps with serious mental health and family problems, saves three dollars for every one dollar invested; and Aggression Replacement Therapy saves six dollars for every one dollar invested (Aos, 2004; Aos et al., 2011; Barnofski, 2009).

School Districts

School districts are responsible for implementing and setting certain policies for all schools, though state and federal policies dictate some discipline code requirements. Data-driven decision making has not been the norm at the school district level, often leading to the current harsh discipline codes and disproportionate outcomes when zero-tolerance policies are initiated (Advancement Project, Alliance for Educational Justice, & GSA Network, 2011). Moving forward, one of the ways to make effective district policy decisions is to use data findings to inform practice. School districts should publically report annual data collection as follows: number of students suspended and expelled; reasons for these out-of-school discipline outcomes; days of lost instruction; on-campus arrests; referrals to juvenile courts; reasons for referrals; bullying data—making these available to review via school level, ethnicity, gender, disability, and poverty (a proxy could represent those who access free or reduced lunch plans); and if available, LGBT status. School districts should then incorporate these data to inform policies and practices surrounding school discipline decisions, student codes of conduct, resource allocation, implemented program effectiveness, and identified school-level disparities (American

Psychological Association, 2006; Losen, Hewitt, & Toldson, 2014; Mitchum & Moodie-Mills, 2014; Morgan et al., 2014).

School districts should be cautious in their use of school resource officers, though this case is much stronger to make for schools with serious crime problems (Kupchik, 2010). Although having school resource officers provides reported feelings of safety and increased positive views of police across school personnel and some student groups (Jackson, 2002; Martinez, 2009), leading to some increases in crime reporting by students (Finn, Townsend, Shively, & Rich, 2005), it has been more consistently found that their presence may reinforce zero-tolerance policies and increase campus arrest rates and referrals to the juvenile courts (Brown, 2006; Dahlberg, 2012; Theriot, 2009). If ongoing and sufficient evidence continues to find this punitive and harmful impact, moving away from the almost common-place presence of police officers in schools nationwide will require significant reform efforts, including the following: reviewing current school–police partnership models; assessing data on need for officers in schools to maintain safety while minimizing juvenile justice system referral; having policies that clearly define the officers' role and engagement in nonemergency situations; and training school personnel on appropriate use of officers (Morgan et al., 2014; Rosiak, 2009).

If school districts determine that the use of school resource officers is warranted by serious crime and safety concerns or other data-driven outcomes, then it is important that they adhere to certain guidelines: recruit and select officers who want to work with children and adolescents, who are committed to maintaining safety while minimizing student involvement with the juvenile courts; provide extensive training on adolescent development, school policies, and working with students in a school setting; monitor officers with ongoing evaluation; and establish memoranda of understanding (MOUs) or memoranda of agreement (MOAs) between the police and school district that formalize these key partnership elements, clearly define roles, responsibilities, and chain of command, and review these agreements regularly by using data and stakeholder feedback (American Psychological Association Zero Tolerance Task Force, 2008; Majd, Marksamer, & Reyes, 2009; Morgan et al., 2014; Rosiak, 2009).

In a related security area, it is important to improve the social and learning environment of schools by decreasing the use of security guards, metal detectors, and surveillance, unless dictated by schools with serious crime problems where these measures are found effective (Addington, 2014; Hirschfield, 2010). Although firm, clear, and consistent rules, appropriate and sufficient punishments for rule breaking, and communication of these to students are vital for improving school safety, an overuse of surveillance and security measures can impede the creation of an inclusive, democratic, or positive social climate (Gottfredson et al., 2005; Kupchik, 2010). It is more useful to invest resources toward prevention programs that teach and reinforce appropriate behavioral skills and positive values, thus building a safer community-focused school (American Psychological Association Zero Tolerance Task Force, 2008; Osher, Sandler, & Nelson, 2001).

When schools or security personnel remove a student from school—be it a suspension, expulsion, or alternative school or program placement—it is imperative that reentry into the classroom be handled with careful planning and integration focused on the student not recidivating. In addition to the more than two million annually suspended students and the 130,000 students annually expelled (U.S. Department of Education, 2014a), hundreds of thousands of students are placed in alternative programming, which may include schools with separate facilities, charter schools, community-based schools, or juvenile detention centers, with stays between 1 and 6 months (Kim, Losen, & Hewitt, 2010). These placements are more likely in urban districts with high minority student enrollment, districts with high poverty concentrations, and disproportionately include students with disabilities (Texas Appleseed, 2007).

After these punitive actions and removals, many students become increasingly alienated from the school and classroom community, with schools often doing little to help with the reintegration and reconnecting with classmates, teachers, and administrators (Zehr, 2002). Schools should develop an individualized reintegration plan for all returning students that connect them and their families to necessary support services. These services can include schools that link the student and family to youth advocate and mentoring programs, as well as develop school-based transition centers that collaborate with child and adolescent community-based providers—mental health, juvenile court, child welfare, family support, and health professionals, among others—to help manage the identified problems and make the transition back to school successful (Gregory, Bell, & Pollock, 2014; Majd, Marksamer, & Reyes, 2009). These duties could be the responsibility of a transition coordinator, who is a school staff member responsible for all reentering students. The coordinator could handle working with other youth-caring systems to ensure reenrollment for the student happens as quickly and as safely as possible; this is particularly important for those returning from juvenile justice facilities (Advancement Project et al., 2011; Morgan et al., 2014).

These alternative education services must be of high quality if they are to be effective in helping to reintegrate a student into their school and community because a majority of students attending these schools are those with behavioral issues who are suspended or expelled from their traditional school (Morgan et al., 2014). In fact, 42 state laws allow or encourage the use of alternative educational placements for students, leading to 64% of school districts having at least one alternative school or program (Carver & Lewis, 2010). Of concern, these programs are disproportionately attended by students of color, those with disabilities, and those with mental health problems (Chlang & Gill, 2010; Ruiz de Velasco et al., 2008), an environment that exacerbates the difficulties (Dishon, Dodge, & Lansford, 2006). Although many school districts offer effective programming and qualified staff—Montgomery County, Maryland, Hillsborough County, Florida, and Orange County, California, for example—the educational quality varies significantly across these alternative placements. School districts must prioritize these schools and programs to be well funded and to offer an array of behavioral health and related services aimed at improving the students' outcomes and successful reintegration into their traditional school classroom (American Psychological Association Zero Tolerance Task Force, 2008; Losen, Hewitt, & Toldson, 2014; Morgan et al., 2014).

State Policies

State legislatures, along with the Federal Congress, are key stakeholders in establishing and perpetuating current zero-tolerance policies, and they greatly influence the utilization of inflexible discipline codes that have led to harsh and disparate outcomes. However, these policy stakeholders are also the solution to many of the unintended problems the policies have wrought. Numerous states, and subsequent local school districts, have taken steps to ameliorate the reasons for these problems through the enactment of new laws and regulations that address the school-to-prison pipeline. More broadly, states can take a number of proactive and important steps toward addressing school discipline problems and the involvement of so many students in out-of-school discipline policies.

An important step that state departments of education can take is requiring, collecting, and disseminating data across all school districts, including charter and alternative education schools, which includes student offenses, suspension and expulsion frequency, bullying, and the extent of disproportionate impact on at-risk student groups (Advancement Project et al., 2011; Center for Civil Rights

Remedies, 2013; Morgan et al., 2014). To do so, a common definition of key disciplinary outcome terms must be determined to ensure accurate and reliable counts. This database would be in addition, though complementary, to an already required data collection: the biennial report of the Office for Civil Rights (CRDC) on school discipline; the Individuals with Disabilities Education Act's requirement of long-term suspension and expulsion data review for those with disabilities and those without them as well as for racial disparities; and the requirement of the Safe and Drug-Free Schools and Communities Title IV, Part A, to report annual truancy rate and violent and drug-related offenses, resulting in out-of-school removal (Elementary and Secondary Education Act, 20 U.S.C. § 4112, 2013; Individuals with Disabilities Education Act, 20 U.S.C. § 1412(a)(22), 2013). A number of information-sharing resources are available to school districts, school resource officers, and juvenile court personnel in managing and adhering to federal laws when collecting, using, and sharing student data across youth-caring systems: the Navigating Information Sharing (NIS) Toolkit (Education Development Center, Inc.) and the Models for Change Information Sharing Toolkit (John D. and Catherine T. MacArthur Foundation).

State legislatures should also review or amend state laws to move away from strict discipline policies, including the following: clearly define school disciplinary actions and terms for disruptive behavior, inappropriate behavior, violent offense, disorderly conduct, disturbing the peace, serious risk, and zero tolerance, among others; reserve school removal only for the most serious and severe disruptive student behaviors; replace rigid disciplinary strategies with graduated systems of discipline, with consequences on par with the student offense through an array of disciplinary alternatives; require school resource officers, if used, to have sufficient training to work with the adolescent population; require sufficient training for teachers and school administrators with regard to behavior management and culturally sensitive pedagogy; and shift or provide funding away from security management and toward preventative and effective school programming to minimize out-of-school discipline outcomes (Advancement Project et al., 2011; American Psychological Association Zero Tolerance Task Force, 2008; Losen, Hewitt, & Toldson, 2014; Morgan et al., 2014).

National Policies

There are numerous areas in which federal laws, rules, and stakeholders had a discerning impact in creating the school-to-prison pipeline.

However, these same stakeholders now have the opportunity to direct a movement away from the pipeline and toward rehabilitative and positive school climates for all students. Leadership across research, data collection, and funding opportunities can shift a tide in policy, particularly one that is already moving, slowly and intermittently, toward the rehabilitative school model direction (Mediratta, 2012). In this regard, it is also important to address current federal laws, some that are shifting policy away from school discipline and others that are reinforcing harmful and difficult outcomes for many students.

The No Child Left Behind Act (NCLB) should be amended in a number of ways: require schools to collect and report data on suspensions, expulsions, school-based arrests, and referrals to juvenile court, disaggregated by those student groups most at risk; provide increased funding for schools to utilize empirically supported alternatives to out-of-school discipline for students who commit nonserious offenses—a major reason for suspensions and expulsions; mandate cross-system collaborations for schools, police districts, juvenile courts, and youth-caring community providers to limit the use of harsh school discipline; decrease the current standardized testing burdens on schools; and base teacher and school evaluations on much broader and diverse evidence. In addition, the issue of "pushing out" lower achieving students, including possible suspended or expelled students before testing dates, from home schools to alternative education programming should be fully investigated, discerned, and remedied (Federal Advisory Committee on Juvenile Justice, 2014; Figlio, 2005; Forum for Education and Democracy, 2008; Majd, 2011).

Other federal laws should be amended to strengthen data collection and practice evaluations. Federal law currently requires states to report test score results (NCLB), graduation rates, and enrollment numbers annually, as well as disaggregated and comparative (to nondisabled students) discipline data for students with special education disabilities (IDEA, 20 U.S.C. § 1418(1)). These laws could be expanded to require discipline data on all students, not just those covered under the Individuals with Disabilities Education Act (IDEA), and include the LGBT student community. It should be noted that the U.S. Department of Education's Office for Civil Rights has recently begun collecting important discipline data for other purposes every 2 years. Some recommend that these data be collected annually (Losen, Hewitt, & Toldson, 2014; Russell, Horn, Kosciw, & Saewyc, 2010).

In addition, the U.S. Departments of Justice and Education could provide additional funding across a variety of important areas. These include an increase in the availability of federal funds to replace exclusionary discipline methods with proven and effective alternatives; funding strategies for comprehensive local stakeholder collaborations, including the schools, police, juvenile courts, and youth-caring systems to investigate the problems and find solutions; improving national data collection and research on effective practices that local school districts and juvenile courts can implement; and determining whether federal funding for K–12 schools can help address disparate local and statewide school district funding (Advancement Project et al., 2011; National Juvenile Justice and Delinquency Prevention Coalition, 2014; Torres & Stefkovich, 2009). In one area, progress has recently been made by a collaboration of 20 federal agencies (Justice, Education, Health and Human Services, Homeland Security, and Treasury, among others) in awarding significant grant dollars to school districts and research organizations through the Comprehensive School Safety Initiative. The focus of the Initiative is three fold: to continue to build a large-scale research effort while identifying empirically sound strategies to increase school safety nationwide through the collection of national-level data; convening stakeholders to identify evidence-based practices and policies; and to conduct innovative research and evaluate pilot projects within school districts (National Institute of Justice, 2014).

In addition, over the past 20 years, nearly one billion federal dollars across numerous agencies have been invested in hiring police to work as resource officers in schools, with more than 17,000 employed annually in nearly half of all elementary, middle, and high schools (Justice Policy Institute, 2011; Thurau & Wald, 2010). Considering the limited evidence to date on the effectiveness of school resource officers in schools, and the emerging evidence of some unintended and harmful consequences to at-risk students by having officers in schools (American Psychological Association Zero Tolerance Task Force, 2008; Brady, Balmer, & Phenix, 2007; Brown, 2006; Dahlberg, 2012; Martinez, 2009; Newman, 2004; Rich-Shae & Fox, 2014; Theriot, 2009), it would be policy wise to slow the proliferation of funding until a definitive impact is known. The Comprehensive School Safety Initiative and research funding is a step in the right direction in helping to clarify the benefits and costs of these types of efforts within the nation's schools.

Legal Remedies

Legal challenges to today's zero-tolerance policies, the criminalization of education, and the school-to-prison pipeline may constitute a broad array of state and federal law, as well as legal theories and strategies used in reform litigation. The complexities, nuances, and local and state law differences make these challenges both difficult and subtle in reforming current practice. A multitude of scholars, researchers, and litigators have employed these reform strategies, along with key advocacy and legal organizations. Three of the key organizations include the Racial Justice Program of the American Civil Liberties Union Foundation, the NAACP Legal Defense Fund and the Educational Fund, Inc., and the Civil Rights Project at UCLA. These organizations, in turn, have led the charge and employed key scholars to publish a primer and current definitive text on reforming the school-to-prison pipeline through the court systems. The text *The School-to-Prison Pipeline: Structuring Legal Reform* (Kim, Losen, & Hewitt, 2010) is the foundation for learning and a necessary tool for activists and litigants wanting to pursue change through the courts, though not an exhaustive review of structural reform litigation on challenging zero-tolerance policies, particularly with relevant recent law.

Because of this text's review quality and breadth of coverage across key school-to-prison pipeline legal problems and potential causes of action, this current book can do no better than to summarize what Kim, Losen, and Hewitt (2010) offer, and to refer the reader to their text for a full review. These authors cover the following material: (1) legal theories that challenge the pipeline where it begins for certain students, in under-resourced public schools through a child's right to education under the U.S. Constitution, federal statutes, and state laws; (2) legal strategies that protect the rights of a number of student groups who are disproportionately impacted—minority students, English language learners, those in foster care, and students with special education disabilities; (3) discourse and strategies to First Amendment and due process challenges to harsh discipline codes and punishments that ensue for students on and off school campuses; (4) rights to alternative education for suspended or expelled students, as well as the rights to a continued quality education during these out-of-school placements and to reenter the home school; (5) the criminal procedural legal rights of students, the implications for having police officers working inside the schools, and challenges to the subsequent criminalization of school misconduct; and (6) legal challenges to the arrest of young people, as well as education rights for those in juvenile justice institutions and their reentry to mainstream education after release. The reader would be wise to review and incorporate this material within their legal and policy initiatives and advocacy efforts, particularly when the concern is the connection from low or inadequate school and community resources to the pipeline.

Effective Interventions and Collaboration

One of the key success strategies for many students caught within the pipeline is addressing risk factors when they are known or identified. Often, this may be trauma from violence, bullying, and/or maltreatment experiences and victimizations, and then subsequent mental health or related school difficulties that increase the risk for involvement with school problems and discipline procedures. These risks and experiences are often connected to later mental health problems, learning difficulties, and/or behavioral problems and some special education disabilities (Grogan-Kaylor, Ruffolo, Ortega, & Clarke, 2008; Lemmon, 2009; Schubert & Mulvey, 2014; Yun, Ball, & Lim, 2011). To do so, coordination across the youth-caring systems needs to be effective, often initiated by or significantly involving school personnel—teachers, counselors, and administrators. Effective interventions and programs can be utilized with these at-risk children and adolescents.

Once youth with trauma histories are identified through screening or assessment, interventions are available and can be provided by community-based services or the school districts. Overall, cognitive-behavioral treatments have been studied more frequently than most other modalities and found to be effective for traumatized children and adolescents—trauma caused by witnessing or being a victim of violence, living in dangerous or unsafe neighborhoods, or maltreatment experiences (Centers for Disease Control and Prevention, 2008). Specifically, the interventions with the strongest empirical support include the Cognitive Behavioral Intervention for Trauma in Schools (CBITS), Trauma Affect Regulation: A Guide for Education and Therapy (TARGET), Seeking Safety, Trauma-Focused Cognitive Behavioral Therapy (TF-CBT), and Skills Training in Affective and Interpersonal Regulation (STAIR) (National Child Traumatic Stress Network, 2009). In addition, the Trauma Recovery and Empowerment Model (TREM) has been found effective for female adolescents, an important consideration because of the apparently strong gender differential impact of maltreatment on certain school problems and delinquency (Huizinga, Miller, & the Conduct Problems Prevention Research Group, 2013). Most of these interventions include a number of the following components: psycho-education, emotional regulation, cognitive processing, family or caregiver involvement, a strengths-based perspective, and personal empowerment training (Cloitre, Koenen, Cohen, & Han, 2002; Cohen, Deblinger, Mannarino, & Streer, 2004; Ford, Courtois, van der Hart, Nijenhuis, & Steele, 2005).

Working across schools, providers, and other child- and adolescent-caring systems has some inherent difficulties. Barriers to coordination across these systems can be substantial, and include, but are not limited to inadequate understanding across stakeholders, too many advocates working at cross purposes on behalf of the children and adolescents, confidentiality concerns across laws and regulations (Family Educational Rights and Privacy Act, Health Insurance Portability and Accountability Act, Federal Drug and Alcohol Confidentiality Laws—42 CFR Part 2, Child Abuse Prevention and Treatment Act, among others), and information-sharing difficulties (Morgan et al., 2014; Stone, D'Andrade, & Austin, 2007; Weinberg, Zetlin, & Shea, 2009). Though vital to coordination efforts, information sharing remains controversial because of concerns among stakeholders as to how certain sensitive information pertaining to matters such as child maltreatment, school problems, or arrest and conviction records may be utilized by other stakeholders (American Psychological Association Zero Tolerance Task Force, 2008; Morgan et al., 2014). Still, significant efforts have been made across some of these systems to improve coordination in child, adolescent, and family information sharing outcomes—with important changes that have occurred in Delaware and Iowa.

In Delaware, governmental structural changes have taken place over the past few years. The state government structure has been coordinated across child and family serving agencies, with the Department of Services for Children, Youth, and Their Families overseeing juvenile justice (Division of Youth Rehabilitative Services), child welfare (Division of Family Services), and mental health (Division of Prevention and Behavioral Health Services). This unique state government organization also allows for innovative and collaborative initiatives. One of these is a vocational system for the City of Wilmington's adolescents who are aging out of foster care that addresses alternative education, demand-driven training systems, targets the neediest young people, and improves service provision. Lessons learned from these efforts are planned for replication in other areas of the state with targeted at-risk populations. Three strategies are being employed: a comprehensive analysis of organizations that serve the target population searching for service gaps and barriers; creation of an interdisciplinary coalition to strategize and integrate the service delivery system; and improving data collection and sharing to ensure that information is comprehensive and accurate (Wilson, Kelly, & Howell, 2012).

Iowa established the Iowa Collaboration for Youth Development, a network of 10 state agencies committed to improving results among at-risk adolescents through the adoption and implementation of positive youth development principles and practices at state and local levels. These efforts work with public–private coalitions in both Dubuque and Buena Vista Counties to strengthen partnerships, build capacity, and integrate services and resources for adolescents, aged 14 to 21, who are involved in or who have aged out of Iowa's child welfare and/or juvenile justice systems. These efforts emphasize engagement by expanding a leadership program called Elevate, aimed at educating policy makers (including schools), foster parents, human service workers, and juvenile court personnel on the challenges of dually involved adolescents and having significantly improved access to necessary disability-related services and high school graduation rates. Training and technical assistance developed through this initiative has been made available to communities throughout the state (Iowa Collaboration for Youth Development, 2013; U.S. Department of Labor, 2009).

Reformation

Reform and change within the schools is vital, and without a continued shift from zero-tolerance discipline policies toward an individualized assessment of safety and risk the future for certain students remains fairly bleak. However, change cannot stop at the schoolhouse doorsteps, for the pipeline is only completed when a student becomes involved, often informally at first, with a local juvenile court. It is under this jurisdictional auspice that delinquency can be adjudicated and the deeper movement through the juvenile justice system ends for some in detention and incarceration facilities. The pipeline needs reform in both the schools and juvenile courts.

REFERENCES

Addington, L. A. (2014). Surveillance and security approaches across public school levels. In G. W. Muschert, S. Henry, N. L. Bracy, & A. A. Peguero (Eds.), *Responding to school violence: Confronting the Columbine effect* (pp. 71–88). Boulder, CO: Lynne Rienner.

Advancement Project, Alliance for Educational Justice, and GSA Network. (2011). *Two wrongs don't make a right: Why zero tolerance is not the solution to bullying*. Washington, DC: Author.

American Academy of Pediatrics, Council on School Health. (2013). Out-of-school suspension and expulsion. *Pediatrics, 131*(3), 1000–1007.

American Psychological Association Zero Tolerance Task Force. (2008). Are zero tolerance policies effective in the schools? An evidentiary review and recommendations. *American Psychologist, 63*(9), 852–862.

Aos, S. (2004). *Washington State's family integrated transitions program for juvenile offenders: Outcome evaluation and benefit-cost analysis.* Olympia, WA: Washington State Institute for Public Policy.

Aos, S., Lee, S., Drake, E., Pennucci, A., Klima, T., Miller, M., . . . Burley, M. (2011). *Return on investment: Evidence-based options to improve statewide outcomes.* Olympia, WA: Washington State Institute for Public Policy.

Arum, R. (2003). *Judging school discipline: The crisis of moral authority.* Cambridge, MA: Harvard University Press.

Barnofski, R. (2009). *Providing evidence-based programs with fidelity to Washington state juvenile courts: Cost analysis.* Olympia, WA: Washington State Institute for Public Policy.

Bazemore, G. (2001). Young people, trouble, and crime: Restorative justice as a normative theory of informal social control and social support. *Youth & Society, 33*(2), 199–226.

Bazemore, G., Leip, L. A., & Stinchcomb, J. (2004). Boundary changes and the nexus between formal and informal social control: Truancy intervention as a case study in criminal justice expansion. *Notre Dame Journal of Law, Ethics and Public Policy, 18,* 521–570.

Beger, R. R. (2003). The "worst of both worlds": School security and the disappearing Fourth Amendment rights of students. *Criminal Justice Review, 28*(2), 336–354.

Berkowitz, M. W., & Bier, M. C. (2005). *What works in charter education: A research driven guide for educators.* Washington, DC: Charter Education Partnership.

Bilchik, S. (1997). *Balanced and restorative justice: A framework for the 21st century.* Washington, DC: Office of Juvenile Justice and Delinquency Prevention, U.S. Department of Justice.

Bradshaw, C., Koth, C., Bevans, K., Ialongo, N., & Leaf, P. (2008). The impact of school-wide positive behavioral interventions and supports (PBIS) on the organizational health of elementary schools. *School Psychology Quarterly, 23,* 462–473.

Bradshaw, C. P., Mitchell, M. M., & Leaf, P. J. (2010). Examining the effects of schoolwide positive behavioral interventions and supports on student outcomes. *Journal of Positive Behavior Interventions, 12*(3), 133–148.

Brady, K. P., Balmer, C., & Phenix, D. (2007). School-police partnership effectiveness in urban schools: An analysis of New York City's impact schools initiative. *Education and Urban Society, 39*(4), 455–478.

Browers, A., & Tornic, C. (2000). A longitudinal study of teacher burnout and perceived self-efficacy in classroom management. *Teaching and Teacher Education, 16*(2), 239–253.

Brown, B. (2006). Understanding and assessing school police officers: A conceptual and methodological comment. *Journal of Criminal Justice, 34*(6), 591–604.

Buffalo Public Schools. (2013). *Developing safe and supportive schools: Buffalo public schools standards for community-wide conduct and intervention supports.* Buffalo, NY: Author.

Buffington, K., Pierkhising, C. B., & Marsh, S. (2010). *Ten things every juvenile court judge should know about trauma and delinquency.* Reno, NV: National Council of Juvenile and Family Court Judges.

Calhoun, A., & Daniels, G. (2008). Accountability in school responses to harmful incidents. *Journal of School Violence, 7,* 21–47.

Carver, P. R., & Lewis, L. (2010). *Alternative schools and programs for public school students at risk of educational failure: 2007–2008.* Washington, DC: U.S. Department of Education, National Center for Education Statistics.

Center for Civil Rights Remedies. (2013). *A summary of new research: Closing the school discipline gap: Research to practice.* Washington, DC: Civil Rights Project.

Center for Civil Rights Remedies. (2014). *Keeping California's kids in school.* Los Angeles, CA: Author.

Centers for Disease Control and Prevention. (2008). *Reducing psychological harm from traumatic events: Cognitive behavior therapy for children and adolescents (individual & group), guide to community preventive services.* Atlanta, GA: Author.

Chestnut Health Systems. (2014). *Global appraisal of individual needs (GAIN).* Normal, IL: GAIN Coordinating Center.

Child Trends. (2007a). *Cognitive-behavioral training program for behaviorally disordered adolescents.* Washington, DC: LINKS Database.

Child Trends. (2007b). *Reconnecting youth.* Washington, DC: LINKS Database.

Chlang, H., & Gill, B. (2010). *The impacts of Philadelphia's accelerated schools on academic progress and graduation.* Cambridge, MA: Mathematica Policy Research.

Cloitre, M., Koenen, K. C., Cohen, L. R., & Han, H. (2002). Skills training in affective and interpersonal regulation followed by exposure: A phase-based treatment for PTSD related to childhood abuse. *Journal of Consulting and Clinical Psychology, 70*(5), 1067–1074.

Cohen, J. A., Deblinger, E., Mannarino, A. P., & Streer, R. (2004). A multisite, randomized controlled trial for children with sexual abuse-related PTSD symptoms. *Journal of the American Academy of Child and Adolescent Psychiatry, 43*, 393–402.

Cornell, D. G. (2007). *The Virginia model for student threat assessment.* Confronting violence in our schools: Planning response, and recovery—A PERI Symposium, University of Virginia.

Cornell, D. G., Shin, C., Ciolfi, A., & Sancken, K. (2013). *Prevention v. punishment: Threat assessment, school suspensions, and racial disparities.* Charlottesville, VA: Legal Aid Justice Center and University of Virginia.

Dahlberg, R. L. (2012). *Arrested futures: The criminalization of school discipline in Massachusetts' three largest school districts.* New York, NY: American Civil Liberties Union.

Dennis, M. L., Feeney, T., Stevens, L. H., & Bedoya, L. (2008). *Global appraisal of individual needs—short screener: Administration and scoring manual.* Normal, IL: Chestnut Health Systems.

Denver Public Schools. (2014). *Parent student policy handbook.* Available at https://www.dpsk12.org/parent_handbook/

Dishon, T. J., Dodge, K., & Lansford, J. E. (Eds.). (2006). *Deviant peer influences in programs for youth: Problems and solutions.* New York, NY: Guilford Press.

Dohrn, B. (2000). "Look out, kid, it's something you did": The criminalization of children. In V. Polakow (Ed.), *The public assault on America's children: Poverty, violence, and juvenile justice* (pp. 157–187). New York, NY: Teachers College.

Donavan, M. S., & Cross, C. T. (2002). *Minority students in special and gifted education.* Washington, DC: National Academy Press.

Durlak, J. A., & Weissberg, R. P. (2007). *The impact of after-school program that promise personal and social skills.* Chicago, IL: Collaborative for Academic, Social, and Emotional Learning.

Eggert, L. L., Thompson, E. A., Herting, J. R., & Nicholas, L. J. (1994). Preventing adolescent drug abuse and high school dropout through an intensive social network development program. *American Journal of Health Promotion, 8*, 202–215.

Eggert, L. L., Thompson, E. A., Herting, J. R., & Nicholas, L. J. (1995). Reducing suicide potential among high-risk youth: Tests of a school-based prevention program. *Suicide & Life-Threatening Behavior, 25*, 276–296.

Fabelo, T., Thompson, M. D., Plotkin, M., Carmichael, D., Marchbanks, M. P. III, & Booth, E. A. (2011). *Breaking schools' rules: A statewide study of how school discipline relates to students' success and juvenile justice involvement.* New York, NY;

College Station, TX: Council of State Governments Justice Center; Public Research Policy Research Institute of Texas A & M University.

Federal Advisory Committee on Juvenile Justice. (2014). *2013 recommendations to the President, Congress, and OJJDP Administrator.* Washington, DC: Author.

Fenning, P., Pigott, T., Engler, E., Bradshaw, K., Gamboney, E., Grunewald, S., & McGrath-Kato, M. (2013). *A mixed methods approach examining disproportionality in school discipline.* Paper presented at the Closing the School Discipline Gap: Research to Practice Conference, Washington, DC.

Ferguson, A. A. (2000). *Bad boys: Public schools in the making of black masculinity.* Ann Arbor, MI: The University of Michigan Press.

Figlio, D. (2005). *Testing, crime, and punishment.* National Bureau of Economics Research, NBER Working Paper #11193, Cambridge, MA.

Finn, P., Townsend, M., Shively, M., & Rich, T. (2005). *A guide to developing, maintaining, and succeeding with your school resource officer program.* Washington, DC: Office of Community Oriented Policing Services, U.S. Department of Justice.

Ford, J. D., Courtois, C., van der Hart, O., Nijenhuis, E., & Steele, K. (2005). Treatment of complex post-traumatic self-dysregulation. *Journal of Traumatic Stress, 18,* 476–477.

Forum for Education and Democracy. (2008). *Democracy at risk: The need for a new federal policy in education, 38.* Washington, DC: Author.

Gonzalez, T. (2015). Socializing schools: Addressing racial disparities in discipline through restorative justice. In D. J. Losen (Ed.), *Closing the school discipline gap: Research for policymakers.* New York, NY: Teachers College.

Gottfredson, G. D., Gottfredson, D. C., Payne, A. A., & Gottfredson, N. C. (2005). School climate predictors of school disorder: Results from a national study of delinquency prevention in schools. *Journal of Research in Crime and Delinquency, 42,* 412–444.

Gregory, A., Allen, J. P., Mikami, A. Y., Hafen, A., & Pianta, R. C. (2012). *The promise of a teacher professional development program in reducing the racial disparity in classroom exclusionary discipline.* Washington, DC: Center for Civil Rights Remedies and the Research-to-Practice Collaborative, National Conference on Race and Gender Disparities in Discipline.

Gregory, A., Bell, J., & Pollock, M. (2014, March). *How educators can eradicate disparities in school discipline: A briefing paper on school-based interventions.* Discipline disparities series: New Research. Bloomington, IN: The Equity Project at Indiana University. Available at http://rtpcollaborative.indiana .edu/briefing-papers

Grisso, T. (2008). Adolescent offenders with mental disorders. *The Future of Children, 18*(2), 143–162.

Grogan-Kaylor, A., Ruffolo, M. C., Ortega, R. C., & Clarke, J. (2008). Behavior of youth involved in the child welfare system. *Child Abuse & Neglect: The International Journal, 32*, 35–49.

Hafen, C. A., Allen, J. P., Mikami, A. Y., Gregory, A., Hamre, B., & Pianta, R. C. (2010). The pivotal role of adolescent autonomy in secondary classrooms. *Journal of Youth and Adolescence, 41*, 245–255.

Hawkins, D. R., Catalano, R. F., Kosterman, R., Abbott, R., & Hill, R. (1999). Preventing adolescent health-risk behaviors by strengthening protection during childhood. *Archives of Pediatrics and Adolescent Medicine, 153*, 226–234.

Hereth, J., Kaba, M., Meiniers, E. R., & Wallace, L. (2012). Restorative justice is not enough. In S. Bahena, N. Cooc, R. Currie-Rubin, P. Kuttner, & M. Ng (Eds.), *Disrupting the school-to-prison pipeline* (pp. 240–264). Cambridge, MA: Harvard Educational Review.

Hirschfield, P. J. (2010). School surveillance in America: Disparate and unequal. In T. Monahan & R. D. Torres (Eds.), *Schools under surveillance: Cultures of control in public education* (pp. 38–54). New Brunswick, NJ: Rutgers University.

Horner, R. H., Sugai, G., Smolkowski, K., Todd, A., Nakasato, J., & Esperanza, J. (2009). A randomized control trial of school-wide positive behavior support in elementary schools. *Journal of Positive Behavioral Interventions, 11*, 133–144.

Huizinga, D., Miller, S., & The Conduct Problems Prevention Research Group. (2013). *Developmental sequences of girl's delinquent behavior.* Washington, DC: Office of Juvenile Justice and Delinquency Prevention, Office of Justice Programs, U.S. Department of Justice.

Iowa Collaboration for Youth Development. (2013). *2013 annual report.* Des Moines, IA: Author.

Jackson, A. (2002). Police-school resource officers' and students' perceptions of the police and offending. *Policing: An International Journal of Police Strategies and Management, 25*, 631–650.

Justice Policy Institute. (2011). *Education under arrest: The case against police in schools.* Washington, DC: Author.

Kamphaus, R. W., & Reynolds, C. R. (2007). *BASC-2: Behavioral and emotional screening system.* Toronto, CA: Pearson.

Kang, K., & Banaji, M. R. (2006). Fair measures: A behavioral realist revision of affirmative action. *California Law Review, 94*, 1063–1085.

Kang-Brown, J., Trone, J., Fratello, J., & Daftary-Kapur, T. (2013). *A generation later: What we've learned about zero tolerance in schools.* New York, NY: Vera Institute of Justice, Center on Youth Justice.

Kim, K. Y., Losen, D. J., & Hewitt, D. T. (2010). *The school-to-prison pipeline: Structuring legal reform.* New York, NY: New York University Press.

Kohli, R. (2012). Racial pedagogy of the oppressed: Critical interracial dialogue for teachers of color. *Equity & Excellence in Education, 45*(1), 181–196.

Kupchik, A. (2010). *Homeroom security: School discipline in an age of fear.* New York, NY: New York University Press.

Latimer, J., Dowden, C., & Muise, D. (2005). The effectiveness of restorative justice practices: A meta-analysis. *Prison Journal, 85*(2), 127–144.

Lemmon, J. H. (2009). How child maltreatment affects dimensions of juvenile delinquency in a cohort of low-income urban males. *Justice Quarterly, 16,* 357–376.

Lohrmann-O'Rourke, S., Knoster, T., Sabatine, K., Smith, D., Horvath, G., & Llewellyn, G. (2000). School-wide application of PBS in the Bangor area school district. *Journal of Positive Behavior Interventions, 2*(4), 283–240.

Losen, D. L., Hewitt, D., & Toldson, I. (2014, March). *Eliminating excessive and unfair discipline in schools: Policy recommendations for reducing disparities.* Discipline disparities series: New Research. Bloomington, IN: The Equity Project at Indiana University. Available at http://rtpcollaborative.indiana.edu/briefing-papers

Luiselli, J., Putnam, R., & Sunderland, M. (2002). Longitudinal evaluation of behavior support interventions in public middle school. *Journal of Positive Behavior Interventions, 4*(3), 182–188.

Macready, T. (2009). Learning social responsibility in schools: A restorative practice. *Educational Psychology in Practice, 25,* 211–220.

Majd, K. (2011). Students of the mass incarceration nation. *Howard Law Journal, 54*(2), 343–394.

Majd, K., Marksamer, J., & Reyes, C. (2009). *Hidden justice: Lesbian, gay, bisexual and transgender youth in juvenile courts.* San Francisco, CA: National Center for Lesbian Rights.

Martinez, S. (2009). A system gone berserk: How are zero-tolerance policies really affecting schools? *Preventing School Failure, 53*(3), 153–157.

Mediratta, K. (2012). Grassroots organizing and the school-to-prison pipeline: The emerging national movement to roll back zero tolerance discipline policies in the U.S. public schools. In S. Bahena, N. Cooc, R. Currie-Rubin, P. Kuttner, & M. Ng (Eds.), *Disrupting the school-to-prison pipeline.* Cambridge, MA: Harvard Educational Review.

Mehan, H. (2012). *In the front door: Creating a college-bound culture of learning.* Herndon, VA: Paradigm.

Mitchum, P., & Moodie-Mills, A. C. (2014). *Beyond bullying: How hostile school climate perpetuates the school-to-prison pipeline for LBGT youth.* Washington, DC: Center for American Progress.

Monroe, C. R. (2005). Why are "bad boys" always black? Causes of disproportionality in school discipline and recommendations for change. *The Clearing House: A Journal of Educational Strategies, Issues, and Ideas, 79*(1), 45–50.

Morgan, E., Salomon, N., Plotkin, M., & Cohen, R. (2014). *The school discipline consensus report: Strategies from the field to keep students engaged in school and out of the juvenile justice system.* Washington, DC: The Council of State Governments Justice Center.

Mulvey, E. P., & Iselin, A. R. (2008). Improving professional judgments of risk and amenability in juvenile justice. *The Future of Children, 18*(2), 35–56.

Muschert, G. W., & Peguero, A. A. (2010). The Columbine effect and school anti-violence policy. *Research in Social Problems and Public Policy, 17*, 117–148.

Muscott, H. S., Mann, E., Benjamin, T. B., Gately, S., Bell, K. E., & Muscott, A. J. (2004). Positive behavioral interventions and supports in New Hampshire: Preliminary results of a statewide system for implementing schoolwide discipline practices. *Education and Treatment of Children, 27*, 453–475.

NAACP. (2005). *Interrupting the school to prison pipeline.* Washington, DC: Author.

National Center for Mental Health and Juvenile Justice. (2007). *Mental health screening within juvenile justice: The next frontier.* Delmar, NY: Author.

National Child Traumatic Stress Network. (2008). *Child welfare trauma referral tool.* Los Angeles, CA: UCLA.

National Child Traumatic Stress Network. (2009). *NCCTS leadership: Evidence-based practices.* Los Angeles, CA: UCLA.

National Institute of Justice. (2014). *Comprehensive School Safety Initiative (CSSI) funding awards.* Washington, DC: Office of Justice Programs, U.S. Department of Justice.

National Juvenile Justice and Delinquency Prevention Coalition. (2014). *Promoting safe communities: Recommendations for the 113th Congress: Opportunities for juvenile justice and delinquency prevention reform.* Washington, DC: Author.

Newman, K. (2004). *Rampage: The social roots of school shootings.* New York, NY: Basic Books.

Osher, D., Bear, G. G., Sprague, J. R., & Doyle, W. (2010). How can we improve school discipline? *Educational Researcher, 39*(1), 48–58.

Osher, D., Coggshall, J., Colombi, G., Wodruff, D., Francois, S., & Osher, T. (2012). Building school and teacher capacity to eliminate the school-to-prison pipeline. *Teacher Education and Special Education: Journal of the Teacher Education Division of the Council for Exceptional Children, 35*(4), 284–295.

Osher, D., Dwyer, K., & Jackson, S. (2004). *Safe, supportive, and successful schools step by step.* Longmont, CO: Sopris West.

Osher, D., Sandler, S., & Nelson, C. (2001). The best approach to safety is to fix schools and support children and staff. *New Directions in Youth Development, 92,* 127–154.

O'Toole, M. E. (2000). *The school shooter: A threat assessment perspective.* Quantico, VA: National Center for the Analysis of Violent Crime, Federal Bureau of Investigation.

Pas, E. T., Bradshaw, C. P., Hershfeldt, P. A., & Leaf, P. J. (2010). A multilevel exploration of the influence of teacher efficacy and burnout on response to student problem behavior and school-based service use. *School Psychology Quarterly, 25*(1), 13–27.

Payne, A. A., Gottfredson, D. C., & Gottfredson, G. D. (2008). Schools as communities: The relationships among communal school organization, students bonding, and school disorder. *Criminology, 41,* 749–777.

Payton, J., Weissberg, R. P., Durlak, J. A., Dymnicki, A. B., Taylor, R. D., Schellinger, K. B., & Pachan, M. (2008). *The positive impact of social and emotional learning for kindergarten to eighth-grade students: Findings from three scientific reviews.* Chicago, IL: Collaborative for Academic, Social, and Emotional Learning.

Person, A. E., Moiduddin, E., Hague-Angus, M., & Malone, L. M. (2009). *Survey of outcomes measurement in research on character education prorams.* Washington, DC: National Center for Educational Evaluations and Regional Assistance, Institute of Education Sciences, U.S. Department of Education.

Psychological Assessment Resources. (2014). *Trauma symptom checklist for children (TSCC).* Lutz, FL: Author.

Rich-Shae, A. M., & Fox, J. A. (2014). Zero-tolerance policies. In G. W. Muschert, S. Henry, N. L. Bracy, & A. A. Peguero (Eds.), *Responding to school violence: Confronting the Columbine effect* (pp. 89–104). Boulder, CO: Lynne Rienner.

Rosenberg, M. S., & Jackman, L. A. (2003). Development, implementation, and sustainability of comprehensive school-wide behavior management systems. *Intervention in School and Clinic, 39,* 10–21.

Rosiak, J. (2009). *Developing safe schools partnerships with law enforcement.* Washington, DC: National Center for Mental Health Promotion and Youth Violence Prevention.

Rudd, T. (2014). *Racial disproportionality in school discipline.* Columbus, OH: Kirwan Institute for the Study of Race and Ethnicity, The Ohio State University.

Ruiz de Velasco, J., Austin, G., Dixon, D., Johnson, J., McLaughlin, M., & Perez, 2008). *Alternative education options: A descriptive study of California continuation high schools.* San Francisco: WestEd.

Russell, S. T., Horn, S., Kosciw, J., & Saewyc, E. (2010). Social policy report: Safe schools policy for LGBTQ students. *Sharing Child and Youth Development Knowledge, 24*(4), 1–22.

SASSI Institute. (2014). *Adolescent substance abuse subtle screening instrument.* Springville, IN: SASSI Institute Headquarters.

Schiff, M. (2013). *Dignity, disparity and desistance: Effective restorative justice strategies to plug the "school-to-prison pipeline."* Paper presented at the Closing School Discipline Gap: Research to Practice Conference, Washington, DC.

Schubert, C. A., & Mulvey, E. P. (2014). *Behavioral health problems, treatment, and outcomes in serious youthful offenders.* Washington, DC: U.S. Department of Justice, Office of Juvenile Justice and Delinquency Promotion, Office of Justice Programs.

Schultz, K. (2008). Interrogating students' silences. In M. Pollock (Ed.), *Everyday antiracism: Getting real about race in school* (pp. 217–221). New York, NY: The New Press.

Sharma, S. (2008). Teacher representations of cultural differences through film. In M. Pollock (Ed.), *Everyday antiracism: Getting real about race in school* (pp. 186–190). New York, NY: The New Press.

Singleton, G. E., & Linton, C. (2006). *Courageous conversations about race: A field guide for achieving equity in schools.* Thousand Oaks, CA: Corwin.

Skiba, R. J., Arrendonda, M. I., & Rausch, M. K. (2014, March). *New and developing research on disparities in discipline.* Discipline disparities series: New Research. Bloomington, IN: The Equity Project at Indiana University. Available at http://rtpcollaborative.indiana.edu/briefing-papers

Skiba, R. J., & Williams, N. T. (2014, March). *Are black kids worse? Myths and facts about racial differences in behavior.* Discipline disparities series: New Research. Bloomington, IN: The Equity Project at Indiana University. Available at http://rtpcollaborative.indiana.edu/briefing-papers

Sleeter, C. E. (2011). *The academic and social value of ethnic studies: A research review.* Washington, DC: National Education Association.

Social and Character Development Research Consortium. (2010). *Efficacy of school-wide programs to promote social and character development and reduce problem behavior in elementary school children.* Washington, DC: National Center for Education Research, Institute of Education Sciences, U.S. Department of Education.

Sprague, J. R., Vincent, C. G., Tobin, T. J., & CHiXapkaid. (2013). Preventing disciplinary exclusions of students from American Indian/Alaska Native backgrounds. *Family Court Review, 51*, 452–459.

Staats, C. (2014). *Implicit racial bias and school discipline disparities.* Columbus, OH: Kirwan Institute for the Study of Race and Ethnicity, The Ohio State University.

Steinberg, M. P., Allensworth, E., & Johnson, D. W. (2013). *What conditions jeopardize and support safety in urban schools? The influence of community characteristics, school composition and school organizational practices on student and teacher reports of safety in Chicago.* Paper presented at the Closing the School Discipline Gap: Research to Practice conference, Washington, DC.

Stone, S., D'Andrade, A., & Austin, M. (2007). Educational services for children in foster care: Common and contrasting perspectives of child welfare and education stakeholders. *Journal of Public Child Welfare, 1*(2), 53–70.

Sugai, G., & Horner, R. (2010). School-wide positive behavior support: Establishing a continuum of evidence-based practices. *Journal of Evidence-based Practices for Schools, 11*(1), 62–83.

Texas Appleseed. (2007). *Texas' school-to-prison pipeline: Dropout to incarceration: The impact of school discipline and zero tolerance.* Austin, TX: Author.

Theriot, M. T. (2009). School resource officers and the criminalization of student behavior. *Journal of Criminal Justice, 37*, 280–287.

Thurae, L., & Wald, J. (2010). Controlling partners: When law enforcement meets discipline in public schools. *New York Law School Law Review, 54*, 977–1020.

Toomey, R. B., & Russell, S. T. (2011). Gay-straight alliances, social justice involvement, and school victimization of lesbian, gay, bisexual, and queer youth: Implications for school well-being and plans to vote. *Youth & Society, 20*, 1–23.

Torres, M., & Stefkovich, J. A. (2008). Demographics and police involvement: Implications for student civil liberties and just leadership. *Education Administration Quarterly, 45*(3), 450–473.

U.S. Department of Education. (2000). *21st annual report to Congress on the implementation of the Individuals with Disabilities Education Act.* Washington, DC: Author.

U.S. Department of Education. (2014). *Civil rights data collection, data snapshot: School discipline, Issue brief No. 1.* Washington, DC: Office for Civil Rights.

U.S. Department of Education. (2015). *Creating safe schools through positive discipline.* National Technical Assistance Training Center on Positive Behavioral Interventions and Supports. Office of Special Education Programs, Washington, DC.

U.S. Department of Labor. (2009). *Vision for youth: Advanced technical assistance forum participating states*. Washington, DC: Author.

Vincent, C. G., Sprague, J. R., & Gau, J. M. (2013). *The effectiveness of school-wide positive behavior interventions and supports for reducing racially inequitable disciplinary exclusions in middle schools*. Paper presented at the Closing the School Discipline Gap: Research to Practice conference, Washington, DC.

Vincent, G. M., Guy, L. S., & Grisso, T. (2012). *Risk assessment in juvenile justice: A guidebook for implementation*. Chicago, IL: MacArthur Foundation, Models for Change: Systems Reform in Juvenile Justice.

Wald, J. W. (2014). *Can "de-biasing" strategies help to reduce racial disparities in school discipline?* Cambridge, MA: Institute for Race & Justice, Harvard Law School.

Welch, W. N. (2003). Individual and institutional predictors of school disorder. *Youth Violence and Juvenile Justice Journal, 1*, 346–368.

Weinberg, L., Zetlin, A. G., & Shea, N. (2009). *A review of literature on the educational needs of children involved in family and juvenile court proceedings*. San Francisco, CA: Judicial Council of California, Center for Children, Families and the Court.

What Works Clearinghouse. (2006a). *Connect with kids*. Washington, DC: Institute of Education Statistics, U.S. Department of Education.

What Works Clearinghouse. (2006b). *Too good for violence*. Washington, DC: Institute of Education Statistics, U.S. Department of Education.

Wilson, J., Kelly, M., & Howell, J. C. (2012). *Juvenile justice system in Delaware 2012: The little engine that could*. Dover, DE: Comprehensive Strategy Group.

Yun, I., Ball, J. D., & Lim, H. (2011). Disentangling the relationship between child maltreatment and violent delinquency: Using a nationally representative sample. *Journal of Interpersonal Violence, 26*(1), 88–110.

Zehr, H. (2002). *The little book of restorative justice*. Intercourse, PA: Good Books.

Chapter 6: Rehabilitative
Juvenile Justice

SCHOOLS TO THE JUVENILE COURTS

Children and adolescents are involved with this country's juvenile courts for many reasons—home difficulties, violence, school problems, peer troubles, offending activities, status offenses, and children's services agency involvement, among others. Most of these young people have experienced difficult lives, often involving trauma, family dysfunction, poverty, and other related delinquency risks (Howell, 2003; Puzzanchera & Robson, 2014). While a majority of these young people enter the juvenile courts each year as low-level or first-time offenders, many are eventually adjudicated delinquent and supervised by the juvenile courts. Once involved in this way, it is likely that the adolescents will continue their delinquent behaviors in large part because of how the juvenile justice system operates, increasing their risk for detention and incarceration. In other words, for many young people, formal juvenile court involvement becomes a vortex, keeping the adolescent involved with the system (Petitclerc, Gatti, Vitaro, & Tremblay, 2013; Petrosino, Turpin-Petrosino, & Guckenburg, 2010). For this reason, along with many others, including the cost of the juvenile justice system and the poor long-term outcomes for most adolescents involved, prevention and diversion is paramount (Mendel, 2011; National Juvenile Justice and Delinquency Prevention Coalition, 2013; Salsich & Trone, 2013).

Delinquency Prevention

Involvement with a juvenile court, outside of maltreatment situations, begins with an adolescent committing an offense and subsequent interaction with law enforcement. Most police contact with young people is unofficial; however, in cases in which there is an official contact and arrests are made, a majority are for noncriminal activities—status offenses, traffic offenses, and nonviolent crimes; only about one-fourth of cases are for violent offenses (Office of Juvenile Justice and Delinquency Prevention, 2014a; Puzzanchera & Robson, 2014). Options for police when making a decision on a youthful offense include the following: questioning, warning, and community release; taking the adolescent to the police station and recording the offense; a referral to a diversion program; issuing a citation and making a formal referral to the juvenile court; or taking the adolescent to a detention center or group home (Lawrence & Hemmens, 2008). Many factors are influential at this decision-making point, including the youthful offender's profile, the police officer's perspectives, organizational policies, specific offense and circumstances, and any community pressures (Martin, 2005).

This first point of contact can be a pivotal time for a child or adolescent. A decision to release a young person or to make a referral for diversion services may provide far greater opportunities for assistance, compared to a formal juvenile court referral, adjudication, detainment, or other possible placements. In fact, most young people who are arrested once are not arrested again. So generally, either inaction or informal actions by the police and juvenile court seem to be appropriate in most nonviolent cases (Mulvey, 2011; Office of Juvenile Justice and Delinquency Prevention, 2014b).

Diversion From the Juvenile Courts

The term "diversion" has come to mean a number of different things for youthful offenders, including nonarrest and release back to the community, addressing the identified problems through rehabilitative means, and any attempt to divert from the juvenile justice system (Griffin & Torbet, 2000). Diversion is an important option for first-time or low-level youthful offenders, particularly for those involved with school-based arrests and referrals to the juvenile courts, because a majority of this population does not pose any serious threat of reoffending (Advancement Project et al., 2011). Beyond this, many of these young people may be effectively assisted because of the diversion efforts in thwarting or decreasing the possibility of offending behaviors, primarily through the identification and treatment of risk factors and related difficulties (Coalition for Juvenile Justice, 2013).

Diversion is particularly helpful for youthful offenders with disabilities, trauma backgrounds, and mental health difficulties. Diversion will prioritize the identification of these problems and lead to possible alternative interventions. Diversionary programming may be offered by a juvenile court or a community-based agency, and may entail a wide array of alternatives, depending on the adolescents' needs, including teen or youth court, truancy intervention programs, respite, shelter care, mentoring, curfew enforcement programs, parent training, restorative justice models, and other alternatives. A number of examples may be useful in describing how these diversion alternatives operate.

The Project Back-on-Track is an after-school diversion program designed for low- and mid-level youthful offenders—for example, those involved in domestic violence, assault, drug, and property offenses—to divert from further juvenile court involvement. This multifaceted program curriculum involves the youthful offenders and their families for 4 weeks, with the provision of individual and group therapy, parent support groups, community service projects, psychoeducational sessions, and adolescent empathy-building sessions. The adolescents participate in 32 hours of programming (2 hr/day, 4 days/week), while parents participate in 15 hours of programming. One-year follow-up evaluations found the program to have significantly decreased the recidivism rate for participants when compared to nonparticipating youthful offenders with similar offending histories (Myers et al., 2000; Office of Juvenile Justice and Delinquency Prevention, 2014b).

The Girls Circle Program is a strengths-based group that works with girls, aged 9 to 18, through the integration of cultural differences, resiliency practices, and skills training to assist in diversion from offending behaviors. The program consists of an 8- to 12-session curriculum, normally held weekly, led by a facilitator who follows a six-step format of gender-specific themes, motivational interviewing techniques, and identified improvement areas—coping with stress, sexuality, drugs or alcohol, decision making, relationships, and trust, among others. Long-term follow-up studies of program participants found significant improvements in alcohol abuse and use, attachment to school, self-harming behavior, social support, and self-efficacy (Irvine, 2005; Office of Juvenile Justice and Delinquency Prevention, 2014b).

The Multidisciplinary Team (MDT) Home Run Program of San Bernardino County, California, is a case management intervention designed to identify the youthful offender's difficulties and provide intense family and individual treatment. The treatment planning process includes the family, school personnel, and other relevant individuals in the adolescent's life. This strengths-based and goal-oriented program targets first-time youthful offenders who are 17 years or younger and at risk for more serious criminal activity. The case management team includes the probation officer, public health nurse, licensed therapist, social service practitioner, school personnel, and volunteers who coordinate, make appropriate referrals, and incorporate, as necessary, interventions such as restitution, restorative justice, community service, counseling, and group therapy (Office of Juvenile Justice and Delinquency Prevention, 2014b).

Mentoring programs have received extensive attention over the past decade as a preventative measure for at-risk youth. The evidence of positive impact is consistently found across two areas (Office of Juvenile Justice and Delinquency Prevention, 2014b). The first is that mentors with a professional background generally promoted more effective outcomes than did mentors without a professional background, though many programs produce positive outcomes. Although it is known that the relationship between the mentor and young person is the most important, the specific processes or program structures need to be identified to know which specific program factors are more effective and why they are more effective (Tolan, Henry, Schoeny, & Bass, 2008; Tolan, Henry, Schoeny, Lovegrove, & Nichols, 2014). The second is with regard to school-based mentoring programs, where the mentor relationship is primarily concerned with school difficulties and challenges for the young person. These programs have a modest impact and improvements on students' absenteeism, school-related misconduct, truancy, and peer support, though no significant improvements were made in academic achievement (Wheeler, Keller, & DuBois, 2010).

Beyond these diversion examples, a key resource for stakeholders is the Models for Change Juvenile Justice Diversion Guidebook. This research-based project has a 16-step model for developing and improving juvenile courts' diversion programs, including type to utilize, eligibility determinations, meeting legal mandates, and implementation effectiveness and fidelity (Models for Change, 2011b).

Truancy and Other Status Offenses

Truancy and other status offenses such as running away, violating curfew, alcohol use, and flagrant disobedience are only crimes if committed by a minor. These difficulties or behaviors come under the purview of a juvenile court after a complaint for a status offense is filed, making diversion from this filing the best alternative for young people. With more than 150,000 status offenses processed annually nationwide—and truancy accounting for more than 36%, running away 11%, and incorrigibility (a filing by parents or legal guardians) 12%—diversion is important to discontinue these offenses (Puzzanchera & Hockenberry, 2010; Salsich & Trone, 2013). Though this is not the norm, for in 2010, 56% of status offenders were adjudicated delinquent, because of which 8% of status offenders were placed into a residential facility, 53% were placed on probation supervision, and 39% were court ordered other punitive sanctions (Levin & Cohen, 2014).

Once adjudicated via a status offense, a juvenile court judge or magistrate can do little other than to court order a young person to not repeat the offense or behavior, something many adolescents find difficult to do, forcing the juvenile court personnel to file court order violations, ongoing supervision, and deeper juvenile justice system involvement (Petrosino, Turpin-Petrosino, & Guckenburg, 2010; Shubick, 2010). In fact, as noted, in 8% of the cases (which is 8,500–12,000 status offenders annually), court order violations led to detention or incarceration of the young person, a situation that exacerbates the problems, moving a status offender toward serious delinquency (Holman & Ziedenberg, 2014; Mendel, 2011). Unfortunately, current federal policies and 33 states still allow status offenders to be incarcerated for court order violations (Levin & Cohen, 2014).

It is important to make available more cost-effective and successful community-based diversion strategies than juvenile court adjudication of status offenders. To be the most effective, these diversion services should be chosen through careful screening and assessment of the young person, be offered at the time of the incident, should work with the family in their home when possible, and have evidence as to their positive impact. Working with families and addressing educational, mental health, trauma, or other issues are best handled by youth-caring systems with expertise in these areas. A number of national stakeholders have identified and proposed standards when working to improve the outcomes for young people with status offenses, with the following recommendations: understand emerging knowledge on adolescent developmental issues; investigate and treat trauma; engage the family; understand gender differences and developmental pathways; redirect students with disabilities toward school rehabilitative services; train first responders on diversion, family impacts, and community resources; implement school responses to truancy; use graduated responses and meaningful incentives for attendance; and not allow adolescents who are adjudicated to waive counsel, thus supporting the use of effective representation (Coalition for Juvenile Justice, 2013).

In particular, schools can increase the risk for student truancy outcomes through the under-identification of special education disabilities, having unsafe or low-quality school environments, low-quality teacher/student relationships, and inadequate and poorly maintained attendance policies (Hammond, Linton, Smink, & Drew, 2007; Heilbrunn, 2007). To minimize these risks and reduce truancy, schools should design responses that are relevant to truancy and the reasons for these outcomes, make prevention services available in and out of school, partner with local youth-caring system providers, and incorporate families in meaningful ways (Baker, Sigmon, & Nugent, 2001). To help address their truancy problem, Rapides Parish, Louisiana, designed a graduated system of interventions within their schools to be utilized by school administrators before a referral for truancy may be made to the local juvenile court. In addition, the Massachusetts Youth Screening Instrument (MAYSI) is utilized along with family engagement to determine the appropriate response to truancy, depending on other factors or difficulties identified, including mental health, trauma, and drug use, among others. These efforts have decreased truancy status offense referrals to the local juvenile court by 40% from 2010 to 2012 (Salsich & Trone, 2013).

Screening and Assessment

Early identification and prevention efforts can desist offending and delinquent acts. Through effective identification, young people in the juvenile courts can be targeted for rehabilitative and not punitive efforts (Models for Change, 2011a; National Institute of Justice, 2014). However, many juvenile courts do not utilize empirically supported and structured decision-making tools, but rely more often on their own intuition on whether the young person poses a community safety risk or is amenable to rehabilitative juvenile court alternatives (Mulvey & Iselin, 2008). With such a large number of youthful offenders troubled by mental health, substance use, and trauma difficulties, it is important for juvenile courts to incorporate the use of appropriate screening tools, along with a complete family and individual assessment. Once identified, subsequent rehabilitative and treatment alternatives should be pursued, through coordination with other adolescent-caring systems (Mulvey, 2005; Vincent, Guy, & Grisso, 2012). Table 6.1 includes some of the more reliable and valid measurement tools that assess offending risk and mental health difficulties identification, including suicide assessment, an under-prioritized problem within the juvenile justice system (Baird et al., 2013).

Two of these screening tools—MAYSI-2 and Youth Level of Service/ Case Management Inventory (Y-LIS)—are utilized both to predict future

TABLE 6.1 Screening and Assessment Tools—Juvenile Courts

Massachusetts Youth Screening Instrument (MAYSI-2): assessment for reoffending risk, mental health, and related problems
Youth Level of Service/Case Management Inventory (Y-LSI): assessment for reoffending risk, mental health, and related problems
Diagnostic Interview Schedule for Children Version 4 (DISC-R): assessment for mental health disorders
Suicidal Ideation Questionnaire (SIQ): screening for suicide risk

offending risk and to identify specific problem areas that may be intertwined with youthful offenders' current behaviors. Such standardized screening tools can assist in identifying offending risk, as well as past and current social and family histories, mental health concerns, and other related problems. The MAYSI-2 is a 52-item standardized instrument with seven subscales that is used to identify mental health needs of adolescents (Grisso, Barnum, Fletcher, Cauffman, & Peuschold, 2001); the Y-LSI is a 42-item checklist with eight subscales, including offense history, family circumstances/parenting, education, peer relations, substance abuse, leisure/recreation, personality/behavior, and attitudes/orientation (Schmidt, Hoge, & Gomes, 2005). In addition to these combined screening tools, the Diagnostic Interview Schedule for Children Version 4 (DISC-R) is a comprehensive, structured interview that assesses more than about three dozen adolescent mental health disorders (Shaffer, Lucas, & Fisher, 2011). The Suicidal Ideation Questionnaire (SIQ) is a 25-item, self-report screening instrument used to assess suicidal ideation in adolescents (Reynolds, 1988). Because of the increased suicidal behavior risks for young people involved with the juvenile justice system, and particularly for those held in detention and incarceration facilities, the use of the SIQ is important.

Coordination Across Youth-Caring Systems

Once problems—mental health, substance abuse, and trauma, among others—have been identified by juvenile court personnel, and best when performed before any formal involvement or adjudication of the young person occurs, the responsibility to offer and pay for these services should be shared across youth-caring and juvenile justice systems.

Coordination efforts are imperative to meet the rehabilitative needs of the young person and to improve the pre- or post-adjudication outcomes (Mears & Aron, 2003). There are a number of effective programs, interventions, and evidence-based therapeutic approaches that should be reviewed for us who are working with adolescents and their families, based on the reasons for involvement with the juvenile courts.

Effective Treatment and Rehabilitation

Trauma and Maltreatment

Elements of effective programs for adolescents with trauma and maltreatment experiences have been identified. These recommended practices include thorough individualized assessment; addressing the entire context of adolescent and family functioning; provision of parental supports and parenting education; a focus on improving the parent–child interaction; involving a multimodal intervention approach; utilization of community supports as available; emphasis on behavior skills development; coordination and integration with school, juvenile court, child welfare, and mental health systems; and focusing on long-term outcomes, including follow-up and relapse prevention (Stagner & Lansing, 2009; Wiig, Spatz-Widom, & Tuell, 2003).

Parental substance abuse is a significant reason for many neglect findings for children and adolescents (Smith & Testa, 2002), and neglect accounts for nearly 80% of annual substantiated maltreatment findings (U.S. Department of Health and Human Services, 2013). An effective approach to parental substance abuse is involving the family in treatment. One intervention for families with adolescents, the Strengthening Families Program, has been found to have a significant impact on decreasing parents' alcohol and drug use (Kumpfer, Whiteside, Green, & Allen, 2010). This program utilizes cognitive behavioral, social learning, and/or family systems theory in involving the whole family with skills training, components that have been found effective across many similarly situated family strengthening interventions (Kaminski, Valle, Filene, & Boyle, 2008; Kumpfer, Alvarado, & Whiteside, 2003).

Behaviorally Based Disorders

The epidemiology and development of behaviorally based disorders have numerous influences, including individual adolescent characteristics, economic (e.g., impact of living in poor neighborhoods) and environmental difficulties (family troubles, conflict), with each area often addressed through different strategies (Kazdin & Weisz, 1998). Cognitive-based, parent training has been found effective and focuses on teaching practical skills to caregivers to address conflict, improve communication, and address interpersonal problems. Cognitive behavioral treatment interventions more broadly utilized with both adolescents and their families have demonstrated effectiveness in reducing aggressive and antisocial behaviors (Barkley, Edwards, & Robin, 1999).

In fact, cognitive behavioral treatments have been found to be some of the more efficient treatments for conduct disorder and related violent adolescent behaviors, as well as for underlying anxiety problems. These interventions improve positive behavioral and other psychological outcomes (Andreassen, Armelius, Egelund, & Ogden, 2006; Connor, 2002; Farrington, 2002; Turner, MacDonald, & Dennis, 2007). Cognitive-behavioral interventions are designed to identify cognitions—thoughts, expressions, and perceptions—and to then alter these cognitions that are distorted in order to reduce maladaptive or dysfunctional thinking, attitudes, or behaviors (Lipsey & Landenberger, 2006; McGuire, 2000). Such approaches may include social skills training, parenting skills training, problem-solving skills, behavioral contracting, anger management, and related efforts (Rapp-Palicchi & Roberts, 2004).

Substance Abuse

Adolescent substance abuse prevention programs should target the enhancement of protective factors and the reduction of risk factors; they should focus on all types of drug abuse, and program characteristics should be designed to be appropriate and effective for the intended community population (Hawkins et al., 2000). Risk factors correlated with adolescent substance abuse include early aggressive behavior, lack of parental supervision, substance use by a caregiver, drug availability, deviant peers, lack of caring adult relationships, traumatic life events, mental health difficulties, academic failure, poor social skills, and poverty; whereas protective factors are often the minimizing or elimination of these risk factors (Frischer, Crome, MacLeod, Bloor, & Hickman, 2007; National Institute on Drug Abuse, 2003).

Families play a key part in reducing the risk of substance abuse, which can be strengthened through skills training, education, and increased involvement among family members (National Institute on Drug Abuse, 2003). Parental skills training can improve rule setting, monitoring, and consistent disciplinary actions (Kosterman, Hawkins,

Spoth, Haggerty, & Zhu, 1997); drug education and information can improve discussions about substance abuse (Bauman et al., 2001); and specific family-focused interventions can improve parenting behaviors (Spoth, Redmond, Trudeau, & Shin, 2002). Schools can also play an important preventative role by increasing adolescent academic (study habits, self-efficacy) and social abilities (peer relationships, drug resistance skills) (Botvin, Baker, Dusenbury, Botvin, & Diaz, 1995; Scheier, Botvin, Diaz, & Griffin, 1999). Effective programs include the Midwestern Prevention Project (MPP); the Strengthening Families Program: For Parents and Youth 10–14; Guiding Good Choices; and the Skills, Opportunity, and Recognition (SOAR) Program (Aos, Phipps, Barnoski, & Lieb, 2001; Hawkins, Catalano, Kosterman, Abbott, & Hill, 1999; Pentz, Mihalic, & Grotpeter, 2006).

Depression and Suicide

Numerous approaches have been utilized to decrease the symptoms and impact of adolescent depression and related suicide risk problems— various individual and group therapeutic modalities, psychopharmacology, and public education, among others. While some of these interventions, primarily psychopharmacology, are important in stabilizing the most serious depressive symptoms, including suicidal ideation and behaviors, others do not appear to be effective in achieving symptom reduction goals—therapy, psychotherapy, and psychoanalysis (March et al., 2004).

Interventions that are more likely to be effective include cognitive-behavioral approaches attuned to adolescents and focused on increasing social activities, problem-solving abilities, cognitive restructuring, psychoeducation for parents and adolescents, and mood and emotion regulation. However, limited long-term follow-up has been completed in research to date, so whether or not lasting effects are achieved is not yet known. In addition, when working with adolescents who have multiple or comorbid problems that significantly complicate treatment planning and coordination efforts, care should be taken, because similarly few long-term intervention outcomes are known (Clark et al., 2001; Curry & Wells, 2005; Horowitz & Garber, 2006).

A number of risk factors correlate with suicidal behaviors; however, an adolescent with an increased risk will not necessarily develop suicidal tendencies. Risk factors include depression and other related mental health problems (substance abuse with a comorbid mental health problem), a prior suicide attempt, a family history of suicide or family violence, firearms in the house, and incarceration (National Institute of Mental Health, 2011; Substance Abuse and Mental Health Services Administration, 2009). When working with adolescents, a number of suicidal behavior signs or symptoms can be identified, thus allowing immediate and concerted preventative actions. These signs include feelings of hopelessness or worthlessness, a decline in or lack of family or social activity participation, changes in sleeping or eating patterns, feelings of rage or need for revenge, consistent exhaustion, low concentration abilities at home and/or school, regular or frequent crying, lack of self-care, reckless or impulsive behaviors, and frequent physical symptoms (Centers for Disease Control and Prevention, 2009; National Institute of Mental Health, 2011).

As the number of risk factors increases for young people, the risk increases; however, this is complicated by the impact of other mental health or substance abuse problems (National Action Alliance for Suicide Prevention, 2013; Shaffer et al., 1996). Depression, and in particular unipolar depression, disruptive behavior disorders, and substance abuse are strongly linked to suicide risk (Conner & Goldston, 2007).

The National Registry of Evidence-Based Programs, supported by the National Institute of Mental Health, has identified a number of suicide prevention programs that are found effective in working with at-risk adolescents or their caregivers in school and group settings. These are as follows: CARE (Care, Assess, Respond, and Empower), a high-school-based program utilizing motivational counseling and social support; CAST (Coping and Support Training), a 12-week program focused on life skills and social support delivered by teachers in a group setting; Emergency Department Means Restriction Education, an adult caregiver program that helps minimize access to adolescent suicidal risks within the home, for example, firearms and prescription drugs; Lifelines Curriculum, a school-wide prevention program that focuses on available resources and on decreasing the stigma of suicidal behaviors; and Reconnecting Youth: A Peer Group Approach to Building Life Skills, a school-based prevention program that teaches skills to build resilience against suicide risk factors and early substance abuse or emotional problems (Substance Abuse and Mental Health Services Administration, 2011).

Probation Supervision Programs

If diversion or rehabilitative treatment does not work, adjudication and probation supervision is often the next step within the juvenile courts. Three of the more widely utilized and successful programs in many probation departments focus on family and adolescent interactions and behavior skill development: Functional Family Therapy (FFT), Multisystemic Therapy (MST), and Intensive Protective Supervision (IPS). The first two programs, FFT and MST, have been found effective in addressing adolescent substance abuse and violence problems, and they are provided in community-based settings in the effort to avoid a residential or detention placement (Alexander et al., 2007; Greenberg, 2008; Henggeler, Mihalic, Rone, Thomas, & Timmons-Mitchell, 2006). Both these programs have significant implementation and continuation costs that may be prohibitive, though their rehabilitative focus is important in continuing the movement away from a punitive court paradigm for troubled adolescents (Little, Popa, & Forsythe, 2005; Welsh, Rocque, & Greenwood, 2014; Willison et al., 2010). The third program, IPS, works with adolescents who have committed status offenses, such as truancy, underage drinking, and so on. This supervision closely monitors these adolescents while working with their families and providing links to necessary therapeutic services such as mental health, substance use, and school deficit-related interventions (Sabol & Listenbee, 2014; Sontheimer & Goodstein, 1993).

Probation departments that are more successful have incorporated graduated sanctions with a focus on positive and incremental youthful offender change, similar to many school districts that utilize these approaches. For example, Orange County, California, has developed their youthful offender probation supervision through a comprehensive three-tier system, utilizing graduated sanctions—a system of increased juvenile court responses to increased youthful offender difficulties or noncompliance—in conjunction with a parallel system of intervention and supervision options to develop the 8% Early Intervention Program. The 8% Program was developed because the juvenile court identified that a small percentage of more serious youthful offenders accounted for a significant amount of juvenile court resources, though many of these adolescents could be diverted from recidivist outcomes. Youthful offenders in this high-risk "8%" group are referred to an intensive, community-based program—the Early Intervention Youth and Family Resource Center; the medium-risk group (22%) is probation supervised and linked to community-based programs, including, as needed, in-home family services, health screenings, substance abuse and mental health treatment, and educational services; and the low-risk group (70%) receives diversion and delinquency prevention programming (Lipsey, Howell, Kelly, Chapman, & Carver, 2010; Schumacher & Kurz, 2000).

Coordination between juvenile courts and school districts is necessary in working with youthful offenders with learning disabilities, unidentified special education needs, and related academic and nonacademic problems. To date, however, limited community-based agency programs have been advocated on behalf of adjudicated adolescents with these difficulties, though there are a few. The TeamChild Model program addresses many of these coordination barriers. This program teams defense attorneys with social workers and other professionals to represent juvenile court-involved youthful offenders with disabilities who are at risk of or are being detained. Through advocacy and case management efforts during the adolescent's formal court involvement, the team addresses education and special education, mental health, vocational, and other needs as problems underlying delinquency and offending. The team works closely with the school districts and educates court personnel on nonjustice-related areas that affect the youthful offender's decision making, academic limitations, and related problem areas. Although not used extensively, this model has been found effective in several communities, including Seattle, Washington, by returning $2 in savings for every $1 spent within 6 months (Washington State Institute for Public Policy, 1998) and in Cleveland, Ohio, by saving $620,000 in placement costs over 18 months for just 41 youthful offenders (Mallett & Julian, 2008).

A significant challenge within juvenile court probation and supervision departments is finding ways to hold youthful offenders accountable for their delinquent behaviors while concurrently acknowledging, identifying, and treating the effects of mental health, substance use, and school-related disabilities with which so many of them struggle. While larger jurisdictions may be in a fiscally secure position to handle such needs, smaller juvenile court jurisdictions often simply cannot. Financial realties can lead to some perplexing dilemmas around who pays for services, who must provide services, how the juvenile court judge handles treatment dispositions, contingencies if the problems are school and special education-related, and contingencies if the needed mental health or substance abuse services are not available within the court or community-based youth-caring systems (Mears & Aron, 2003; Models for Change, 2011a).

Juvenile Drug and Mental Health Courts

The increased recognition and identification of youthful offenders' disability-related problems over the past 20 years has coincided with a move toward a rehabilitative paradigm within the juvenile courts and has prompted and expanded the number of juvenile drug courts (approximately 500) and juvenile mental health courts (approximately 75) nationally (Bureau of Justice Assistance, 2003; Office of Juvenile

Justice and Delinquency Prevention, 2014b). Both juvenile drug and mental health courts selectively divert youthful offenders from the regular juvenile courts to work in tandem with community-based service providers, thereby having the judge oversee the therapeutic treatment of the adolescent, and often the family, while maintaining adjudication authority (McNiel & Binder, 2007). However, such courts often lack standardization, with projected youthful offender outcomes such as divergent as substance use elimination, reduction of delinquent acts, adhering to a probation plan, and improving school performance, among others (Sloan & Smykla, 2003).

Although public and stakeholder support is increasing for diversionary and therapeutic alternatives for youthful offenders with mental health and substance abuse problems, evaluation of such programs' efficacy cannot yet be completed because of limited data (Wormer & Lutze, 2010). A majority of the evaluations of the juvenile drug courts have focused on substance use reduction, and the results are inconclusive, with some showing reductions in use that are significant but with no clear consistency of effect (Hiller et al., 2010; Kirchner & Kirchner, 2007; Latessa, Shaffer, & Lowenkamp, 2002). Juvenile mental health courts, which focus primarily on treatment engagement and improving community safety, simply have not been evaluated sufficiently to know whether there is an impact (Cocozza & Shufelt, 2006; Office of Juvenile Justice and Delinquency Prevention, 2014b). Before relying on or expanding these therapeutic juvenile court dockets, research designs must be improved and long-term assessments should be completed. Diversion of these young people prior to delinquency adjudication, and coordination with community-based mental health and substance abuse providers, may be a much more efficient and effective alternative.

Intensive Case Management/Wraparound

Intensive case management, also called the "wraparound model," is a flexible, multifaceted intervention strategy that is used to maintain youthful offenders in their homes and out-of-correctional institutions or residential care. These highly structured programs, significantly more intense in supervision and service delivery than traditional case management services, have been found effective for adolescents with low-level offenses and with a smaller number of adolescents with more serious offenses (Brown, Borduin, & Henggeler, 2001; Burchard, Bruns, & Burchard, 2002). Though designed differently, these programs often entail collaborative efforts with community-based agency services. In addition, intensive case management programs develop individualized and specific treatment plans for the adolescent and family, building numerous redundant and collaborative safety supports (National Wraparound Initiative Advisory Group, 2003). To be the most effective, it is important that these services have consistent staff working with the adolescent and family, use a strengths-based paradigm, and incorporate cultural competence in treatment delivery (Bruns et al., 2004; Office of Juvenile Justice and Delinquency Prevention, 2014b).

Some research indicates that intensive case management services can be effective for youthful offenders with serious emotional problems and comorbid problems across numerous settings (home, school, and community), tackling the difficult problem of allotting costs among various systems of care through shared cost agreements. Improved youthful offender outcomes include significant reductions in residential and psychiatric facility days, as well as lower arrest rates, which reduce costs of care across both juvenile justice and mental health systems. However, although a number of well-established programs, including Wraparound Milwaukee, Clark County, Washington Connections Program, and California's Repeat Offender Prevention Program, have demonstrated efficacy, broader empirical support is necessary to determine in which settings these interventions are the most effective. Efforts to determine the effectiveness of these programs are important, for they hold promise to vastly improve community-based services for these adolescents and possibly divert detention and incarceration placements (Kamradt, 2000; Mendel, 2003; Models for Change, 2011a).

JUVENILE JUSTICE FACILITIES

Detention

The detention of youthful offenders is best limited to those youthful offenders who have committed a serious offense and who pose a clear danger to public safety due to a high risk of their reoffending. However, detaining and incarcerating adolescents in and of itself do little to improve delinquent behaviors or offending outcomes, and, in certain circumstances, it causes harm by negatively affecting youthful offenders and increasing their recidivism risk (Loughran et al., 2009; Winokur, Smith, Bontrager, & Blankenship, 2008).

The Annie E. Casey Foundation has assumed a leadership role through advocacy and training efforts with the Juvenile Detention Alternatives Initiative (JDAI). The JDAI works to decrease the use of detention through collaboration across child welfare, mental health, schools, and social service agencies, builds community-based rehabilitative alternatives, and utilizes standardized assessment instruments and data collection within juvenile courts to direct decision making. Results, depending on the length of implementation, have been very positive in more than 150 jurisdictions in 35 states in which the initiative has been involved. These results include the lowering of detention populations and reoffending rates, sometimes by more than 40%, and state incarceration placements by more than 34%, thus often freeing up limited juvenile justice system resources to be used for more productive and cost-effective programming. For example, in Albuquerque, New Mexico, JDAI reduced the detention population by 44% through reorganization of the juvenile court's resources, and expanding innovated, community-based treatment alternatives. Ultimately, juvenile court staff members in this jurisdiction were reassigned from the two closed secure detention facilities that were no longer needed for front-end delinquency diversion and treatment services, shifting emphasis to prevention (Annie E. Casey Foundation, 2009, 2012).

It is critically important for detention and incarceration personnel to identify, as early as possible, a youthful offender's disability problems or related difficulties. In fact, studies of the effects stemming from the utilization of mental health screening tools (the MAYSI-2) found that in nine detention centers in three states, staff increased efforts to obtain mental health services and suicide precautions for adolescents in the facilities (Models for Change, 2011a). Unfortunately, this is far from the norm in such facilities (Sedlak & McPherson, 2010).

Within the detention facilities, a number of specific programs and interventions have been found effective—aggression replacement training, cognitive behavioral therapy, and the Family Integrated Transitions Program. Aggression replacement training uses certain cognitive behavioral techniques to identify anger triggers, improve behavioral skills, and increase adolescent pro-social skills; cognitive-behavioral therapy focuses on skill building and step-by-step curriculum to affect change; and the Family Integrated Transitions Program uses a combination of interventions (MST, relapse prevention) to address adolescent mental health and substance abuse problems and to ease transitions back to the community after detention facility release (Aos, 2004; Lipsey & Landenberger, 2006). In addition, reviews find that programming that addresses mental health problems is more successful than programming that takes a punitive-only approach, with these programs having a more positive impact when delivered by mental health professionals and not detention center staff (Greenberg, 2008).

Incarceration

Many youthful offenders do not receive services while incarcerated and that may assist in mitigating their prior offending behavior or address their disabilities (Schubert & Mulvey, 2014). Many, but not all, incarceration facilities use punitive approaches; however, recognition is growing that a rehabilitative approach better achieves important public policy goals of decreasing youthful offender recidivism and, subsequently, increasing community safety. There is evidence that incarceration facilities that identify adolescent problems and provide disability treatment services can have a significant impact on decreasing reoffending (Garrido & Morales, 2007; Texas Appleseed, 2011). Behavior contracting and programming, token economies, level systems, individual counseling, skill building (e.g., improving anger management skills), group counseling, education, vocational training, and combinations of these services have shown some effectiveness as rehabilitative interventions. In addition, though, research indicates that when such rehabilitative interventions are utilized, they must be well designed, of high quality, and of sufficient duration in order to have an impact (Hoge, 2001; Lipsey, 2009). Some incarceration facilities that have incorporated appropriately designed and implemented therapeutic components have been able to effectively decrease youthful offender recidivism rates (Armelius & Andreassen, 2007; Greenwood & Turner, 2009).

Missouri is a leading example of how to move away from serious youthful offender incarceration toward a rehabilitative model. Over the past 20 years, the Missouri Division of Youth Services first closed the larger state incarceration institutions (called training schools), divided the state into five regions, and developed a continuum of programs—day treatment, nonsecure group homes, medium-secure facilities, and secure care facilities—within each region. None of the secure care facilities hold more than 30 to 36 youthful offenders; further, the adolescents are then placed into even smaller cohorts that live together, receiving individualized, rehabilitative care. Recidivism rates for youthful offenders are less than 10% annually (Justice Policy Institute, 2009; Mendel, 2003, 2011).

A number of states have recognized the exorbitant and often unnecessary costs of youthful offender incarceration and have taken steps to readjust fiscal allotments. Ohio created a system that incentivizes the counties to use community-based rehabilitative and diversion efforts rather than state incarceration for many youthful offenders by capping the state allocation, and in the process has saved between $11 and $45 in commitment costs for every $1 spent on the Reclaim Ohio program

(Latessa, Lovins, & Lux, 2014). Similar efforts in reallocating Illinois state dollars to the local county jurisdictions have saved an estimated $18 million by decreasing state juvenile incarcerations by more than 50% (Illinois Department of Human Services, 2008). Even New York, by reallocating state funds at the local level, closed six state-run youthful offender residential facilities, with a portion of the local funds made available for diversion and rehabilitative efforts (New York Juvenile Justice Coalition, 2009).

Effective Education in the Facilities

Contact with the juvenile justice system, from arrests to incarceration, has been clearly established to harm student education progress and school outcomes (Aizer & Doyle, 2013; Sweeten, 2006), with only 3 in 10 incarceration facility-released youthful offenders engaged in school or work 12 months after reentry (Zajac, Sheidow, & Davis, 2013). Part of the problem is that education within the incarceration facilities is often ineffective for youthful offenders. When a young person is placed in pre-adjudication detention with lengths of stay that range from a few days to a few months, or a correctional facility where lengths of stay range from 3 to more than 36 months, the obligation to continue education services remains and is particularly necessary for those students with special education disabilities and subsequent Individualized Education Plans (Advancement Project et al., 2011; Boundy & Karger, 2011). However, with more than one-third of incarcerated youthful offenders who receive special education services, many of these adolescents' needs are not met (Musgrove & Yudin, 2014).

Coordination between the juvenile courts' detention facilities and schools is challenged by poor school records transfers, instructional communication, and appropriate coursework (Brooks & White, 2000). Within longer-term correctional facilities, the education services and instructional strategies vary widely: The programs are often less rigorous than traditional schools, not aligned with grade-level standards, and often not monitored by state education officials, and pre-release planning is not conducted leading to enrollment barriers and loss of academic credit (Bahena, Cooc, Currie-Rubin, Kuttner, & Ng, 2012; Mears & Travis, 2004; Morgan, Salomon, Plotkin, & Cohen, 2014).

Educational programming within the institutions is the most effective when educational plans are coordinated with home schools, when higher-quality teachers are employed, and when correctional and educational staff work together in their efforts throughout the educational instruction. In addition, schools within these facilities can improve their learning environment and education outcomes by moving away from harsh discipline protocols and incorporating appropriate restorative practices, focusing on social-emotional learning and development, offering flexible and individualized curriculum, incorporating positive behavior protocols to engage students, building social skills, and promoting positive relationship building across students and staff (Child Trends, 2007; Hereth, Kaba, Meiners, & Wallace, 2012; Karger, Rose, & Boundy, 2012; Osher, Bear, Sprague, & Doyle, 2010). Specific programs that are effective, in both traditional and alternative schools, include School-Wide Positive Behavior Interventions and Supports, a tiered and graduated management approach that focuses on positive steps in managing difficult behaviors; professional development of teachers and administrators; and increased conflict resolution and cultural competency training for teachers and staff (American Psychological Association Zero Tolerance Task Force, 2008; Browers & Tomic, 2000; Gregory, Allen, Mikami, Hafen, & Pianta, 2012; Losen, Hewitt, & Toldson, 2014).

Almost all youthful offenders released from these facilities return to their communities, and without continued education and a quick and seamless reentry into their school, the chances for reoffending and school dropouts significantly increase (Sweeten, Bushway, & Paternoster, 2009; Sentencing Project, 2012). To avoid these poor outcomes, it is important to designate a transition coordinator in the school to work with the juvenile courts, families, and school staff; develop reenrollment guidelines within the school system; and have returning students reenroll as soon as possible from institutional release (Morgan, Salomon, Plotkin, & Cohen, 2014). The U.S. Departments of Education and Justice strongly recommend that formal procedures be established through statutes. This includes memoranda of understanding (MOUs) and/or practices that ensure successful navigation across youth-caring systems as well as meaningful planning that is focused on reentry of youthful offenders into their communities and home school (U.S. Department of Education & U.S. Department of Justice, 2014).

REFERENCES

Advancement Project, Education Law Center–PA, FairTest, The Forum for Education and Democracy, Juvenile Law Center, & NAACP Legal Defense and Educational Fund, Inc. (2011). *Federal policy, ESEA reauthorization, and the school-to-prison pipeline.* Washington, DC: Author.

Aizer, A., & Doyle, J. (2013). *Juvenile incarceration, human capital and future crime: Evidence from randomly-assigned judges* (NBER Working Paper 19102). Cambridge, MA: National Bureau of Economic Research.

Alexander, J., Barton, C., Gordon, D., Grotpeter, J., Hansson, K., Harrison, R., . . . Sexton, T. (2007). Functional family therapy: Blueprints for violence prevention, book three. In D. S. Elliott, *Blueprints for violence prevention series.* Boulder, CO: Center for the Study and Prevention of Violence, Institute of Behavioral Science, University of Colorado.

American Psychological Association Zero Tolerance Task Force. (2008). Are zero tolerance policies effective in the schools? An evidentiary review and recommendations. *American Psychologist, 63*(9), 852–862.

Andreassen, T. H., Armelius, B., Egelund, T., & Ogden, T. (2006). *Cognitive-behavioural treatment for antisocial behavior in youth in residential treatment (Protocol).* Oslo, Norway: Cochrane Database of Systematic Reviews, Issue 1.

Annie E. Casey Foundation. (2009). *Two decades of JDAI: A progress report. From demonstration project to national standard.* Baltimore, MD: Author.

Annie E. Casey Foundation. (2012). *Expanding JDAI's focus to reduce commitments and placements.* Baltimore, MD: Author.

Aos, S. (2004). *Washington State's family integrated transitions program for juvenile offenders: Outcome evaluation and benefit-cost analysis.* Olympia, WA: Washington State Institute for Public Policy.

Aos, S., Phipps, P., Barnoski, R., & Lieb, R. (2001). *The comparative costs and benefits of programs to reduce crime (version 4.0).* Olympia, WA: Washington State Institute for Public Policy.

Armeluis, B. A., & Andreassen, T. H. (2007). *Cognitive-behavioural treatment for antisocial behavior in youth in residential treatment.* Oslo, Norway: The Campbell Collaboration.

Bahema, S., Cooc, N., Currie-Rubin, R., Kuttner, P., & Ng, M. (2012). *Disrupting the school-to-prison pipeline.* Cambridge, MA: Harvard Educational Review.

Baird, C., Healy, T., Johnson, K., Bogie, A., Dankert, E. W., & Scharenbroch, C. (2013). *A comparison of risk assessment instruments in juvenile justice.* Washington, DC: Office of Juvenile Justice and Delinquency Prevention, Office of Justice Programs, U.S. Department of Justice.

Baker, M. L., Sigmon, J. N., & Nugent, M. E. (2001). *Truancy reduction: Keeping students in school.* Washington, DC: Office of Juvenile Justice and Delinquency Prevention, Office of Justice Programs, U.S. Department of Justice.

Barkley, R. A., Edwards, G. H., & Robin, A. L. (1999). *Defiant teens: A clinician's annual for assessment and family interventions.* New York, NY: Guilford Press.

Bauman, K. E., Foshee, V. A., Ennett, S. T., Pemberton, M., Hicks, K. A., King, T. S., & Koch, G. G. (2001). The influence of a family program on adolescent tobacco and alcohol. *American Journal of Public Health, 91*(4), 604–610.

Botvin, G., Baker, E., Dusenbury, L., Botvin, E., & Diaz, T. (1995). Long-term follow-up results of a randomized drug-abuse prevention trial in a white middle class population. *Journal of the American Medical Association, 273,* 1106–1112.

Boundy, K. B., & Karger, J. (2011). The right to a quality education for children and youth in the juvenile justice system. In F. Sherman & F. Jacobs (Eds.), *Juvenile justice: Advancing research, policy, and practice* (pp. 286–309). Hoboken, NJ: Wiley and Sons.

Brooks, C. C., & White, C. (2000). *Curriculum for training educators of youth in confinement.* Washington, DC: U.S. Department of Justice.

Browers, A., & Tornic, C. (2000). A longitudinal study of teacher burnout and perceived self-efficacy in classroom management. *Teaching and Teacher Education, 16*(2), 239–253.

Brown, T. L., Borduin, C. M., & Henggeler, S. W. (2001). Treating juvenile offenders in community settings. In J. Ashford, B. Sales, & W. Reid (Eds.), *Treating adult and juvenile offenders with special needs* (pp. 445–464). Washington, DC: American Psychological Association.

Bruns, E. J., Walker, J. S., Adams, J., Miles, P., Osher, T., Rast, J., & VanDenBerg, J. (2004). *Ten principles of the wraparound process.* Portland, OR: National Wraparound Initiative, Research and Training Center on Family Support and Children's Mental Health, Portland State University.

Burchard, J. D., Bruns, E. J., & Burchard, S. N. (2002). *The wraparound process. Community-based treatment for youth.* Oxford, UK: Oxford University Press.

Bureau of Justice Assistance. (2003). *Juvenile drug court: Strategies in practice.* Washington, DC: Bureau of Justice Assistance, U.S. Department of Justice.

Centers for Disease Control and Prevention. (2009). *Suicide prevention: Youth suicide.* Atlanta, GA: National Center for Injury Prevention and Control, Division of Violence Prevention.

Child Trends. (2007). *Cognitive-behavioral training program for behaviorally disordered adolescents.* Washington, DC: LINKS Database.

Clark, G. N., Hornbrook, M., Lynch, F., Polen, M., Gale, J., Beardslee, W., . . . Seeley, J. (2001). A randomized trial of a group cognitive intervention for preventing depression in adolescent offspring of depressed parents. *Archives of General Psychiatry, 58,* 1127–1134.

Coalition for Juvenile Justice. (2013). *National standards for the care of youth charged with status offenses.* Washington, DC: Author.

Cocozza, J. J., & Shufelt, J. L. (2006). *Juvenile mental health courts: An emerging strategy*. Delmar, NY: National Center for Mental Health and Juvenile Justice.

Conner, K. R., & Goldston, D. B. (2007). Rates of suicide among males increase steadily from age 11 to 21: Developmental framework and outline for prevention. *Aggression and Violent Behavior, 12*, 193–207.

Connor, D. F. (2002). *Aggression and antisocial behaviour in children and adolescents: Research and treatment*. New York, NY: Guilford Press.

Curry, J. F., & Wells, K. C. (2005). Striving for effectiveness in the treatment of adolescent depression: Cognitive behavior therapy for multisite community intervention. *Cognitive and Behavioral Practice, 12*, 177–185.

Farrington, D. P. (2002). Developmental criminology and risk-focused prevention. In M. Maguire, R. Morgan, & R. Reiner (Eds.), *The Oxford handbook of criminology* (pp. 657–701). Oxford, UK: Oxford University Press.

Forman, J., & Domenici, D. (2011). *What it takes to transform a school: Inside a juvenile justice facility*. Faculty Scholarship Series, Paper 3608. New Haven, CT: Yale University.

Frischer, M., Crome, I., Macleod, J., Bloor, R., & Hickman, M. (2007). *Predictive factors for illicit drug use among young people: A literature review*. London: Home Office Online Report.

Garrido, V., & Morales, L. A. (2007). *Serious (violent and chronic) juvenile offenders: A systematic review of treatment effectiveness in secure corrections*. Philadelphia, PA: The Campbell Collaboration Reviews of Intervention and Policy Evaluations (CT-RIPE), Campbell Collaboration.

Greenberg, P. (2008). Prevention and intervention programs for juvenile offenders. *The Future of Children, 18*(2), 185–210.

Greenwood, P., & Turner, S. (2009). Overview of prevention and intervention programs for juvenile offenders. *Victims & Offenders, 4*(4), 365–374.

Gregory, A., Allen, J. P., Mikami, A. Y., Hafen, A., & Pianta, R. C. (2012). *The promise of a teacher professional development program in reducing the racial disparity in classroom exclusionary discipline*. Washington, DC: Center for Civil Rights Remedies and the Research-to-Practice Collaborative, National Conference on Race and Gender Disparities in Discipline.

Griffin, P., & Torbet, P. (Eds.). (2000). *Desktop guide to good juvenile probation practice*. Washington, DC: Office of Juvenile Justice and Delinquency Prevention, National Center for Juvenile Justice.

Grisso, T., & Barnum, R. (2000). *Massachusetts youth screening instrument-2: User's manual and technical report*. Worchester, MA: University of Massachusetts Medical School.

Grisso, T., Barnum, R., Fletcher, K., Cauffman, E., & Peuschold, D. (2001). Massachusetts Youth Screening Instrument for mental health needs of juvenile justice youths. *Journal of the American Academy of Child and Adolescent Psychiatry, 40,* 541–548.

Hammond, C., Linton, D., Smink, J., & Drew, S. (2007). *Dropout risk factors and exemplary programs: A technical report.* Clemson, SC: National Dropout Prevention Center/Network and Communities in Schools.

Hawkins, J. D., Catalano, R. F., Kosterman, R., Abbott, R., & Hill, K. G. (1999). Preventing adolescent health-risk behaviors by strengthening protection during childhood. *Archives of Pediatric and Adolescent Medicine, 153,* 226–234.

Hawkins, J. D., Herrenkohl, T. I., Farrington, D. P., Brewer, D., Catalano, R. F., Harachi, T. W., & Cothern, L. (2000). *Predictors of youth violence.* Washington, DC: Office of Juvenile Justice and Delinquency Prevention, Office of Justice Programs, U.S. Department of Justice.

Heilbrunn, J. Z. (2007). *Pieces of the truancy jigsaw: A literature review.* Denver, CO: National Center for School Engagement.

Henggeler, S. W., Mihalic, S. F., Rone, L., Thomas, C., & Timmons-Mitchell, J. (2006). *Blueprints for violence prevention, book 6: Multisystemic therapy.* Boulder, CO: Center for the Study and Prevention of Violence, University of Colorado.

Hereth, J., Kaba, M., Meiniers, E. R., & Wallace, L. (2012). Restorative justice is not enough. In S. Bahena, N. Cooc, R. Currie-Rubin, P. Kuttner, & M. Ng (Eds.), *Disrupting the school-to-prison pipeline* (pp. 240–264). Cambridge, MA: Harvard Educational Review.

Hiller, M. L., Malluche, D., Bryan, V., DuPont, M. L., Martin, B., Abensur, R., . . . Payne, C. (2010). A multisite description of juvenile drug courts: Program models and during-program outcomes. *International Journal of Offender Therapy and Comparative Criminology, 54*(2), 213–235.

Hoge, R. D. (2001). *The juvenile offender: Theory, research and applications.* Norwell, MA: Kluwer Plenum.

Holman, B., & Ziedenberg, J. (2014). *The dangers of detention: The impact of incarcerating youth in detention and other secure facilities.* Washington, DC: Justice Policy Institute.

Horowitz, J. L., & Garber, J. (2006). The prevention of depressive symptoms in children and adolescents: A meta-analytic review. *Journal of Consulting and Clinical Psychology, 24*(3), 401–415.

Howell, J. C. (2003). *Preventing and reducing juvenile delinquency: A comprehensive framework.* Thousand Oaks, CA: Sage.

Illinois Department of Human Services. (2008). *Redeploy Illinois annual report: Implementation and impact.* Chicago, IL: Author.

Irvine, A. (2005). *Girls circle: Summary of outcomes for girls in the juvenile justice system*. Santa Cruz, CA: Ceres Policy Research.

Justice Policy Institute. (2009). *The costs of confinement: Why good juvenile justice policies make good fiscal sense*. Washington, DC: Author.

Kaminski, J. W., Valle, L. A., Filene, J. H., & Boyle, C. L. (2008). A meta-analysis review of components associated with parent training program effectiveness. *Journal of Abnormal Psychology, 36*, 567–589.

Kamradt, B. (2000). Wraparound Milwaukee: Aiding youth with mental health needs. *Juvenile Justice Journal, 7*(1), 14–23.

Karger, J., Rose, D., & Boundy, K. (2012). Applying universal design for learning to the education of youth in detention and correctional facilities. In S. Bahema, N. Cooc, R. Currie-Rubin, P. Kuttner, & M. Ng (Eds.), *Disrupting the school-to-prison pipeline* (pp. 119–140). Cambridge, MA: Harvard Educational Review.

Kazdin, A. E., & Weisz, J. R. (1998). Identifying and developing empirically supported child and adolescent treatments. *Journal of Consulting and Clinical Psychology, 66*, 19–36.

Kirchner, R., & Kirchner, T. (2007). *Model program for multi-jurisdictional, rural settings*. Technical report. Nevada: Administrative Office of the Courts for Nevada, Western Regional Drug Court.

Kosterman, R., Hawkins, J. D., Spoth, R., Haggerty, K. P., & Zhu, K. (1997). Effects of a preventive parent-training intervention on observed family interactions: Proximal outcomes from preparing for the drug free years. *Journal of Community Psychology, 25*(4), 337–352.

Kumpfer, K. L., Alvarado, R., & Whiteside, H. O. (2003). Family-based interventions for substance abuse and prevention. *Substance Use & Misuse, 38*, 1759–1787.

Kumpfer, K. L., Whiteside, H. O., Greene, J. A., & Allen, K. C. (2010). Effectiveness outcomes of four age versions of the strengthening families program in statewide field sites. *Group Dynamics: Theory, Research, and Practice, 14*(3), 211–229.

Latessa, E. J., Lovins, B., & Lux, J. (2014). *Evaluation of Ohio's Reclaim programs*. Cincinnati, OH: University of Cincinnati, School of Criminal Justice.

Latessa, E. J., Shaffer, D., & Lowenkamp, C. (2002). *Outcome evaluation of Ohio's drug court efforts*. Technical report. Cincinnati, OH: Center for Criminal Justice Research, University of Cincinnati.

Lawrence, R., & Hemmens, C. (2008). *Juvenile justice: A text/reader*. Thousand Oaks, CA: Sage.

Levin, M., & Cohen, D. (2014). *Kids doing time for what's not a crime: The over-incarceration of status offenders.* Austin, TX: Texas Public Policy Foundation: Policy Perspective.

Little, J. H., Popa, M., & Forsythe, B. (2005). *Multisystemic therapy for social, emotional, and behavioral problems in youth aged 10–17.* Campbell Systematic Reviews. Oslo, Norway: The Campbell Collaboration.

Lipsey, M. W. (2009). The primary factors that characterize effective interventions with juvenile offenders: A meta-analytic overview. *Victims and Offenders, 4*(4), 124–147.

Lipsey, M. W., Howell, J. C., Kelly, M. R., Chapman, G., & Carver, D. (2010). *Improving the effectiveness of juvenile justice programs.* Washington, DC: Center for Juvenile Justice Reform, Georgetown University.

Lipsey, M. W., & Landenberger, N. A. (2006). *Cognitive-behavioural programs for juvenile and adult offenders: A meta-analysis of controlled intervention studies.* Oslo, Norway: The Campbell Collaboration.

Losen, D. L., Hewitt, D., & Toldson, I. (2014, March). *Eliminating excessive and unfair discipline in schools: Policy recommendations for reducing disparities.* Discipline disparities series: New Research. Bloomington, IN: The Equity Project at Indiana University. Available at http://rtpcollaborative.indiana.edu/briefing-papers

Loughran, T., Mulvey, E., Schubert, C., Fagan, J., Pizuero, A., & Losoya, S. (2009). Estimating a dose-response relationship between length of stay and future recidivism in serious juvenile offenders. *Criminology, 47*(3), 699–740.

Mallett, C., & Julian, L. (2008). Alternatives for youth's advocacy program: Effectively reducing minority youth's detention and incarceration placements in Cleveland, Ohio. *Juvenile and Family Court Journal, 59*(3), 1–17.

March, J., Silva, S., Petrycki, S., Curry, J., Wells, K., Fairbank, J., . . . Treatment for Adolescents With Depression Study (TADS) team. (2004). Fluoxetin, cognitive-behavioral therapy, and their combination for adolescents with depression: Treatment for Adolescents With Depression Study (TADS) randomized controlled trial. *Journal of the American Medical Association, 292*(7), 807–820.

Martin, G. (2005). *Juvenile justice: Process and systems.* Thousand Oaks, CA: Sage.

McGuire, J. (2000). *Cognitive-behavioural approaches: An introduction to theory and research.* London: Home Office Communication Directorate.

McNiel, D. E., & Binder, R. L. (2007). Effectiveness of a mental health court in reducing criminal recidivism and violence. *American Journal of Psychiatry, 164*(9), 1395–1403.

Mears, D. P., & Aron, L. Y. (2003). *Addressing the needs of youth with disabilities in the juvenile justice system: The current state of knowledge.* Washington, DC: Urban Institute, Justice Policy Center.

Mears, D. P., & Travis, J. (2004). *The dimensions, pathways, and consequences of youth reentry.* Youth Reentry Roundtable Series. Washington, DC: Urban Institute.

Mendel, R. (2003). *Less hype, more help: Reducing juvenile crime, what works—and what doesn't.* Washington, DC: American Youth Policy Forum.

Mendel, R. A. (2011). *No place for kids: The case for reducing juvenile incarceration.* Baltimore, MD: Annie E. Casey Foundation.

Models for Change. (2011a). *Does mental health screening fulfill its promise?* Models for Change: Systems Reform in Juvenile Justice. Chicago, IL: John D. and Catherine T. MacArthur Foundation.

Models for Change. (2011b). *Juvenile diversion handbook.* Models for Change: Systems Reform in Juvenile Justice. Chicago, IL: John D. and Catherine T. MacArthur Foundation.

Morgan, E., Salomon, N., Plotkin, M., & Cohen, R. (2014). *The school discipline consensus report: Strategies from the field to keep students engaged in school and out of the juvenile justice system.* Washington, DC: The Council of State Governments Justice Center.

Mulvey, E. P. (2005). Risk assessment in juvenile justice policy and practice. In K. Heilbrun, N. E. S. Goldstein, & R. E. Redding (Eds.), *Juvenile delinquency: Prevention, assessment, and intervention* (pp. 209–231). New York, NY: Oxford University Press.

Mulvey, E. P. (2011). *Highlights from pathways to desistance: A longitudinal study of serious adolescent offenders (Juvenile justice fact sheet).* Washington, DC: Office of Juvenile Justice and Delinquency Prevention, Office of Justice Programs, U.S. Department of Justice.

Mulvey, E. P., & Iselin, A. R. (2008). Improving professional judgments of risk and amenability in juvenile justice. *The Future of Children, 18*(2), 35–58.

Musgrove, M., & Yudin, M. K. (2014). *An open letter to juvenile justice correctional facilities.* Washington, DC: Office of Special Education and Rehabilitative Services, U.S. Department of Education.

Myers, W. C., Burton, P. R., Sanders, P. D., Donat, K. M., Cheney, J., Fitzpatrick, T., & Monaco, L. (2000). Project back-on-track at 1 year: A delinquency treatment program for early-career juvenile offenders. *Journal of American Child and Adolescent Psychiatry, 39*(9), 1127–1134.

National Action Alliance for Suicide Prevention. (2013). *Suicidal ideation and behavior among youth in the juvenile justice system: A review of the literature.* Washington, DC: Author.

National Institute of Justice and Office of Juvenile Justice and Delinquency Prevention. (2014). *NCCD compares juvenile risk assessment instruments: A summary of the OJJDP-funded stud.* San Diego, CA: Author.

National Institute of Mental Health. (2011). *Suicide: A major, preventable mental health problem*. Washington, DC: National Institutes of Health, U.S. Department of Health and Human Services.

National Institute on Drug Abuse. (2003). *Preventing drug use among children and adolescents: A research-based guide for parents, educators, and community leaders, second edition*. Washington, DC: National Institutes of Health, U.S. Department of Health and Human Services.

National Juvenile Justice and Delinquency Prevention Coalition. (2013). *Promoting safe communities: Recommendations for the 113th Congress*. Washington, DC: Author.

National Wraparound Initiative Advisory Group. (2003). *History of the wraparound process. Focal point bulletin*. Portland, OR: National Wraparound Initiative, Research and Training Center on Family Support and Children's Mental Health, Portland State University.

New York Juvenile Justice Coalition. (2009). *Re-direct New York: Reinvesting detention resources in community treatment*. New York, NY: Author.

Office of Juvenile Justice and Delinquency Prevention. (2014a). *Easy access to juvenile court statistics*. Washington, DC: Office of Justice Programs, U.S. Department of Justice.

Office of Juvenile Justice and Delinquency Prevention. (2014b). *Model programs guide*. Washington, DC: Office of Justice Programs, U.S. Department of Justice.

Osher, D., Bear, G. G., Sprague, J. R., & Doyle, W. (2010). How can we improve school discipline? *Educational Researcher, 39*(1), 48–58.

Pentz, M. A., Mihalic, S. F., & Grotpeter, J. K. (2006). The Midwestern prevention project: Blueprints for violence prevention, book two. In D. S. Elliott (Ed.), *Blueprints for violence prevention series*. Boulder, CO: Center for the Study and Prevention of Violence, Institute of Behavioral Science, University of Colorado.

Petitclerc, A., Gatti, U., Vitaro, F., & Tremblay, R. E. (2013). Effects of juvenile court exposure on crime in young adulthood. *Journal of Child Psychology and Psychiatry, 54*(3), 291–297.

Petrosino, A., Turpin-Petrosino, C., & Guckenburg, S. (2010). *Formal system processing on juveniles: Effects on delinquency*. Oslo, Norway: Campbell System Review.

Puzzanchera, C., & Hockenberry, S. (2010). *Juvenile court statistics, 2010*. Pittsburgh, PA: National Center for Juvenile Justice.

Puzzanchera, C., & Robson, C. (2014). *Delinquency cases in juvenile court, 2010*. Washington, DC: Office of Juvenile Justice and Delinquency Prevention, Office of Justice Programs, U.S. Department of Justice.

Rapp-Palicchi, L., & Roberts, A. R. (2004). Mental illness and juvenile offending. In A. R. Roberts (Ed.), *Juvenile justice sourcebook: Past, present, and future* (pp. 289–308). New York, NY: Oxford University Press.

Reynolds, W. (1988). *Manual for the suicidal ideation questionnaire.* Odessa, FL: Psychological Assessment Resources.

Sabol, W. J., & Listenbee, R. L. (2014). *Changing lives: Prevention and intervention to reduce serious offending.* Washington, DC: Office of Juvenile Justice and Delinquency Prevention, Office of Justice Programs, U.S. Department of Justice.

Salsich, A., & Trone, J. (2013). *From courts to communities: The right response to truancy, running away, and other status offenses.* New York, NY: Vera Institute of Justice.

Scheier, L., Botvin, G., Diaz, T., & Griffin, K. (1999). Social skills, competence, and drug refusal efficacy as predictors of adolescent alcohol use. *Journal of Drug Education, 29*(3), 251–278.

Schmidt, F., Hoge, R., & Gomes, L. (2005). Reliability and validity analysis of the youth level of service/case management inventory. *Criminal Justice and Behavior, 32*(3), 329–344.

Schubert, C. A., & Mulvey, E. P. (2014). *Behavioral health problems, treatment, and outcomes in serious youthful offenders.* Washington, DC: Office of Juvenile Justice and Delinquency Prevention, Office of Justice Programs, U.S. Department of Justice.

Schumacher, M., & Kurz, G. (2000). *The 8% solution: Preventing serious, repeat juvenile crime.* Thousand Oaks, CA: Sage.

Sedlak, A. J., & McPherson, K. (2010). *Survey of youth in residential placement: Youth's needs and services.* Washington, DC: Westat Corporation.

Sentencing Project. (2012). *Youth re-entry.* Washington, DC: Author.

Shaffer, D., Gould, M. S., Fisher, L. A., Trautman, P., Moreau, D., Kleinman, M., & Flory, M. (1996). Psychiatric diagnosis in child and adolescent suicide. *Archives of General Psychiatry, 53*, 339–348.

Shaffer, D., Lucas, C., & Fisher, P. (2011). *Diagnostic interview schedule for children version four.* New York, NY: DISC Development Group.

Shram, P. J., & Gaines, L. K. (2005). Examining delinquent nongang members and delinquent gang members: A comparison of juvenile probationers at intake and outcomes. *Youth Violence and Juvenile Justice, 3*(2), 99–115.

Shubick, C. (2010). What social science tells us about youth who commit status offenses. *Child Law Practice, 29*(9), 133–141.

Sloan, J., & Smykla, J. O. (2003). Juvenile drug courts: Understanding the importance of dimensional variability. *Criminal Justice Policy Review, 14*(3), 339–360.

Smith, B. D., & Testa, M. F. (2002). The risk of subsequent maltreatment allegations in families with substance-exposed infants. *Child Abuse & Neglect*, *26*(1), 97–114.

Sontheimer, H., & Goodstein, L. (1993). Evaluation of juvenile intensive aftercare. *Justice Quarterly*, *10*, 197–227.

Spoth, R. L., Redmond, D., Trudeau, L., & Shin, C. (2002). Longitudinal substance initiation outcomes for a universal preventive intervention combining family and school programs. *Psychology of Addictive Behaviors*, *16*(2), 129–134.

Stagner, M. W., & Lansing, J. (2009). Progress toward a prevention perspective. *The Future of Children*, *29*(2), 19–38.

Sweeten, G. (2006). Who will graduate? Disruption of high school education by arrest and court involvement. *Justice Quarterly*, *23*(4), 462–480.

Sweeten, G., Bushway, S., & Paternoster, R. (2009). Does dropping out of school mean dropping into delinquency? *Criminology*, *47*(1), 47–91.

Substance Abuse and Mental Health Services Administration. (2009). *Addressing suicidal thoughts and behaviors in substance abuse treatment*. Washington, DC: Center for Mental Health Services, U.S. Department of Health and Human Services.

Substance Abuse and Mental Health Services Administration. (2011). *Best practices registry for suicide prevention*. Washington, DC: National Registry of Evidence-Based Practices and Programs, U.S. Department of Health and Human Services.

Texas Appleseed. (2011). *Thinking outside the cell: Alternatives to incarceration for youth with mental illness*. Austin, TX: Disability Rights Texas National Center for Youth Law.

Tolan, P. H., Henry, D. B., Schoeny, M. S., & Bass, A. (2008). *Mentoring interventions to affect juvenile delinquency and associated problems*. Campbell Systematic Reviews. Oslo, Norway: The Campbell Collaboration.

Tolan, P. H., Henry, D., Schoeny, M. S., Lovegrove, P., & Nichols, E. (2014). Mentoring programs to affect delinquency and associated outcomes of youth at risk: A comprehensive meta-analytic review. *Journal of Experimental Criminology*, *10*, 179–206.

Turner, W., MacDonald, G. M., & Dennis, J. A. (2007). *Cognitive-behavioural training interventions for assisting foster carers in the management of difficult behaviour*. Oslo, Norway: Cochrane Database of Systematic Reviews, Issue 1.

U.S. Department of Education & U.S. Department of Justice. (2014). *Guiding principles for providing high-quality education in juvenile justice secure care settings*. Washington, DC: Author.

U.S. Department of Health and Human Services. (2013). *Child maltreatment 2012.* Washington, DC: U.S. Government Printing Office.

Vincent, G. M., Guy, L. S., & Grisso, T. (2012). *Risk assessment in juvenile justice: A guidebook for implementation.* Models for Change: Systems Reform in Juvenile Justice. Chicago, IL: MacArthur Foundation.

Washington State Institute for Public Policy. (1998). *Watching the bottom line: Cost-effective interventions for reducing crime in Washington.* Olympia, WA: Evergreen State College.

Welsh, B. C., Rocque, M., & Greenwood, P. W. (2014). Translating research into evidence-based practice in juvenile justice: Brand-name programs, meta-analysis, and key issues. *Journal of Experimental Criminology, 10,* 207–225.

Wheeler, M. E., Keller, T. E., & DuBois, D. L. (2010). Review of three recent randomized trials of school-based mentoring. *Social Policy Report, 24*(3), 1–27.

Wiig, J., Spatz-Widom, C., & Tuell, J. A. (2003). *Understanding child maltreatment & delinquency: From research to effective program, practice, and systematic solutions.* Washington, DC: Child Welfare League of America.

Willison, J. B., Brooks, L., Salas, M., Dank, M., Denver, M., Gitlow, E., Roman, J. K., & Butts, J. A. (2010). *Reforming juvenile justice systems: Beyond treatment.* Portland, OR: Reclaiming Futures, Portland State University.

Winokur, K. P., Smith, A., Bontrager, S. R., & Blankenship, J. L. (2008). Juvenile recidivism and length of stay. *Journal of Criminal Justice, 36,* 126–137.

Wormer, J., & Lutze, F. E. (2010). *Managing and sustaining your juvenile drug court.* Reno, NV: National Council of Juvenile and Family Court Judges.

Zajac, K., Sheidow, A. J., & Davis, M. (2013). *Transition age youth with mental health challenges in the juvenile justice system.* Washington, DC: Technical Assistance Partnership for Child and Family Mental Health, Substance Abuse and Mental Health Services Administration, U.S. Department of Health and Human Services.

Chapter 7: Shifting the Paradigm to Student Success

The school-to-prison pipeline took a generation to build; it will take significant coordinated efforts across many stakeholders to dismantle it nationwide. However, the decriminalization of our nation's education system and subsequent movement back to a rehabilitative paradigm in our schools and juvenile courts is quite possible, as evidenced by school districts, state legislatures, and other stakeholders who are leading the way to safer and more inclusive schools for all students. These changes have been made across schools, school districts, and some states, with policy makers working within the legislature and regulatory process, and others coordinating efforts across youth-caring delivery systems. A few examples can illuminate the importance of emulating these experiences and outcomes.

SCHOOL DISTRICTS/SCHOOLS

The Cleveland, Ohio, Public School District reacted to a fatal 2010 in-school shooting by increasing school security, hiring more school police, and tightening the discipline codes to expand zero-tolerance policies. However, the result was a significant increase in out-of-school discipline actions for students and poorer statewide academic rating standards. Prior to this student shooting incident, the school district had been moving away from zero-tolerance policies in three ways: one, incorporating school student support teams—responsible for reviewing relevant data and prioritizing student concerns, designing interventions, and making necessary educational adjustments; two, shifting from the use of in-school suspensions to student planning centers that provide support and appropriate student interventions to inhibit the escalation of misbehaviors by focusing on social, behavioral, and academic causes; and three, establishing additional restorative practices throughout the schools. As these reform efforts were returned after the school shooting adjustment period, student suspensions decreased by 25% and improved academic success has been occurring across the student body over the past 2 academic years (Morgan, Salomon, Plotkin, & Cohen, 2014).

In the Albuquerque, New Mexico, Public School District, a collaborative stakeholder team was formed to address the school-based student difficulties that led to juvenile court involvement and detention placement. An agreed-upon strategic plan included the following: a redefinition of "challenging and disruptive student behavior" to lessen the number of low-level offenses referred for discipline; identifying the reasons for referrals to juvenile court probation; reviewing special education, suspension, and administrative discipline policies; revising the handling of minor student infractions without the use of a police report; mapping service and treatment gaps; and implementing a pilot program for at-risk delinquency middle schoolers. This program (Prevention Intervention Program for Youth [PIPY]) focuses on student transitions back to school from discipline outcomes and detention center placement, offers wraparound services, and improves coordination and communication across the school and juvenile court personnel. These efforts led to a 53% decrease in school-based arrests and formal juvenile court referrals, as well as a decrease in recidivism over time (Bershad & Kitson, 2012).

The San Francisco Unified School District adopted district-wide policies to improve professional staff development on the use and implementation of restorative practices. These trainings include monthly learning communities, cross-district sharing of experiences, and data analysis. After 3 years, student suspensions dropped by more than 34% during the 2011 to 2012 academic year due to these and other related efforts to improve school climate and student academic outcomes (Morgan et al., 2014).

During the 2012 to 2013 academic year, the Los Angeles, California, Public School District incorporated a new School Climate Bill of Rights. This policy guarantees the implementation of restorative justice practices, minimizes the role of school resource officers in school discipline, prioritizes a safe learning environment for all students, and bans suspensions of students for willful defiance. Willful defiance violations accounted for 48% of the 700,000 suspensions in the states during the 2011 to 2012 academic year, greatly contributing to the disproportionate impact on students of color. Before this policy, the school district had a zero-tolerance policy for students who defied any school administrator's or teacher's directive. Today, school personnel must keep the student on campus and find alternative interventions and supports (Garcia, 2013).

The Denver, Colorado, Public School District has made significant changes to its education and discipline protocols over the past 10 years. The School District reformed its discipline code to move away from zero-tolerance policies and fully incorporate restorative justice practices; reformed its relationship with school police to minimize the risk of campus-based violations and arrests by differentiating discipline from crime issues and using de-escalation techniques whenever possible; and has continued to refine and amend these reforms with ongoing data collection and evaluation. These efforts have caused a decrease from 2003 to 2013 of out-of-school suspensions by 32%, expulsions by 44%, and referrals to law enforcement by 42%, with greater improvements made for students of color (Padres & Jovenes Unidos & Advancement Project, 2014).

The Baltimore, Maryland, City Public School District began reform efforts in 2010 through the formation of a stakeholder work group—school system, school police, Maryland Office of the Public Defender, State's Attorney's Office, and interested advocacy organizations—to assess the problems and school discipline data. This analysis found three themes: inconsistent interpretation of the district's student discipline code leading to outcome disparities; a majority of the school-based arrests were for misdemeanors—disorderly conduct and disturbing school activities; and most of these referrals were not adjudicated by the juvenile court, leaving the young person without additional service or treatment provisions. From there, the chief of the Baltimore City's School Police trained officers on the use of discretion and diversionary alternatives to arrest, worked most closely with those officers with the highest numbers of arrests, and significantly lowered the arrest numbers in subsequent academic years (Shriver Center, 2014).

Garfield High School in the Los Angeles Public School District, predominantly Hispanic and Latino, has made a significant turnaround from a school that suspended and expelled 683 students (from the 2,500 total student body) in the 2008 to 2009 academic year to only one suspension totally in the 2011 to 2012 academic year; correspondingly raising their Academic Performance Index score by 160 points and increasing graduate rates from 62% to 71%. This was accomplished through supportive leadership and a focus on teacher training and shared decision making, parent and community engagement through the school's parents center and use of parent volunteers on campus, personalized student curricula and use of small learning communities, a shift toward focusing on academic success through Positive Behavioral Interventions and Supports (PBIS) and Response to Intervention (RtI) programming, the use of data-driven decision making and a school-wide information system, and a shift toward progressive discipline policy with the focus on keeping all students in school and replacing suspensions with referrals for services (Labre, Stern-Carusone, Rosiak, Becker, & Wright, 2013).

LEGAL REFORM

Advocacy litigation can be particularly effective for federally protected student groups. For example, a 7th District Federal Court ruled against the Milwaukee Public Schools and the Wisconsin Department of Public Instruction in finding that detailed requirements were necessary for action plans and programmatic interventions, as well as ongoing monitoring and reporting of relevant data, for students with special education disabilities who were repeatedly suspended or retained at grade level. This decision has led to a significant decrease in these students' suspension rates (*Jamie S. v. Milwaukee Public Schools*, 519 F. Supp. 2d 870 (E.D. Wis. 2007)). Individual states have also taken on the responsibility to address the school-to-prison pipeline.

Florida's state legislature set new policies and guidelines for local school districts and juvenile courts through the establishment of the Florida Civil Citation Alternative in 2012. This Act encourages schools to decrease the use of expulsion and court referral alternatives through the implementation and expansion of restitution, civil citations, teen court, restorative justice, and other similar rehabilitative programming. It also directs that zero-tolerance school policies are not to be used for minor misbehaviors, misdemeanors, or school disturbances. Thus, as an alternative, a civil citation is an arrest that provides first-time, low-level offenders with an opportunity to have intervention services and not formal juvenile court processing. Almost all of Florida's counties have implemented this new policy shift with 96% of first-time offenders successfully completing their civil citation intervention plans (Morgan et al., 2014; Roberts, 2012).

Colorado has shown strong state leadership through the passage of comprehensive legislation in 2012. This law, and subsequent regulations, requires school districts throughout the state to adhere to the following changes: implement proportionate discipline that minimizes the use of out-of-school placement and referrals to law enforcement;

eliminate the involvement of minor student misbehaviors with the juvenile justice system if the reasons for these student issues are developmental; implement delinquency prevention interventions, including counseling, restorative justice, and peer mediation, among others; and collect and utilize data on school-based arrests and court referrals, disaggregated by student age, race, gender, and school (CO 12-1345).

Over the past few years, the state legislature of California has enacted a number of new laws governing schools districts and student discipline. Both school district superintendents and principals have been provided discretion to use alternatives to student expulsions or suspensions (AB 383-2013; 2537-2012); public schools can no longer readmit students if for no reason other than contact with the juvenile justice system (SB 2011-2012), and they provide school administrators with flexibility for truancy violations, not requiring automatic juvenile court referrals after four truancies per student in an academic year (AB 2616-2012).

Massachusetts has also recently enacted similar legislation. Since 2012, school districts are now required to do the following: collect and report data on school suspensions and expulsions; improve due process and hearing notification for students at risk of suspension or expulsion; provide educational services to students suspended or excluded from school for more than 10 consecutive school days; create additional alternative educational programs; have school administrators exhaust all other available resources before removing a student from school; and disallow students to be excluded from school for more than 90 days in 1 academic year (MA, HB-4332, 2012).

COLLABORATION/INFORMATION SHARING

In the Union Springs, New York, School District, efforts to prevent school and community offending behaviors and violence have led to successful partnerships across stakeholders. By bringing together directors of education, law enforcement agencies, and child and adolescent treatment providers, a multidisciplinary screening and assessments system was implemented. This system effectively screens children and adolescents who are at risk for arrest, truancy, substance abuse, and school discipline, including suspensions and expulsions. Over the years, the system has been institutionalized within the community and can identify these young people at early ages, thus involving qualified professionals who can use the assessment in their treatment and diversion efforts. The school district uses its data aggregation system to help the partnership plan services, which helps consenting families share students' school, juvenile court, and other related confidential information, leading to effective, coordinated services (Bershad & Kitson, 2012).

The Shelby County School District in Tennessee has coordinated a multisystem approach with 200 of its schools to decrease the number of school-based referrals to the juvenile justice system. This effort, titled S.H.A.P.E., offers student offenders who have committed certain violations—assault, disorderly conduct, and trespassing, among others—3 months of individualized services utilizing both restorative practices and mentoring/academic tutoring, as necessary. To coordinate these services, a memorandum of understanding (MOU) was established among the school district, City of Memphis, Memphis Police Department, juvenile court, prosecutor's office, and public defender's office, with these efforts lowering the number of school to court referrals from 1,000 in 2007 to 281 in 2013 (James-Garner, 2013).

Expanding the existing database of student information and maximizing its use was vital to improving and evaluating an implemented Positive Behavioral Intervention System in the Pueblo City School District in Colorado. By using an interactive software system, student discipline and related data can be mapped, examined, and aggregated with other school data (academic, school schedule), and individual students', classes, time of day, or location can be examined. School personnel track this information daily and longitudinally, providing reports to decision makers and administrators, and thus more effectively monitor students who traditionally were disproportionately involved with school discipline. This group included students with emotional, behavioral, intellectual, and academic difficulties or disabilities. This system has allowed an accurate analysis of PBIS that is incorporated across 25 schools within the district, with a 38% decrease in office referrals after program implementation (Bershad & Kitson, 2012).

While in Los Angeles, California, the public schools have established an information-sharing system for school districts, county agencies, and other stakeholders involved in the education of young people who are formally involved with the juvenile courts. This system ensures information sharing across the education systems and service providers and includes the following available information: demographic, contacts for all parties, legal status, and information on academic records, attendance, school discipline records, testing scores, mental and physical health information, and other related concerns (Morgan et al., 2014).

In a broader, though similar, reformation, the Clayton County Juvenile Justice Collaborative in Georgia addressed a serious increase in school-based truancy and disruptive behavior referrals to the juvenile court that occurred during the later 1990s till 2003 when almost 3,000 referrals were made. Through a significant effort that was led by Clayton County Court Judge Steven Teske, an agreement was finalized among the school districts, juvenile court, and law enforcement that explicated the criteria for school-based referrals utilizing a graduated sanction philosophy because of which only a third offense can result in a court referral. In addition, a system of care and point of access was established for those students with chronic difficulties, focused on identifying and treating the underlying causes. Referrals from the public schools to the juvenile court decreased by more than 73% from 2003 to 2011 (Teske, 2011).

These reformation efforts are difficult, and moving systems to work together and collaborate poses significant political, legal, and administrative coordination. Judges at both the state and local levels can be particularly effective in leading these cooperative and necessary changes across the school districts and juvenile courts. Without effective judicial leadership, these efforts often fail. Judicial officials are uniquely positioned to convene stakeholders and leaders from law enforcement, education, community-based providers, and other necessary stakeholders to diagnose the problems and spearhead local solutions. Because of the need for judicial leadership, the National Council of Juvenile and Family Court Judges (NCJFCJ) is leading these efforts through its School Pathways to Juvenile Justice System technical assistance training and other related nationwide efforts (National Council of Juvenile and Family Court Judges, 2014).

Some of the more difficult issues in collaboration across school districts, juvenile courts, and community-based service providers include sharing data and coming to an agreement on how to do so effectively and efficiently. Two resource tools are available that provide basic guidance as well as examples of documents that deal with federal laws and oversight policies. The first is the Navigating Information Sharing (NIS) Toolkit (National Center for Mental Health Promotion and Youth Violence Prevention, 2013) that is available to schools, school resource officers, and other school partners. The second is the Models for Change Information Sharing Toolkit (John D. and Catherine T. MacArthur Foundation, 2008) that provides guidance to juvenile courts and school districts, as well as community-based providers, on how to improve information sharing across systems. Summaries of pertinent federal laws are provided along with case-study scenarios, as well as standard data-sharing agreements that can be modified to fit local jurisdictions.

CONCLUSION

A society is judged not by the success of its most prominent or able-bodied, but by how it treats its most disadvantaged. When looking at a majority of today's schools' criminalization of education and punitively focused juvenile courts, it is difficult to draw any conclusion other than the truth that we have failed many of these children and adolescents. It is possible to dismantle established policies that were based on fear, a tough-on-crime philosophy, and a dearth of empirical data that led to the school-to-prison pipeline. We now know that the zero-tolerance movements in our schools and juvenile courts do not work and the pipeline can be dismantled.

REFERENCES

Bershad, C., & Kitson, J. (2012). *Supportive school discipline: Snapshots from the safe schools/healthy schools initiative.* Newton, MA: Education Development Center.

Garcia, M. (2013). *Resolution: 2013 school discipline policy and school climate bill of rights.* Los Angeles, CA: Los Angeles School District.

James-Garner, A. (2013). *School House Adjustment Program Enterprise (SHAPE): 2012–2013 outcome and evaluation study.* Shelby County, TN: Shelby County Schools Office of Safety and Security, Department of Research, Planning, and Improvement.

John D. and Catherine T. MacArthur Foundation. (2013). *Models for change: Information sharing tool kit.* Chicago, IL: Author.

Labre, M., Stern-Carusone, J., Rosiak, J., Becker, B., & Wright, C. (2013). *A snapshot of James A. Garfield High School, Los Angeles Unified School District.* Newtown, MA: Education Development Center.

Morgan, E., Salomon, N., Plotkin, M., & Cohen, R. (2014). *The school discipline consensus report: Strategies from the field to keep students engaged in school and out of the juvenile justice system.* Washington, DC: The Council of State Governments Justice Center.

National Center for Mental Health Promotion and Youth Violence Prevention. (2013). *Navigating information sharing: You can share information to help youth involved in multiple systems.* Waltham, MA: Education Development Center.

National Council of Juvenile and Family Court Judges. (2014). *School pathways to the juvenile justice system project: A practice guide.* Reno, NV: Author.

Padres & Jovenes Unidos & Advancement Project. (2014). *Lessons in racial justice and movement building: Dismantling the school-to-prison pipeline in Colorado and nationally.* Denver, CO: Author.

Roberts, T. (2012). *Civil citation.* Tallahassee, FL: Florida Department of Juvenile Justice.

Shriver Center. (2014). *Exploring strategies to stem the school-to-prison pipeline for students with disabilities.* Chicago, IL: Sargent Shriver National Center on Poverty Law.

Teske, S. (2011). A study of zero tolerance policies in schools: A multi-integrated systems approach to improve outcomes for adolescents. *Journal of Child and Adolescent Psychiatric Nursing, 24,* 88–97.

Index

reform
  efforts, 192–193, 197
  legal, 194–195
  schools, 27
  strategies, 145, 148
rehabilitation
  alternatives, 54–55
  authority through effective, 7
  effective treatment and, 168–171
  juvenile justice system efforts, 2
  movement toward, 30, 191
  policy changes from, 2
  punitive policies compared to, 177
  rehabilitative discipline
    philosophy, 121–123, 126, 128
  retribution compared to, 28
reintegration, into schools, 140–141,
    179, 192
release
  barriers to community reentry
    upon, 59–60
  from juvenile justice facilities, 58
resegregation, of schools, 16, 23
resiliency, 83–84
resources
  inequitable distribution of, 99
  information sharing, 142
Response to Intervention (RtI), 194
restorative justice, 122, 129, 135, 164,
    192–193
restorative practices, 128–130, 135
retribution, 28
risk factors, 6, 75–84
  adult criminal justice system, 59
  community, 83
  comorbidity across, 53
  cross-system, 79–80
  delinquency, juvenile justice
    system and, 80–81
  family, 82
  homelessness, 3, 60, 76
  individual, 81–82
  learning disabilities, 49, 81
  maltreatment victimization/
    trauma, 76–77, 81–82

mental health problems, 3, 50, 80,
    81
  poverty, 75–76, 82
  protective factors and, 83–84
  recidivism, 57
  resiliency and, 83–84
  screening for, 136–138
  special education disabilities,
    78–79, 81
running away, 94

Safe and Drug-Free Schools and
    Communities Title IV, Part A,
    142
safe school districts, 18
Safe Schools Act (1994), 23, 24
safety resource officers (SROs). *See*
    police
Sandy Hook Elementary School,
    Connecticut, 18
San Francisco Unified School
    District, 192
School Climate Bill of Rights, 192
school districts, 138–141, 191–194
  safe, 18
School Pathways to Juvenile Justice
    System, 197
schools. *See also* police
  academic and learning needs
    focus of, 2
  academic disengagement, 22, 43,
    45
  alternative, 22, 56, 141
  classroom and, 131–132
  corporal punishment in, 15
  declining funding for, 16
  delayed graduation, 25
  discipline in, 2–3, 16–26
  disturbing, 46
  dropping out of, 26, 44, 56–57, 58,
    90
  education in juvenile justice
    facilities, 178–179
  from education to discipline in, 2,
    16–17

Printed in the United States
By Bookmasters